Tarzan, Jungle King
of Popular Culture

Tarzan, Jungle King of Popular Culture

DAVID LEMMO

McFarland & Company, Inc., Publishers
Jefferson, North Carolina

ISBN (print) 978-1-4766-6695-2
ISBN (ebook) 978-1-4766-2622-2

LIBRARY OF CONGRESS CATALOGUING DATA ARE AVAILABLE

British Library cataloguing data are available

Front cover: Poster art for the 1932 film
Tarzan the Ape Man (MGM/Photofest)

Printed in the United States of America

*McFarland & Company, Inc., Publishers
Box 611, Jefferson, North Carolina 28640
www.mcfarlandpub.com*

To Rachael Wenban

Acknowledgments

The author wishes to pay his respects to the many people who helped in the creation of this book:

George T. McWhorter, who proofread the original manuscript and added information while attending to his duties at the University of Louisville Ekstrom Library's Edgar Rice Burroughs Memorial Collection. Rachael Wenban, who took the time from a busy schedule to proofread. Ralph Brown, who allowed me to scan and photograph items from his incredible Tarzan archives. Katie Brown, who read through the manuscript and offered constructive comments and encouragement. Bill Hillman, for his help and fantastic website *ERBzine*—an amazing wealth of information. Bruce Bozarth, for his amazing website ERBLIST.com, and his help finding information. Delinda Buie of the University of Louisville Ekstrom Library for delivering manuscript chapters to George McWhorter. Henry Garfield, friend, author and a great writing teacher. Bob Roehm of the University of Louisville Ekstrom Library for his help and enthusiasm. Brian "Shaggy" Smith, for encouragement and reading through chapters. Mike Sirota, another friend, a great writing teacher and Tarzan fan. James M. Waxon, a friend and fan who added information used in the book. Robert Zeuschner, for his Burroughs bibliography and help finding information.

Table of Contents

Preface

First appearing in 1912, Tarzan of the Apes is a multimedia super-star whose social impact and cultural heritage extends beyond mere entertainment. As the seminal 20th century superhero, his contribution to the explosion of popular culture is worldwide—he stands at the head of a line of early archetypes such as the Shadow and Doc Savage, who were later combined by writers to create new ones such as Superman and Batman. Today he takes on his greatest foe, his own media incarnations, competing against himself while influencing American culture and philosophy.

The Ape-Man also helped pioneer (starting in 1916) the pervasive fandom movement. Before World Cons, Comic-Cons and the *Star Trek* phenomena, Tarzan fandom was aiding in the acceptance of popular culture as a valid subject of academic study. Since then, the incredible growth and influence of pop culture has turned fandom from a loose-knit organizations of "geeks" into a mainstream phenomenon that generates billions in revenue and ensures the future legacies of archetypes like Tarzan.

The Lord of the Jungle has along the way adapted to the pop culture pantheon he helped create. He's a century-old example of the tendency of media archetypes to change, combine and recombine in response to shifting audience tastes and sensibilities. Many fans are defining life and personal experiences based on fictional characters and universes, as people have long done with historical or religious figures.

I discovered Tarzan during the mid–1950s while reading the daily and Sunday newspaper comics sections, and also in the pages of Dell Comics' *Tarzan*. By the time I was 11, I was a great fan of the Tarzan movies, and then I made the discovery there were also great novels. Later in life I became a bookseller, specializing in, among other things,

Preface

the works of Edgar Rice Burroughs. I worked for the Holmes Book Company in Oakland, California, and utilized their considerable research collection. I also learned a lot on the subject by working book fairs hosted by the Antiquarian Booksellers' Association of America.

Of the many works I read in preparation for the telling the story of Tarzan's transcendence in world of pop culture, Irwin Porges' *Edgar Rice Burroughs: The Man Who Created Tarzan* is highly recommended. In researching Tarzan's "life," I delved into the movies and TV episodes, the comics, and magazines articles, combed the vast downtown Los Angeles library, and explored the Internet. And then there's *ERBzine*, the official Edgar Rice Burroughs tribute and weekly webzine site, with over 15,000 pages of archives. *ERBzine* has it all: documents, photographs, artwork and lots of information.

After I had written a first draft of this book, George T. McWhorter, creator and curator of the Edgar Rice Burroughs Memorial Collection in the University of Louisville, went through it, fixing things up here and there and adding information.

Introduction: A Continuity of Popular Culture

The origins of popular culture date back to the latter part of the 1700s, a period of urban growth, industrialization, mass media and technological development. During the 19th century, mass culture continued to develop with increasing urban populations, large-scale organizing of industry (including the division of labor) and the developing worldwide communications systems. By the early 20th century, mass communication had created a vast audience of media consumers that was ripe for the appearance of superheroes.

Fans of Sherlock Holmes may be said to have organized the first fandom conventions when they organized mourning events after the fictional detective was (supposedly) killed off in 1893, and some of the first Holmes fan fiction appeared as early as 1897. The first official Tarzan fan club, the Tribe of Tarzan Club, was organized in 1916 out of Staunton, Virginia, by a boy named Herman Newman. Science fiction and fantasy fandom dates back to the 1930s, and the World Science Fiction Convention—Worldcon—began in 1939, with *Star Trek* fandom, Comic-Con International San Diego, San Diego Comic Fest, Anime, SteamPunk and Manga all decades in the future.

Superheroes are now everywhere in American popular culture, in comics, movies, television, books, video games, merchandise, advertising and fan activities. Their origin can be traced through a study of the first multimedia superstar of the 20th century, Tarzan of the Apes, whose influence on American and world popular culture extends beyond the commercialism of books, movies, comics and mass-marketed merchandise, inspiring personal philosophies on life, politics and the activities of the fandom movement.

Introduction: A Continuity of Popular Culture

The comics, movies and memorabilia have made billions of dollars for the superhero industry. Popular culture changes constantly, forming branches and blending interdependent elements that influence us in many ways. After World War II, cultural and social forces, aided by mass media innovations, changed the meaning of popular culture by the blending of so-called lowbrow and highbrow tastes. Collecting memorabilia could now become an interesting and affordable hobby, a mere pastime or, in extreme cases, a complex nightmare of fan consciousness. Thousands of dollars are spent on memorabilia including rare comic books, movie posters, toys, recordings, books and costumes, supporting an industry that continues the legacies of their superheroes.

People can relate to superheroes not only because they are saviors of the planet, but also because they are in many ways like us. A shift toward relatable superhero existentialist angst developed during the early 1960s with Marvel Comics' Stan Lee. The doubts, fears and confusions of 1960s Marvel characters such as Spider-Man, the Hulk, and the X-Men reveal the people behind the masks of the infallible superheroes that had come before. This new type of superhero shifted the paradigm and commandeered popular culture so that by the mid–1960s, King Kong, the Lone Ranger, Spider-Man and the Hulk were considered counterculture icons by college students, alongside real public figures such as Martin Luther King, Jr., Rosa Parks and Robert Kennedy. Also during the 1960s, artist Roy Lichtenstein compiled comic book panels into pop art portraits, including word balloons, and these comics-inspired works of art aided in the legitimizing and publicizing of comics as an art form. From the 1960s onward, popular culture skyrocketed, in great part because of the many forms of organized fandom, to its present position as an industry dealing in billions of dollars, and collectively the greatest show on earth.

But popular culture has been infiltrated by a superhero craze, feeding our hunger even more for being something we can never be. Fandom has been seen as a dysfunction, an excess, like being caught between childhood and adulthood. And because popular culture is self-documenting, it has been seen by others as a type of religious faith. Fandom activities include conventions and other events and exhibitions; collecting memorabilia; publishing books, videos, fanzines and newsletters; congregating on forums and discussion boards; fan fiction; fan art and costuming; gaming; archiving; and role-playing.

Does the seeming triviality of pop culture represent a decline into meaninglessness in culture? If so, then the study of comparative religious and mythological archetypes and motifs, taught in schools and universities for centuries, could also be seen as a waste of time. Like many scholars and professors of ancient religion and myth, thousands of superhero and comic book fans remain undaunted by the accusations. Comic-Con International San Diego, a convention for the fantastic, attracts around 125,000 attendees each year and is so important that major Hollywood personalities make appearances and promote their superhero and action films. Grade school children have superheroes of their own, for example the star of Dav Pilkey's Captain Underpants books. Pre-schoolers are amused by Sesame Street's Super Grover. Yet, lest one regard superheroes and comics as juvenile pulp, Michael Chabon's 2000 novel *The Amazing Adventures of Kavalier and Klay* (based loosely on the lives of comics creators Joe Shuster and Jerry Siegel) won a Pulitzer Prize and is being adapted into a motion picture.

Many believe that popular culture can make the world a better place by mobilizing fans into communities that promote creative outlets and activities for social good, such as charity projects. Artist Phil Yeh of Winged Tiger Press created the *Cartoonists Across America & the World* project, painting more than 1800 murals in 49 American states and 15 other countries since 1986. Yeh enlists the aid of local children. These murals promote cooperation and creative activities designed to educate and inspire youth to reject violence, prejudice and other destructive elements facing young people.

Noting the cultural importance of popular culture, many editors, publishers, artists and writers have become archivists of the comics. Superheroes and other characters are also here to stay inside the pages of hardback and trade paperback book reprints of classic comic strip and comic book stories. This insures that we have a sampling of the past incarnations of comics heroes. But there has been another postmodernist cultural shift, a loose, unified theory of a continuity of popular culture. Superheroes, like archetypes of ancient mythology, or even historical figures, are not bound by any particular time or perspective of any one generation of fans, and they are malleable to historical changes and interpretations.

Sherlock Holmes is in the unique position, as of this writing, of being the hero of motion pictures taking place in the 19th century (where he originated in print media), one that takes place during the great man's elderly, declining years, and also the subject of two television series, *Sherlock* and *Elementary*, both bringing Holmes and Watson into the 21st century. The Holmes and Watson of the recent movies and TV series are certainly not the Holmes and Watson of Sir Arthur Conan Doyle's original stories. For that matter, neither are the Holmes and Watson provided by Basil Rathbone and Nigel Bruce in 1940s movies. Yet they are all Sherlock Holmes.

Tarzan is also over a century old. His many media manifestations have their own story arcs and historical perspectives, but these motifs stay within the overall concept of the Ape-Man as laid down in the original novels written by Edgar Rice Burroughs. In some fantastic, improbable way, one person, a superhero, has had all of these adventures. A mere mortal could not survive them, nor even have enough time or energy to do it all. The continuity of popular culture can be said to be the same for Superman, Batman and Wonder Woman. All three are nearing the 80-year mark and exhibit signs of becoming (modern) myths, as with (ancient myths) Hercules, Athena and Odysseus, whose individual stories also differ and are often contradictory, but the archetype itself remains recognizable and embedded in world popular culture.

It is one thing to have Tarzan, in one of his old movies, introduce himself by saying, "Me, Tarzan." In the novels of Burroughs, it is something very different when Tarzan declares, "I am Tarzan of the Apes." Both are recognizably Tarzan but they are two distinct versions of this icon.

A continuity of popular culture also benefits from a once scarce but now popular genre in books, movies, graphic novels, gaming, Internet and other forms of storytelling. The crossover genre mixes characters, real or fictitious, from a variety of media sources. Thus, for example, Tarzan shares an adventure with Arthur Conan Doyle (creator of Sherlock Holmes), Nikola Tesla (scientific genius) and the Frankenstein Monster, in Dark Horse Comics' *Tarzan: The Modern Prometheus.*

Also fitting within a continuity of popular culture is the genre of the secret "real lives" of fictitious characters such as Sherlock Holmes, Tarzan, Dr. Fu Manchu, Doc Savage and others—a pantheon, a family of superheroes and villains living secret lives behind the fiction of books and movies about them.

Boundaries that once separated so-called high and low culture have merged, changing the perspectives of media studies, cultural studies and popular culture itself. Established disciplines, having loosened a hold on an intellectual rigor mortis, bred an explosion of academic interest in popular culture, which encompasses such diverse media as books, movies, college courses, conventions, theater, comic books, radio, graphic novels and documentaries. The Internet has been described as a locus of communal activity for fandom. Prior to the Internet, fandom was, to a large extent, dependent on people gathering at various geographical locations. The Internet changed this within the framework of huge conventions and events, and fandom has become an interlocking global village, which includes amateur press associations and networking into sub-organizations and communities within various factions of fandom.

While we're considering Tarzan of the Apes in the terms of fandom, multimedia and a continuity of popular culture, it turns out that he was a secret agent 40 years before the appearance of James Bond. The Ape-Man has also been involved in international political chaos that includes fighting in World War I, battling an invasion of communists during the late 1930s and serving the Allies as a British RAF officer, Colonel John Clayton, in a novel set during World War II.

The Ape-Man battled the Axis in another time, as another Tarzan, in another media—motion pictures. In the 1943 film *Tarzan Triumphs*, Nazis invade the jungle and Johnny Weissmuller's Tarzan, after uttering that immortal line, "Now, Tarzan make war!" goes out and thrashes them. The film was released 14 months after America's entrance into the war, and has an ironic ending. Tarzan's chimpanzee friend Cheta, monkeying with a radio, manages to contact a unit of Nazis; a German officer mistakes Cheta for Hitler and blurts out a frantic "Heil Hitler!"

1

"Your son deserted Thursday. Letter will follow."

Tarzan of the Apes, mighty hunter and warrior—the titled English lord who was raised by apes is part ancient mythology and part Native American tradition, combined over time into a modern pop culture archetype. The Ape-Man of Edgar Rice Burroughs' imagination first appeared over a century ago, when advances in science and a growing population were merging to create what eventually became the super-media of the 21st century. Springing into life in 1912, this foster son of a she-ape exploited many forms of entertainment, becoming both the first multimedia superstar and the first seminal superhero to emerge in the 20th century.

The saga begins in April 1861. Conflict over secession from the Union exploded at the Battle of Fort Sumter near Charleston, South Carolina, beginning the American Civil War. George Tyler Burroughs was mustered into the Union Army on April 19. Born in Warren, Massachusetts, in 1833, he was of English stock on his paternal side (he was related to Edmund Rice, an early Massachusetts Pilgrim) and Pennsylvania Dutch on his mother's side. He and Mary Evaline Zieger had been planning to marry, but now that the war intervened they would have to put their personal wishes aside.

George Tyler Burroughs fought at Sudley Springs and survived the Battle of Bull Run, considered the first major land battle of the conflict. Commissioned as a lieutenant in the infantry, George told friends in a letter, "I must say that I feel thankful for this war because I believe that this Institution of slavery will now receive its death blow."[1] His son's literary creation Tarzan would later share this revulsion with slavery and a willingness to fight it.

George and Mary Evaline Zieger decided to resume their life together and were married on February 24, 1863, while the war still raged. In July the Battle of Gettysburg became known as the bloodiest of the war but also a turning point, representing the end of Robert E. Lee's key invasion plans to mount an assault on Washington. Mary, an adventurous spirit herself, followed George from front to front and wrote a book titled *Memoirs of a War Bride*. The original handwritten manuscript is preserved by the family of Edgar Rice Burroughs. The

Poster for *Tarzan and the Slave Girl* (1950). Edgar Rice Burrough's literary Tarzan would share the author's revulsion with slavery (Ralph Brown collection).

influence of Mary's adventurous spirit would later appear in many of Edgar's feisty female characters, including Jane (Porter) Clayton, Tarzan's wife.

Mary and George (now a captain) witnessed the fall of Richmond in April 1865. Under orders to destroy armories, supply warehouses and bridges, retreating Confederate soldiers set fire to them. The fires spread out of control and burned large areas of Richmond. The old traditions were besieged for North and South alike, and something that had been present all along, embedded within the fabric of the war, was emerging in new forms. Linus Yale, Jr., for example, had invented the cylinder lock in 1861; the machine-gun was patented the next year by Richard Gatling. The emerging new form was another revolution in science and technology, a revolution eventually based on electricity and oil, and ushering in the future.

On July 22, 1865, George Tyler Burroughs received an honorable discharge from the army with the title of brevet major. He went on to join various military organizations and in 1867 became one of the 13 Original Companions of the Illinois Commandery, a member of the Grand Army of the Republic and a Freemason. George, Mary and their two boys George, Jr., and Harry moved to Chicago in 1868. Major Burroughs went into the distillery business, as distillation had many scientific functions used in power generation, transportation, heating and alcohol. Mary raised the children and managed the house with a cook and two Irish maids. The major ran the house with military efficiency.

From October 8 through 10, 1871, Chicago burned. The firestorm killed 300 people and destroyed 17,000 buildings, leaving 100,000 citizens homeless. The Burroughses' West Side neighborhood was spared from the flames, and from atop their rented Washington Boulevard townhouse George, Mary and the two boys watched helplessly.

In 1872 Frank Coleman Burroughs was born to George and Mary. Edgar Rice Burroughs was born at home on September 1, 1875. He was Mary's fifth son after George, Jr., Harry, Frank and a son who had died. With a bright and imaginative mind, Eddie, at age five, wrote his thoughts down on paper and rhymed: "I'm Dr. Burroughs come to town, To see my patint [*sic*] Maria Brown...."[2]

By age six, Eddie had developed an interest in letter writing, communicating mostly to family who were away. With Mary's common sense and moderation and the major's stoic conservatism, Edgar Rice Burroughs got as good an education from his family as he did in school. In 1882 he entered Brown School on the Chicago West Side, where he was a mediocre scholar with no outstanding activities. Here he met Emma Hulbert, daughter of hotel businessman Alvin Hulbert. (The Hulbert family were neighbors of the Burroughses.) Edgar and Emma formed a friendship.

Edgar continued writing letters and poems and drew cartoons. The boy drew and wrote in the margins of pages within his textbooks, his attention straying from schoolwork. Bored with the stories his mother had been telling him all of his very young life, he created his own imaginative tales and told them to *her*. Edgar's correspondences with his brothers reveal a friendly, sympathetic relationship. For example, his brother George wrote and praised him for having read *Tales of Ancient Greece*.

The eight-year-old's interest in myth and the fantastic would become more important later, in the early 20th century world that would be rushing toward the future. In 1883, Gottlieb Daimler had just patented the gasoline combustion engine; George Eastman patented the invention of roll film in 1884, which would eventually replace glass plates. Advances in technology, especially in communications, and the expansion of population were slowly merging to create the mass marketing of media, soon to play an important part in the American Dream, and in the creation and sustained popularity of Tarzan.

Edgar Rice Burroughs, shown on a 1990s poster for an annual gathering of Tarzan fans, was born September 1, 1875, in Chicago, Illinois (Ralph Brown collection).

In 1885, George Tyler Burroughs sent George, Jr., and Harry to Yale University. Also that year, the major's distillery business caught fire and burned; its market shares and revenues dropped. He then invested in the American Battery Company, manufacturing and selling storage batteries. Science marched on, and so did Major Burroughs, fire or no fire.

Edgar read the works of Jack London, George Barr McCutcheon and Zane Grey and the travel adventures of Richard Halliburton. He kept up the friendship with Emma Hulbert and they spent more time together. When he was 12, a diphtheria epidemic spread through Chicago, and the boy's parents took him out of public school and placed him in a private girls' school (the only private school available on the West Side at the time). Edgar's father was stern and authoritarian in their relationship, and Edgar was expected to endure the temporary embarrassment of continuing his studies in a girls' school.

In 1889, author and charity worker Nellie Bly, working for the *New York World* newspaper, circumnavigated the earth in 72 days, six hours, 11 minutes and 14 seconds, breaking the fictional record of Phileas Fogg in Jules Verne's novel *Around the World in Eighty Days*. Alfred Russell Wallace published his book on natural selection, *Darwinism*. Edgar Rice Burroughs, 14 years old, began proposing marriage to Emma Hulbert.

Edgar attended Harvard School, learning Greek and Latin grammar before turning to a study of English. Then fierce labor wars erupted in Chicago, with the lingering memory of the Haymarket Square riot of 1886. When an influenza epidemic hit the city, Edgar was dispatched to his brothers' ranch in Idaho. Edgar's brothers George and Harry were in the cattle business with Lew Sweetser, a Yale classmate of their father's. In the 1890s, the population of the United States surpassed 60 million. The population of Idaho at the time was approximately 15,000, with ranching and mining the principal industries. The Sweetser-Burroughs ranch was located along the Raft River Valley in Cassia County, in the southeastern part of the territory. Edgar did chores, grubbed sagebrush, drove a team of broncos, delivered mail on horseback and hauled freight with a horse team and wagon. He awoke at 4 a.m. each morning and arose from the floor of a log cabin to begin his work. The boy had an instinct for handling horses, including the notorious Whiskey Jack, a cranky, violent black gelding.

Cassia County in the 1890s was still untamed, frontier America.

Burroughs had a sensitive and understanding inclination towards animals, a trait shared with Tarzan in his novels. Moe Gollub created the cover art for this Dell *Tarzan* comic book, Number 8, 1951.

Edgar met men who were bred rough and violent: Blanco, who, though he had a stammer, always managed to curse up a storm; Texas Pete, forever fixing for a fight, was shot by Sheriff Gum Brown over a minor violation. On a visit to the ranch, a Burroughs family friend was shocked by the boy's stories of his encounters with horse thieves, cattle rustlers and other bad men. In the next mail delivery, he received a railroad ticket from his father with orders to return to Chicago at once. Edgar was told that he would be sent to Phillips Academy in Andover, Massachusetts, and educated with people of his own station in life. The academy was then over 100 years old, and excellent preparation for Yale. In September 1891 Edgar was sent to Phillips Academy; he later wrote, "From murderers, horse thieves and bad men I was transported to Phillips Academy. I presume there must have been another epidemic somewhere."[3]

Among Edgar's classmates were Irenee du Pont, future president of the du Pont Corporation, and Hiram Bingham, later a governor and then a U.S. Senator. In the first semester he studied mathematics, English, history, Latin and chemistry; he was elected president of his class. But Edgar didn't excel; he was uncomfortable in the strict environment, especially with memories of his Idaho ranch stint still lingering. At the beginning of the second semester he received a notice that his academic performance had better improve or he would be dropped. When the warning was ignored, the principal, Dr. Cecil F. P. Bancroft, dismissed Edgar from the Academy.

Edgar's father told him that more discipline was in order and escorted the 16-year-old to Orchard Lake Michigan Military Academy, which had been founded by Brevet Major J. Sumner Rogers. Edgar had an interest in the readings and studies of Caesar's *Commentaries*, the works of Gibbons and the Romans in general. Duties included roadwork and ditch-digging. When Capt. Charles King took over as commandant, the standards of discipline were expected to improve. King was a famous author of novels about army life in the west. As a teenager during the Civil War he had volunteered as an army orderly; he later attended West Point and then fought Apaches and the Sioux.

Edgar was rebellious as ever. George Tyler Burroughs became concerned, especially after receiving an April 16, 1892, telegram from Capt. King: "Your son deserted Thursday. Letter will follow."[4]

Captain King informed the major that Edgar had received a number of negative reports. Nevertheless, Edgar eventually became one of the Academy's top horse riders, sometimes performing bareback. Despite the hassles and discipline problems, Edgar realized he liked the vigorous life of the Military Academy.

While still a student, Edgar's lifelong fascination with automobiles surfaced at the 1893 World's Columbian Exposition in Chicago. Advances in science stood out as the main attraction; electricity was the star of the show. Edgar, working for his father's business, drove an electric automobile throughout the fairgrounds. Back at school, he found time to draw, sometimes in letters, sometimes just for relaxation.

In 1894 the first commercial exhibition of motion pictures in history took place in New York City, using ten Kinetoscopes. Motion pictures would later play a key part in the development of popular culture and, through Tarzan, in the life of Edgar Rice Burroughs himself. But in 1895, Edgar failed the examination for entrance to West Point. He was stunned at his inability to meet the standards set by his father.

George Tyler Burroughs gave his underage son permission to join the military and on May 13, 1896, Edgar enlisted as a private in the Regular Army, assigned to Troop B 7th Regiment, U.S. Cavalry. "The Bloody Seventh" had fought at the Little Bighorn in 1876 and at Wounded Knee in 1890, and stopped the Pullman strike in Chicago in 1894. The recruiting sergeant told Edgar it was the worst assignment in the United States Army.

Edgar was sent to Fort Grant, territory of Arizona, in the parched environment northeast of Tucson at the foot of the Pinaleno Range. Fort Grant was built in 1872 during the Army's war with Apaches. It was now a dusty collection of tents and adobe and rough-timbered buildings surrounding a parade ground. Edgar was assigned to Company B, where his bunkmates included many foreigners and black soldiers. Their main duty was keeping Native Americans contained in the reservations. Edgar worked under the supervision of black sergeants and became impressed with the fort's African-American soldiers. He also found himself drawn to Native American colleagues and the Army's Apache scouts, particularly Corp. Josh.

With unfaltering loyalty to his creative predispositions, Edgar wrote letters, especially to Emma, as their romance continued growing. He also continued drawing, doing a series of sketches of Army life that featured Native Americans, Chinese immigrants, horses being branded, a stagecoach, horseback drills and a whiskey drinker. Edgar's service with the 7th Regiment ended in March 1897 because he had a condition of irregular and intermittent heart action, especially after exertion. Edgar was deeply disappointed. It was all he could do to face his father.

Edgar's brother Harry set him up in a stationery store in Pocatello, Idaho, with a large newsstand and cigar counter. When the business failed, Edgar returned to Chicago and worked for his father's American Battery Company. Edgar and Emma went to parties and the theater.

Edgar's creative imagination often clashed with the harsh realities of making a living, leaving him impatient, restless and impulsive. He did manage to produce some political cartoons. On the flyleaf of a copy of Charles Darwin's *The Descent of Man,* he drew a large ape with the notation "grandpa," as a joke for his grandfather Abner Tyler Burroughs.

In 1898, the total world population was about 1,440,650,000; Rudolf Diesel was granted a U.S. patent for his internal combustion engine; a mail order buggy could be purchased for $20; radium was discovered by the Curies and G. Bemont; J.B. Dunlop introduced the pneumatic rubber tire. And as the 20th century dawned, Americans were spending more money.

Edgar and Emma Centennia Hulbert were married in January 1900. William McKinley was re-elected president in November of that year on his Full Dinner Pail campaign.

Ed did three booklets of poetry, drawings and cartoons for his brother Harry's children Evelyn and Studley. He also produced a 12-page illustrated poem with a homemade hardcover, bound together with a shoelace. Titled *Snake River Cotton-Tail Tales,* this gift to his niece and nephew was one of his more accomplished works.

In 1903, after Edgar's three-year stint working at his father's American Battery Company, the couple packed up their belongings and left for Idaho, where Edgar became an employee of the Sweetser-Burroughs Mining Company. He described the area as the most beautiful in the country, surrounded by snow-capped mountains and populated with grizzly bears, deer and mountain sheep. The dredge ran on three eight-hour shifts. No mother lode was discovered at the Stanley Basin dredge. Another gold-dredging operation located on the Snake River did better but was not productive enough. When the company folded, Edgar and Emma rode a freight wagon to Salt Lake City, where Edgar worked as a railroad police officer at the Union Pacific yards. Some of his drawings of this period reflect his experiences as a policeman.

Unable to comfortably support himself and his wife on his meager earnings, Edgar began developing a distrust of so-called civilization, and this distrust would appear years later in his Tarzan novels. In the summer of 1905, the couple moved back to Chicago—493 West Jackson

Boulevard in the West End. For the first time since 1885, all brothers were living in Chicago. Frank was a sales manager of Hawtin Engraving; Harry was assistant manager of Automatic Electric; George, Jr., took over the presidency of the American Battery Company upon their father's retirement. Edgar had salesman jobs, hating them all. An intelligent man with a pattern of vapid jobs, he sometimes seemed self-defeating.

In 1908, Robert Peary was in the middle of an expedition to reach the North Pole; liquid helium was made for the first time; tungsten proved to be well adapted for filaments in incandescent lamps; 150,000 cars were on the streets of America; and Edgar and Emma had their first child, Joan. Their son Hulbert was born on August 12, 1909. After many jobs and a failed business venture, Edgar was given a position placing ads in pulp fiction magazines for a patent medicine called Alcola, supposedly a cure for alcoholism. Edgar went through the magazines, reading some of the stories. His conclusion: "I made up my mind that if people were paid for writing such rot as I read in some of those magazines that I could write stories just as rotten."[5]

In 1911, Edgar's brother Frank, who worked for Champlin-Yardley, got him a job at the stationers. However, the pulp magazine "rot" that had rekindled his creative instincts remained in the forefront of Edgar's mind. A young man whose life experiences had included that of cowboy, miner and cavalry soldier might be expected to write about what he knew. But Edgar Rice Burroughs had an exceptionally developed imagination and an above-average education that included an interest in astronomy. In 1895, scientist Percival Lowell had made critical observations of Mars popular in a book titled *Mars*. Edgar also read Lowell's early 20th century works.

Another influence was his drive to succeed, fueled by frustration at having been cut loose from the Army because of a heart condition. A superhuman version of himself was in order. His first literary protagonist was John Carter, a gentleman from Virginia whose profession was that of fighting man. His story was published in six parts in *All-Story* magazine, beginning in February 1912, with the title "Under the Moons of Mars." After being transmigrated to Mars and becoming superhuman, Carter has incredible adventures and meets the love of his life, Dejah Thoris, princess of Helium. Edgar used the *nom de plume*

Normal Bean, a name that humorously indicated that the author was not crazy. Somehow between author and typesetter, the byline became Norman Bean. In his *Billion Year Spree: The True History of Science Fiction*, English author Brian W. Aldiss stated, "With this first effort, Burroughs brought the novel with an interplanetary setting into science fiction to stay."[6]

After the publication of his first story, Edgar spent evenings at the Chicago Public Library researching 13th-century English history. He was writing a swashbuckler about a war and a lost prince of England (a fictitious son of Henry III). Titled "The Outlaw of Torn," this story was rejected by *All-Story* editor Thomas Newell Metcalf, who urged Edgar not to be discouraged. But Edgar was now having doubts about his ability to make a living writing fiction. He was 35, and his paychecks from the stationers weren't covering living expenses. In the spring of 1912 he got a job at the A.W. Shaw Company, as a department manager for a business magazine.

He also continued his Chicago Public Library research. But now his subjects were along the lines of ancient myth (Romulus and Remus, Hercules, Odysseus) and Henry M. Stanley's *In Darkest Africa*. His personal experiences with Native Americans were added to the mix. These elements culminated in the creation of both the first multimedia superstar and the first seminal superhero to emerge in the 20th century.

2

Edgar's Improbable Tale

Myths and legends of ancient world cultures are possibly the earliest examples of popular culture. First spread orally, these tales appeared over thousands of years as art, on urns, carved into stone walls, sculpted, as body ornaments, sung, as prose, poetry, theater and movies. According to the British Library, the *Diamond Sutra*, printed in China in 868 A.D., is the world's earliest dated printed book. Movable type was invented in China in 1041. By 1400, European popular art prints were published in great numbers. Johannes Gutenberg produced his first book on a printing press with movable type in 1453. But books, because of the expense to produce them, took at least a century to become part of a growing mass media, to become popular culture. Newspapers developed around 1612, not attaining mass media status until the 19th century.

Physicists Michael Faraday (1791–1867) and James Clerk Maxwell (1831–1879) advanced the sciences of electromagnetism and electrochemistry with their separate laboratory and theoretical work, and the influences of their work led to electric lights, telephones, phonographs, radio, trains and television, and eventually to hydro-electric power plants, computers and crafts that explore the universe. Many of these inventions have fundamentally changed our global society, especially the easy public access to communication in its myriad forms. This scientific revolution, alongside the expanding population of the early 20th century, fueled conditions that would eventually lead to the supermedia we have today.

In 1912, mass media was driven mostly by the whims of the population. The mass duplication of items and, more importantly, the demand for said items continued and was encouraged to develop by shrewd businessmen. This included the many forms of printing, record pressing, film duplication and radio. The appeal for more motion pic-

Burroughs was fascinated with the role human heredity would play for a child reared by animals. This 1933 children's coloring book from Saalfield Publishing Company depicts the she-ape Kala caring for the baby John Clayton, later to be known as Tarzan of the Apes.

tures created the star system. In 1912, Lon Chaney, "The Man of a Thousand Faces," began his screen career in minor parts. Gilbert M. "Bronco Billy" Anderson, who appeared in about 60 short movies, is considered the Western film genre's first real star.

In 1912, Edgar Rice Burroughs' creative imagination strayed to ways not in keeping with his life experiences. He frequently said that

the ancient myth of Romulus and Remus first inspired him. Edgar was fascinated with the idea of the effects human heredity would play on a child reared by animals. He wanted to experiment with the idea of the mental development of a person raised by beasts but nevertheless learns to develop the mental powers of a human being. Other inspirations were the ancient Greek heroes Hercules and Odysseus.

Edgar also drew from his personal experiences with Native Americans to create his "improbable" character, including Tarzan's use of a bow and arrows, dexterity with a rope and his donning of adornments and a loincloth. He also recalled having read a story about a sailor, shipwrecked on the coast of Africa, who had been befriended by great apes.

During Edgar's teenage years, his Harvard School education had included a strong emphasis in

Burroughs drew upon his personal experiences with Native Americans to create his improbable character. Child's bow and arrow set, probably from the thirties or forties (photograph by author).

22

Greek and Latin grammar and the study of themes from ancient literature. The book *Tarzan and Tradition* by Professor of Classics Erling B. Holtsmark makes the point that Burroughs' tales were conceived and written in a manner that reflects his classical influences, placing him in the modern form of classical heroic myth.

On the eighth line of Edgar's conceptual manuscript, the first name he chooses for his protagonist appears to have been Zantar. He tried Tublat-zan (Tublat was Tarzan's foster father), but didn't like that either. Finally he came up with the name Tarzan, which in the language of the mangani (ape-like hominids) means "white skin."

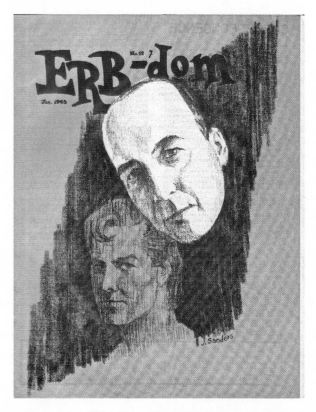

With the successful publication of two stories—especially the Tarzan tale—Burroughs eased the constraints of trying to live up to his father's expectations. The fanzine above is from January 1965, its cover symbolizing Tarzan looming in the background of Burroughs's life.

Tarzan, Jungle King of Popular Culture

After the rejection of "The Outlaw of Torn," Edgar was still dubious about his career as a writer. But his latest tale, *Tarzan of the Apes*, was enthusiastically bought by *All-Story* magazine. Editor Thomas Newell Metcalf gave it advance publicity, plugging it in the magazine as a build-up to its publication. The October 1912 issue of *All-Story* magazine contained Edgar's masterpiece, presented as a "book" marked "complete in this issue." The cover depicts an almost naked young man on the back of a raging lion, his legs locked around the body, one arm around the feline's throat and the other wielding a large knife. The man's hair is long and black, and his eyes stand out stark and fierce, like the lion's.

The artist who created the first image of Tarzan, Clinton Pettee (born in 1872), also added a man in the background who is immobile in fear, with wide, terrified and unbelieving eyes. This instantly casts the Ape-Man in the heroic role. The eyes of Pettee's Tarzan also reveal the agile mind of a seeker of knowledge. Indeed, by the end of Edgar's first Ape-Man tale, Tarzan's education has progressed: He speaks mangani, French and English. Edgar's first two Tarzan novels set the precedent of the cliffhanger ending. And, with the Ape-Man, the classical hero had returned in a modern, pop cultural form—a culmination of ancient symbolic archetypes.

Tarzan stepped out of the realms of literature, intervening in the life of Edgar Rice Burroughs to exorcise the dominating influence of Major George Tyler Burroughs. The major's satisfaction with Edgar's two published stories, especially the Tarzan tale, made Edgar feel better about the fact that he had failed to live up to his father's military expectations, and his own feelings of inferiority after having been turned down by West Point and let loose by the U.S. Cavalry because of a weak heart.

3

Letters Still Come In About "Tarzan"

The pulp magazine appearance of Tarzan prompted a flood of letters praising the tale. But *All-Story* magazine's circulation was only around 200,000. In an effort to make more money out of his latest creation, Edgar mailed packets of the *All-Story* issue with *Tarzan of the Apes* to book publishing houses. *All-Story* editor Thomas Newell Metcalf, discussing reader reaction with Edgar, told him they were already inquiring about a sequel.

In February 1913 Edgar was busy working on *The Gods of Mars*, his second John Carter tale, when his father died. Edgar was pleased that the major had had the satisfaction of sharing in his youngest son's success. The old soldier had been especially impressed by the Tarzan story. On February 28, Edgar and Emma became the parents of a third child, John Coleman. Edgar's decision to become a full-time writer, combined with a diligent work ethic, eventually produced the above-mentioned *The Gods of Mars*, one of his best novels; *The Monster Men*, a Frankensteinian science fiction adventure; and a third John Carter of Barsoom exploit, *The Warlord of Mars*.

Four months after the publication of *Tarzan of the Apes*, letters were still arriving at *All-Story* magazine in surprising numbers, praising the story and demanding a sequel. The *New York Evening World* newspaper serialized it in 46 daily installments; a typical center-page advertising illustration was accompanied by a headline such as "A Forest God Youth and a Yankee Heroine Who Met in a Primitive World."[1] The serialization made more people aware of Tarzan. Edgar was just beginning to understand the true power of his greatest creation.

To get even more exposure for his efforts, Edgar carefully watched the trends of the motion picture business, which included using 19th-century fictional literary figures as subjects for entertainment. The first Alice in Wonderland film had been released in 1903; a Sherlock Holmes movie appeared in 1909; Thomas Edison produced the first cinema version of *Frankenstein* in 1910. And in 1913, the year Edgar Rice Burroughs realized the marketing potential of Tarzan, Robert Louis Stevenson's *Dr. Jekyll and Mr. Hyde* was filmed by Universal. It starred King Baggot, generally known as "the first king of the movies."[2]

To Edgar's surprise, his next Tarzan story was turned down by *All-Story* editor Metcalf, and Edgar decided to take control of his career. He sold *The Return of Tarzan* to rival *New Story Magazine*, edited by A.L. Sessions. In this sequel to *Tarzan of the Apes*, Tarzan has been living in Paris, becomes more educated, joins the French War Ministry as a secret agent, returns to his jungle home and eventually marries Jane Porter.

Though Burroughs was a new writer, he had a sharp business sense, and now had two magazines competing for his stories. Bob Davis, chief

Burroughs' next Tarzan story was turned down by *All Story* magazine. He sold *The Return of Tarzan* (1913) to rival *New Story Magazine*. This later Armed Forces Edition dates from 1943 (Ralph Brown collection).

editor at Munsey Publications, wasn't happy about the Ape-Man sequel being published somewhere other than in *The All-Story*. He was determined this would not happen again and that meant offering more money for Edgar's stories.

While Tarzan and Jane were happily married and going to England at the end of *The Return of Tarzan*, Edgar was, as usual, hard at work. The once-rejected "The Outlaw of Torn," about a 13th-century Norman outlaw, was published in *New Story Magazine* from January through May of 1914. Edgar made more money on this sale than he would have in earlier years, and earned more out of second serial rights to his stories. He gave many interviews to the press and wrote letters to editors of newspapers on various issues, exploiting another part of the media to promote his name, literary career and his unique position, through Tarzan, in world popular culture.

When *All-Story* became a weekly and needed more stories, Edgar's imagination went into overdrive. He introduced the Pellucidar series in *At the Earth's Core*, which appeared in *All-Story Weekly* magazine from April 4 through April 25, 1914. Taking place at the center of the Earth and teeming with prehistoric monsters, most of the Pellucidar stories describe the adventures of inventor Abner Perry, his friend David Innes and Dian the Beautiful of Amoz. Meanwhile, Munsey Publications merged *All-Story Weekly* with *The Cavalier*, creating the magazine *The All-Story Cavalier Weekly*. Bob Davis, in control of this project, revitalized Edgar's interest in writing more sequels.

The third Tarzan tale, *The Beasts of Tarzan*, was published in *All-Story Cavalier Weekly* from May 16 through June 13, 1914. A fan favorite, the storyline has the Ape-Man reverting, by necessity, to his mangani, his non-human self, before re-emerging in his cultured John Clayton, Lord Greystoke, persona.

While tapping into his inexhaustible storehouse of ideas, Edgar was also a husband and father, taking the family on a train trip to San Diego, California. He also transported an automobile on the train. They stayed at the famous Hotel del Coronado for six months. Edgar was still in a working frenzy during this vacation, writing *The Mucker*, *The Girl from Farris's* and *The Lad and the Lion*.

Back home in Chicago, Edgar and Emma bought their first house; it was on Augusta Street, in a suburb of Oak Park. His outpouring of words continued for *All-Story Weekly*: the lost island adventure *The Cave Girl*; the reincarnation tale *The Eternal Lover*; the pre–World War I political thriller *The Mad King*; the second Inner-World adventure of David Innes and Dian the Beautiful *Pellucidar*; and *Thuvia, Maid of Mars*, the fourth in the Barsoom (Mars) series, but without John Carter as its protagonist.

Newspapers were serializing *Tarzan of the Apes*, resulting in its publication as a book in June 1914 by A. C. McClurg of Chicago. Above, Fred J. Arting's frontispiece for the first edition.

In an important and shrewd move, Edgar also signed up with International Press Bureau, a syndication agency that dispersed his stories to newspapers throughout the U.S. Other newspaper chains were already serializing *Tarzan of the Apes* and this resulted in more readers wanting the story in book form. *Tarzan of the Apes* was published as a book in June 1914 by A.C. McClurg of Chicago. The dust jacket, created by Fred Arting, featured a black silhouette of Tarzan against a greenish jungle background. Publisher Alexander McClurg was a local Civil War hero, and the old soldier's publishing house had its own bookstore on Wabash Avenue. Reviewers called the tale everything from extraordinary to wildly ridiculous. Yet fans had spoken and Tarzan's career as the seminal 20th-century superhero took off.

4

Tarzan Takes on a Pop Cultural Life of His Own

Determined to be in charge of his new career, Edgar Rice Burroughs negotiated important changes in the contract of his second book, *The Return of Tarzan*. For starters, he received a better advance. His profits would come to him first rather than to his agent, and he would also receive royalties from the "popular reprints" of his books by A. L. Burt Publishers. And, with an eye toward the movie industry, he insisted that all moving picture and drama rights were owned by himself.

Sweetheart Primeval, a sequel to *The Eternal Lover*, appeared in *All-Story Cavalier Weekly* in January 1915. *The Return of Tarzan*, released in book form on March 10, is noteworthy for the dust jacket art by renowned American artist N.C. Wyeth; the original painting resides in the Burroughs family archives. One of the book's inside line-drawings, the work of exalted Tarzan-Burroughs artist J. Allen St. John, has Tarzan, in immaculate gentleman's dress, roaring the victory cry of the mangani over the prone body of the count. But the Ape-Man looks stiff, like a butler with his hands out holding a tray, and exclaiming, "Oh, I say, sorry, old chap."

In May 1915, Edgar's second Inner World novel, *Pellucidar*, began running in *All-Story Cavalier Weekly*. *The Man-Eater* ran from November 15 to 20 in *The Evening World*, a New York City newspaper.

Also in 1915, D.W. Griffith's Civil War motion picture epic *The Birth of a Nation* amazed and outraged audiences. Cecil B. DeMille's *The Cheat* was another indication of the trend toward a technically better quality of films. Edgar chose the Authors Photo-Play Agency in New York to promote a motion picture sale of *Tarzan of the Apes*. He also began formulating plans for his own filmmaking company. This proposed company was an early example of his drive for self-incorporation and the later creation of his financial empire.

The Son of Tarzan appeared in *All-Story Weekly* magazine from December 4, 1915, through January 8, 1916, with the cover art of the first installment by P.J. Monahan. There is a ten-year period in this story in which the Ape-Man is living mostly in England. Given Tarzan's previous work with the French War Ministry as a secret agent (*The Return of Tarzan*), the reader can't help wondering if British Intelligence had ever utilized his skills during this ten-year hiatus from jungle life. The subject of Tarzan's status as a secret agent will arise later. But by this time in his career Edgar felt that he couldn't do anything else with the Ape-Man, and decided to stop writing the adventures. That same year, *The Beasts of Tarzan* appeared in book form with a stark, gorgeous J. Allen St. John dust jacket depicting the Ape-Man, a mangani and a sheeta (panther).

Edgar, always the family man and a lover of automobiles, took Emma, the kids and their Airedale (named Tarzan) on a vacation with intentions of driving to Maine. Their Packard Twin Six touring car was followed by a chauffeur-driven three-quarter-ton Republic truck that included a portable kitchen; this vehicle pulled a trailer with trunks, tents, bedding and even a bathtub. In Michigan, news of a polio outbreak in the East prompted Edgar and Emma to change their itinerary, and they decided to go to California again. After a change of chauffeurs, they trekked toward the Great Plains, Rocky Mountains and the deserts of the Southwest. In Missouri, Edgar made a point of visiting Hannibal, the boyhood home of Mark Twain.

Onward to California: The travelers tried crossing the Rockies near Pikes Peak and Colorado Springs, but the overloaded truck couldn't make the climb. They had to backtrack and cross over Raton Pass into New Mexico. Twenty years earlier, Edgar had been on horseback in this parched environment with the 7th U.S. Cavalry, trying to find the Apache Kid and his "gang of cutthroats."[1] In September 1916 they made it to Southern California, where Edgar moved the family into a rented house at 355 South Hoover Street in downtown Los Angeles. The more Edgar lived in Southern California extrapolating on his ideas in the form of fiction, the better he liked it. He was hooked, especially on Los Angeles itself, which he envisioned as a city of the future.

While temporally living in Los Angeles, Edgar met *Wizard of Oz* creator L. Frank Baum; during the Burroughs family's yearly stays in California, the two became good friends. Also, the November 1916 death of Jack London, one of Edgar's favorite authors, reignited an ambition that had been fermenting in his mind: to become a rancher-writer, as London himself had wanted.

Tarzan continued taking on a life of his own. Readers and editors still demanded more Ape-Man adventures despite Edgar's intention to retire him after *The Son of Tarzan*. The property was very profitable and Edgar was enticed into going to New York for business meetings with Bob Davis of Munsey Publications. Davis put on the pressure for more Tarzan. Edgar gave in to the pressure and the opportunity to make some more money. While in New York he visited the Consolidated Magazine Corporation, founded by a wealthy hat-maker who published magazines such as *The Blue Book*, *The Green Book* and *The Red Book*. There Edgar pitched some ideas that Davis hadn't liked. *Blue Book* editor Ray Long liked them. One was about an isolated biological environment and the unusual effects of evolution on the environment; this would produce a three-part *Blue Book* serial and, later, one of Edgar's best novels: *The Land That Time Forgot*. Edgar and Long also struck a deal for a series of Tarzan short stories, *New Stories of Tarzan*, which began running in *The Blue Book* in September 1916. These tales take place during Tarzan's adolescent years, before he'd met any Europeans or Americans. They are fascinating depictions of the personal lives of the ape-like hominids that adopted the baby John Clayton. The stories also reveal, in even more dramatic fashion than in *Tarzan of the Apes*, the predicament of being a human raised by animals; of being different, a member of the tribe but an outsider all the same. Many Tarzan fans (including this book's author) have stated that as a child or adolescent, they found these *Jungle Tales of Tarzan* (the book title) not to their liking, even unsettling, but as adults enjoyed the book very much.

Meanwhile, back over at the Munsey Company, *All-Story Weekly* published *Tarzan and the Jewels of Opar*, which ran from November 18 through December 16, 1916. Scholars disagree over its place in the

Tarzan book chronology; does it take place before, during or after *The Son of Tarzan*? Many fans argue that Tarzan's amnesia is his subconscious way of ridding himself of the awesome responsibilities of being the wealthy Duke of Greystoke. Others take the view that the amnesia is Edgar's subconscious way of removing Tarzan from civilization. Aaron Clayton, writing in *Global Perspectives on Tarzan: From King of the Jungle to International Icon*, wrote, "In Burroughs' second novel, *The Return of Tarzan*, the titular hero establishes himself as a gentleman financially by discovering the hidden African city of Opar. Tarzan steals a small fortune from the primitive inhabitants, who are unaware of the limitless wealth. Several novels later in *Tarzan and the Jewels of Opar*, Tarzan returns to Opar to restock his precious metals in order to reestablish his fortune after making some poor financial investments. His actions hauntingly predict the future of American colonialism whereby corporations simply extract valuable resources from third world countries to circumvent the fiscal and social costs of conquering other nations."[2]

In *Tarzan and the Jewels of Opar*, the plundering of the lost city by competing factions ends with the Ape-Man recovering his human memory and ferociously insuring that only he knows the location of Opar. Later, he and Jane spot vultures feasting nearby. Investigating, they discover the corpse of an enemy, and amidst his grisly remains they find the stolen Jewels of Opar.

Also during 1916, during the Burroughs family's Southern California stay, L. Frank Baum convinced Edgar to join a men's club, the Uplifters, that met for lunches, dinners and other activities. This elite group, founded by Baum in 1914, included influential businessmen and celebrities; for Edgar, it was a potential avenue of exploitation for his activities. Back home in Chicago, he learned of the Tribe of Tarzan Club. Headed by a boy named Herman Newman, this fan-based organization out of Staunton, Virginia, held regular meetings. Edgar made sure that Newman's club was publicized in the pages of *All-Story* magazine. The beginnings of the fandom aspect of media (the insertion of fans into the history and fabric of popular culture), rooted in the earlier Sherlock Holmes fan activities, would blossom in the U.S.

In February 1917, Germany torpedoed American shipping lanes, sinking the SS *Housatonic* in the Bay of Biscay and the SS *California* off the coast of Ireland. Two years before they had sunk the RMS *Lusitania*, also off Ireland's coast. The Zimmerman Telegram inviting Mexico to align with Germany against America raised fears of German submarine attacks on seagoing commerce. In the face of all of this (and much more), Congress declared war on Germany in April 1917.

If America was going to war, Edgar, determined as ever, would not sit by watching the action. He got reference letters from author Emerson Hough (*The Covered Wagon*) and his old schoolmaster, the formidable Charles King, now brigadier general in the Wisconsin National Guard, and the 42-year-old Edgar Rice Burroughs campaigned for a commission in the U.S. Army. On July 19 he became a captain in the Illinois Reserve Militia, Second Infantry.

Major George Tyler Burroughs would have approved.

On the 1917 business front, Edgar's friendship with L. Frank Baum and membership in the Uplifters provided the connection he needed to further promote his imaginative works. He met William Selig of the Selig Polyscope Company, who had produced a film version of Baum's first Oz story. Wheeler-dealer Edgar made a deal with Selig for a motion picture of a story slated for *All-Story Weekly* magazine, *The Lad and the Lion*.

Edgar wrote the screenplay for the movie, which starred Vivian Reed and Will Machin. The release of this film fired Edgar's enthusiasm for the movie business, and in the back of his mind he still wanted to make his own films.

Meanwhile, the series of short Tarzan tales continued in the pages of *Blue Book* magazine. *The Cave Man* (a jungle adventure sequel to *The Cave Girl*) ran in four issues of *All-Story Weekly*. The first tale in the Barsoom saga, *A Princess of Mars*, appeared in book form; A.C. McClurg, adorned with a dust jacket and illustrations by Frank E. Schoonover (1877–1972). Schoonover had studied art at Philadelphia's Drexel Institute, and his instructor was illustrator and author Howard Pyle, founder of the Brandywine School style of illustration.

And Tarzan continued his own inexorable rise in the mass-media jungle. Edgar accepted a generous offer from the National Film Corp. for a motion picture version of the first Tarzan story: A $5000 advance on royalties (a record in those days), $50,000 in company stock and five percent of the film's gross earnings. Filming took place in Louisiana

Burroughs took a generous offer for the motion picture rights to the first Tarzan story. Promotional card with Elmo Lincoln playing the Ape-Man, teaching himself to read a children's primer in the 1918 production of *Tarzan of the Apes* (Ralph Brown collection).

and Los Angeles; the movie also incorporated previously shot footage from Brazil and Peru. Young Gordon Griffith played Tarzan as a child, ex-police officer Elmo Lincoln portrayed the adult Tarzan, and Enid Markey became the first celluloid Jane. Released in January 1918, the movie *Tarzan of the Apes* became a smash hit and, despite Lincoln's "caveman" presence and lack of Tarzanic agility, was one of first films to make over a million dollars at the box office.

Three months later, the April 1918 publication of the book *Tarzan and the Jewels of Opar* featured a striking dust jacket of the Ape-Man battling a lion and eight interior halftone sepia plates by J. Allen St. John. In an early example of a continuity of popular culture, the book also included approximately 7300 words not in the magazine version, adding more ammunition for fan and scholar proponents of contro-

Tarzan of the Apes was a smash hit and was one of the first films to make over $1,000,000 at the box office. Another promotional card from 1918, with Enid Markey and Elmo Lincoln as Jane and Tarzan.

versies surrounding the story, discussed earlier. As the Ape-Man's adventures grew in popularity, inexpensive reprints of the first five Tarzan books were published by A.L. Burt. Affordable hardback reprints were the forerunners of paperbacks and book club editions. Tarzan's influence was also becoming worldwide, increasing Edgar's income. Methuen and

By 1918, Tarzan and Burroughs were both on their way to global fame. This fanzine was published some years later by writer and Burroughs scholar James Van Hise.

Tarzan, Jungle King of Popular Culture

Company Ltd. of London started their Tarzan blitz with the first three novels. The Ape-Man had created a multimedia business for Edgar: in pulp magazines, first-edition books, newspaper serializations, mass-marketed hardback reprints, foreign editions and now motion pictures. In September 1918, another Tarzan movie appeared. *The Romance of Tarzan*, also starring Elmo Lincoln and Enid Markey, had been rushed into production and released to theaters.

By 1919, Edgar and Emma had made the decision to move to Southern California. Friends from Chicago's White Paper Club hosted a farewell banquet at the La Salle Hotel. The Burroughs family took a Santa Fe train to Los Angeles, where they stayed at the Alvarado Hotel until moving into a rented house at 1729 North Wilton Avenue. Edgar spent much of his time searching for a ranch to buy. And his imagination worked overtime on what to do with Tarzan. With the book publication of *Jungle Tales of Tarzan* (the short stories which had first appeared in *Blue Book*), the six books said all that Edgar had to say on the subject. But the subject just wouldn't go away. The public demanded more.

Tarzan of the Apes had arrived upon the world stage as a growing population and advances in science created a super-media with easy access to his adventures even during times of war and cultural upheavals. Edgar was not only aware of the incredible multimedia potential of Tarzan, but that Tarzan had become a self-perpetuating, independent entity from himself. The idea, the concept, the meme (transmitters of ideas and belief information) of Tarzan of the Apes was here to stay: an instant popular culture icon in a growing American media.

5

Edgar Rice Burroughs, Inc.

The World War I–era thriller *Tarzan the Untamed* chronicles the Ape-Man's revenge for the murder of his wife Jane Clayton (the body burned beyond recognition) and many Waziri warriors. German soldiers are responsible, and the Ape-Man ferociously helps the British in their war effort. *Tarzan the Untamed* appeared in *Red Book Magazine* from March through August 1919. Anti-German propaganda of those times certainly influenced the patriotic Edgar Rice Burroughs while he was writing *Tarzan the Untamed*, and it shows in the bitter, vengeful tone of the story. Edgar knew that Tarzan was popular in the German market and asked his book publisher make changes in the text so as not to offend his readers in Germany. The book did not appear in Germany until a publishing house not connected to Edgar Rice Burroughs, Inc., found an English edition of it and released it to the German public.

This caused a backlash against Tarzan, Burroughs and his books. In a letter to the German press, Edgar apologized for his flare-up of patriotism. The letter had practically no effect. Criticisms from the German press continued, calling out for nationalistic pride. By 1925, German author Stefan Sorel had written *Tarzan der Deutschenfresser* (*Tarzan the German-Devourer*), an anti–Tarzan-Burroughs publication that outraged Germans seven years after the war. Sorel's book claimed that the Tarzan books represented stupidity, and that Burroughs was one of the basest of German-devourers living in the Anglo-Saxon countries. It took years for the situation to cool off.

Edgar's *Tarzan the Untamed* not only has the Ape-Man aiding the British against the Germans during World War I, but his connection to British Intelligence is revealed, the second in a chain of events throughout the saga indicating that John Clayton, Lord Greystoke, Tarzan of the Apes is also a secret agent.

The limb bent beneath the weight of the two

The World War I–era thriller *Tarzan the Untamed* first appeared in pulp magazine form in 1919. Above, a J. Allen St. John plate from the 1920 first edition book of *Tarzan the Untamed*, page 18, depicting a neighborly dispute over boundaries.

Meanwhile, in Southern California, Edgar was still looking for a ranch. He had his eye on Mil Flores, the 540-acre estate of the late Gen. Harrison Gray Otis, located in the San Fernando Valley foothills of the Santa Monica Mountains.

Otis, a member of the Republican National Convention responsible for the nomination of Abraham Lincoln for president, was born in Marietta, Ohio, in 1837. Joining the Union Army during the Civil War, he fought as a private in William McKinley's 23rd Ohio Infantry. Twice wounded in battle, he was promoted several times, rising to the rank of brigadier general. Otis and his wife Eliza, a poet and philanthropist, moved their family to Los Angeles in 1876. Otis bought a half-interest in the *Los Angeles Times* newspaper, becoming president and editor-in-chief.

The area that Edgar wished to buy from the Otis family was originally part of the San Fernando Valley discovered on August 5, 1769, by a military party lead by Governor Gaspar de Portola. The San Fernando Mission was founded by Spanish missionary Padre Ferminde Francisco Lasuen de Arasqueta (1736–1803). The padre had been granted an appointment as president of the California missions, replacing Junipero Serra in 1785. On September 8, 1797, the elderly father-presidente established the San Fernando Rey de Espana.

By 1810 Spain was forced to stop sending funds to the military in California because of the Hidalgo Revolution in Mexico. This began a series of events that culminated in the Treaty of Guadalupe Hidalgo. Not only did the Mexican-American War end, but the U.S. took legal control of Texas, New Mexico and California. In 1865 the San Fernando Valley Spanish land grants were bought by the Los Angeles Farming and Milling Company. By the 1870s, the mission region was turned into a wheat farm operation. The Los Angeles Suburban Homes Company, purchased the land in 1909 and Gen. Otis, an investor in the company, took control of over 500 acres. The Owens Valley Aqueduct project was later completed, supplying water to the San Fernando Valley.

On March 1, 1919, Edgar paid $125,000 for the estate. He renamed it Tarzana Ranch. Edgar had realized his dream of becoming a gentleman farmer, as his literary hero Jack London had wanted to do. Among the responsibilities associated with his new undertaking: cows, horses, goats, pigs, farm equipment, hens, bunk houses (for employees), barns, corrals, orange, lemon, apricot and walnut trees, and a house with 18 rooms and six baths. "It is really a very decent sort of dump,"[1] Edgar quipped to his old friend Bert Weston, with his usual self-deprecating sense of humor.

On March 29, 1919, the hardback book edition of *Jungle Tales of Tarzan*, with dust jacket and illustrations by J. Allen St. John, was published by A.C. McClurg. Also, the release of the first two Tarzan motion pictures renewed Edgar's ideas of forming his own motion picture production company. Other ideas for expanding the public range of his creations swirled around in his head. He had only to seize opportunities as they arose.

In May, Edgar was surprised to receive a letter from the American Jewish Congress in Washington, D.C. The Congress, "recognizing his tolerance and humanity,"[2] requested that Edgar sign a card supporting the Jewish Bill of Rights, organized to put a legal stop to discrimination against Jews. A motif of the excesses of organized religion runs through many of Edgar's novels, from the fanaticism of the Oparians and their human sacrifices in the Tarzan stories, to the First Born of the Martian series and their cannibalistic rites. Edgar readily agreed to support the American Jewish Congress, having "always been perplexed by intolerance and inhumanity that all religions—Jews, Christians, Muslims, Pagans, etc., exhibit toward each other."[3]

In August 1919, a pulp magazine character swashbuckled his way through the pages of *All-Story Weekly* magazine in a Johnston McCulley story titled *The Curse of Capistrano*. This was the world's introduction to Zorro, the Spanish aristocrat who by night becomes the masked, sword-wielding enemy of despots and the protector of downtrodden Mexican peasants. How Tarzan of the Apes fits into, and inspires, the superhero pantheon existing today begins here, in 1919, seven years after the Ape-Man's first appearance. Zorro is number two, after Tarzan, of a series of extraordinary heroes of mainstream media and, much later, the vast superhero pantheon of 20th- and 21st-century popular culture. Though no influence of Burroughs on McCulley contributed to the creation of Zorro, there are thematic, pop cultural and archetypal bindings. Both Zorro and Tarzan are of the aristocratic class, outstanding athletes (especially Tarzan), fight on behalf of the victims of evil, and use another identity. Adding to this, the ancient motif of a special weapon is a characteristic of both. Zorro's legendary swordsmanship has gotten him out of many jams. Tarzan of the Apes, as a child, discovers the knife of his dead human father, enabling him to fight and kill animals much bigger and stronger than himself; as an adult, he is like a ferocious leopard with the mind of a man.

Edgar, the family man, never neglecting Emma and their children or his activities as a gentleman farmer, was very busy during 1919. Nevertheless, his business blitz continued. The first hardback edition of *The Warlord of Mars*, published by A.C. McClurg, appeared in September. He also negotiated a movie version of *The Oakdale Affair*, based on his 1918 *Blue Book* story. Released in October, the film starred Evelyn Greeley as Edgar's adventurous heroine, another tough female character inspired by his mother, Mary Evaline Burroughs. By the end of 1919 two million copies of the books of Edgar Rice Burroughs had been sold in the U.S. Foreign sales grew, royalties in England beginning to rival the American figures.

Tarzan was clearly the catalyst of this popularity and the continuing rise of Edgar's income.

Picking up where *Tarzan the Untamed* left off, *Tarzan and the Valley of Luna* ran in *All-Story* magazine from March 20 through April 17, 1920. The Ape-Man, after many adventures involving spies, is debriefed and informed by an Intelligence officer that his wife Jane, thought to have been killed by the Germans, actually escaped their clutches. Tarzan goes off to track her down.

On April 5, 1920, Edgar's mother Mary Evaline Burroughs (born 1840), died while visiting Edgar and Emma at their Tarzana Ranch in California. Edgar loved his mother deeply but, through his grief, kept up with his attentions to family, the ranch and business endeavors. Released on April 30, the A. C. McClurg hardback book edition of *Tarzan the Untamed* featured a striking dust jacket and moody, noir-like interior illustrations by J. Allen St. John. That same year there was a 78 RPM recording by Ernie Mayne, *Tarzan of the Apes*,[4] which became a British Music Hall (vaudeville) song.

Also in 1920, another movie debuted: *The Revenge of Tarzan* starred ex-fireman Joseph C. Pohler, whose name was changed to Gene Pollar. He was offered a salary of $100 a week. Evelyn Fariss, hired to play Jane Clayton, backed out after discovering that real lions were being used on the set. Karla Schramm ended up portraying Jane; Tarzan's friend Lieutenant Paul D'Arnot was played by Franklin Coates. Theater managers nationwide were sent an Exploitation Campaign Book that included promotional suggestions and striking window display illustrations. In one, an obviously nude Ape-Man battles a lion while Jane, aghast, cowers in fear. In the film, however, Pollar, with his blocked haircut and an over-the-shoulder leopard skin, emerged as the "clean-cut" Ape-Man—not quite the image created by Burroughs. On the other hand, neither was Elmo Lincoln (in the first two movies), who was more of a "caveman" Tarzan. Writing in *The Burroughs Bulletin* periodical about *The Revenge of Tarzan,* a fan calling himself Lord Passmore of Ghenzi (Lord Passmore was a name the Ape-Man sometimes used) reported, "Actually, the film did so well at the box office that Universal offered Gene Pollar a two-year contract at $350 per week to make more Tarzan films. But the Weiss brothers at Numa Pictures got greedy and refused to let him go unless Universal paid them $800 per week (out of which they offered Pollar his customary $100). The result was that Pollar's acting career came to a screeching halt after one film, and he went back to New York City to his fireman's job where he remained until 1944, dreaming of what might have been."[5]

Besides the third celluloid adventure of Edgar's Ape-Man, there was a British theatrical production combining elements from the novels *Tarzan of the Apes* and *The Return of Tarzan.* Starring as Tarzan was Ronald Adair, who had previously been a heavyweight boxer and spent 18 years as a vaudeville performer. Ivy Carlton appeared as Jane and the apes were portrayed by actors in costume. Interestingly, the ten-year-old Tarzan was played by a young girl, Gwen Evans. A critique of the play noted that both the parts of Tarzan and Kala (the Ape-Man's foster mother) were performed well, the actor portraying Kala standing out from the rest. One can enjoy the irony of one of the two best performances in the play being given by a guy in an ape suit: Edward Sillward as Kala!

Tarzan again appeared on movie screens in 1920 in a 15-chapter serial version of *The Son of Tarzan,* another box office and critical success. The National Film Corp. had paid Edgar an enormous $20,000 plus a percentage for the rights. In the early part of the film, Tarzan and Jane's son was played by Gordon Griffith, who had been cast as the child Tarzan in the 1918 motion picture *Tarzan of the Apes*. In *The Son of Tarzan*, the role of the adult character, Korak, went to an actor from Hawaii named Kamuela Searle. He insisted on doing his own stunts, and all went well until the filming of a scene where Korak, tied to a wooden pole, is rescued and carried off to safety by an elephant. The pachyderm, frightened by the crowds and noises of the production company, slammed the pole-bound Searle to the ground. Searle, severely injured, was hospitalized. Searle's stand-in, his back to the camera, played the character in subsequent scenes. Tarzan was portrayed by P. Dempsey Tabler, an aging singer who had studied opera in Leipzig, Germany. He came off as the "stuffy" Ape-Man with his large waistline and an awful, ill-fitting toupee.

One of the literary Ape-Man's greatest adventures, *Tarzan the Terrible*, blasted through the pages of *Argosy All-Story Weekly* February through March of 1921. The hardback book edition of *Tarzan the Terrible*, released in June 1921, was adorned with an action-packed dust jacket illustration and interior plates by J. Allen St. John. Tarzan, using information given to him by British Intelligence, tracks Jane to a lost prehistoric valley. After many fantastic adventures they are reunited with their son Jack Clayton, Korak the Killer, who had been fighting on the British side during World War I.

In September, the British Tarzan stage play made its way to New York and the Broadhurst Theater on Broadway, with Ronald Adair reprising his role of the Ape-Man. The drawbacks of staging a play on this subject (including the use of real lions on stage) was reflected in American audiences' lack of support. A September 8, 1921, *New York Tribune* review noted: "The role of Tarzan laid too great a responsibility upon Ronald Adair."[6] After two epic literary adventures in a row, it was beginning to become obvious that the film and stage incarnations of the Ape-Man paled in comparison.

Continuing his disciplined writing and business schedules, Edgar wrote *The Efficiency Expert*, published in *All-Story* magazine from October 8 to 29, 1921. On the last day of October, *The Mucker* appeared in book form from A.C. McClurg, with dust jacket and illustrations by J. Allen St. John.

The next Tarzan motion picture, *The Adventures of Tarzan* (1921), heralded the return of Elmo Lincoln in the role. In his book *Kings of the Jungle*, David Fury wrote, "Elmo was draped in animal skins and looked like he was wearing a fur coat...."[7] This December release also starred Louise Lorraine as Jane, Lillian Worth as La of Opar and Maceo Bruce Sheffield as the Waziri Chief, presumably Tarzan's friend Muviro, a great character from the novels.

A series of dangerous incidents involving the use of animals during the filming of Tarzan movies had begun with the injuries to Kamuela Searle in *The Son of Tarzan*. During the filming of *The Adventures of Tarzan*, three lionesses escaped and attacked several actors, five of whom were severely mauled and then rushed to a hospital. Cameras were destroyed during the melee. Lincoln himself was later pounced on by a lion, sustaining injuries that required several weeks of recuperation.

Edgar was pleased that his 1921 domestic royalties alone were around $100,000. And Tarzan was still the foundation of his success. (In 1922, Universal Pictures, founded by Carl Laemmle, bought the film rights to Tarzan for $40,000.) Though Edgar had become weary of writing Ape-Man adventures, there was no doubt about the source of his fame and fortune. Nevertheless, his fertile imagination continued producing other works still popular with the public. *Argosy All-Story Weekly* magazine ran *The Chessmen of Mars* as a seven-part serial starting on February 18, 1922. In this tale of Barsoom, Gahan of Gathol and Tara of Helium (the daughter of John Carter and Dejah Thoris) share incredible adventures that include a giant game of chess played in an arena with gladiators fighting to the death for possession of a square.

Concerned about the destruction of the natural world in the name of progress, Edgar gave an Arbor Day ecology and conservation speech to the Uplifters business group. Arbor Day, organized by Secretary of Agriculture J. Sterling Morton in 1872, is celebrated on the last Friday of April; groups and individuals plant trees and take care of any that might need help. Also, the difficulties and dangers surrounding the use of animals in motion pictures prompted Edgar to write an article in the June issue of the magazine *Hollywood Screenland*, promoting the humane treatment of animals. *The Girl from Hollywood*, serialized in *Munsey's Magazine* from June through November of 1922, depicts the seducing allure of a nefarious subculture of Hollywood's film business.

Cocaine, alcohol, morphine addiction, adultery and murder plague the characters.

The first book appearance of *At the Earth's Core* (published by A.C. McClurg, dust jacket and illustrations by J. Allen St. John) was released on July 22, 1922. But despite Edgar's continuing success, the financial burden of owning a ranch became too great. In August he considered subdividing 50 acres of his land into business and residential lots. By September, plans to develop Tarzana into a town with its own post office were released to the public.

Again, Tarzan came to Edgar's financial rescue. The first authorized Tarzan merchandise, by New York toy manufacturers Davis & Voetsch, was only the beginning of an eventual trend that would become a Tarzan multimedia frenzy.

It is interesting to speculate whether Edgar's lack of interest in writing more Tarzan stories was the result of his belief that he had exhausted the character's potential and/or a subconscious resentment that like his father, Major Burroughs, the Ape-Man was continually getting him out of difficulties. Six months before the publication of the next story in the Tarzan saga, Edgar wrote to editor Bob Davis telling him that he was disappointed, and doubted that it was good enough. Nevertheless, Davis planned to publish the tale in the fortieth anniversary issue of *Argosy All-Story Weekly*. P. J. Monahan's cover illustration would be accompanied by the announcement **Triumphant Return of Tarzan of the Apes**.

Edgar wasn't convinced; "My readers have been too good to me to deserve another Tarzan story as rotten as this last one...."[8]

The seven-part serial *Tarzan and the Golden Lion* ran from December 9, 1922, through January 20, 1923. This science fiction Tarzan tale involves a genetic mixing of species resulting in a tribe of intelligent gorillas and their half-ape, half-human slaves. In its 400-word introduction, Edgar states: "The life of Tarzan of the Apes is symbolic of the evolution of man and the rise of civilization, during which mankind gained much in its neverending search for luxury; but not without the sacrifice of many desirable characteristics, as well as the greater part of its liberty."[9]

On January 15, 1923, Edgar held an auction, selling his livestock and farm equipment but keeping the riding horses. By March he had

In the novel *Tarzan and the Golden Lion,* the Ape-Man adopts a lion cub whose mother had been killed. The grown feline becomes his devoted companion. The cover of this Tarzan/Burroughs fanzine from 1965 is by Reed Crandall, a Will Eisner Comic Book Hall of Fame Inductee (Ralph Brown collection).

48

finally incorporated and created Edgar Rice Burroughs, Inc., to handle his enterprises and cut down on taxes. This was one of the best decisions of his life; it insures the financial security of his descendants to this day. The first book edition of *Tarzan and the Golden Lion*, published by A.C. McClurg, with dust jacket and eight interior plates by J. Allen St. John, hit the bookstores on March 24, 1923.

From May 5 through June 2, the five-part serial *The Moon Maid* appeared in *Argosy All-Story Weekly*. In this inventive tale, Earthman Julian the Fifth crash-lands his spaceship on the moon and becomes involved with the title character Nah-ee-lah, and they have fantastic adventures beneath the lunar surface. This imaginative novella would spawn two sequels; the three stories were later combined into a novel, which is considered one of Edgar's greatest works. Also, this politically and socially charged novel is epic in its scope, spanning many generations, and is an early example of the future-history subgenre of science fiction, along with Olaf Stapledon's *Last and First Men* (1930) and Isaac Asimov's Foundation series (1951–1986).

On August 10, 1923, *The Girl from Hollywood* was published as a book by the Macauley Company with the dust jacket illustrated by P.J. Monohan. On September 5, *Pellucidar*, the second Inner-World story, was released in book form by A.C. McClurg with dust jacket and interior sepia plates by J. Allen St. John. Along with his busy writing schedule and media deals, Edgar spent much of his time developing the town of Tarzana. He hired broker H.B. Currier to negotiate the sub-dividing of a portion of his land for homes; the Tarzana Tract. The announcement of sales to the public ran in newspapers on September 27, 1923.

6

The Tarzan Gravy Train

Tarzan and the Ant Men, a science fiction adventure, ran in *Argosy All-Story Weekly* from February 2 through March 15, 1924. Tarzan and Jane are grandparents in this tale, a "Tarzanic" version of Jonathan Swift's classic novel *Gulliver's Travels*. There is even a scientist who is able to shrink the giant Ape-Man down to Lilliputian size.

Returning to the business of his ranch, Edgar sold the house and 120 acres to promoters of the El Caballero Country Club. Edgar became its managing director. By June 1924, the Burroughs family had moved from the ranch to 544 South Gramercy Place, Los Angeles. That same month, another of Edgar's best stories, *The Land That Time Forgot*, was published in book form by A.C. McClurg with a striking dust jacket and four sepia plates by J. Allen St. John. The Burroughs children were growing up fast. Joan was accepted into the Marta Oatman School of the Theatre in Los Angeles; Hulbert attended Los Angeles High School, and Jack, the youngest, became a student at John Burroughs Junior High. Edgar's writing schedule continued through all of the negotiations involved with the sub-dividing of Tarzana Ranch, attentions to his family and his media concerns. A Western titled *The Bandit of Hell's Bend* ran in *Argosy All-Story Weekly* from September 13 through October 18, 1924.

With his interests in the movie picture business still strong, Edgar rented parts of his Tarzana property to various movie companies making Westerns, notably *Terrible Terry* starring William Duncan. Duncan, a producer, director, writer and actor in serials, joined American Vitagraph Studios, making $1,000,000 a year, more than Mary Pickford or Douglas Fairbanks.

September 30 marked the A.C. McClurg book publication of *Tarzan and the Ant Men*, wrap-around dust jacket and sepia frontispiece by J. Allen St. John. But the strain of Edgar's business activities plus a rift between the writer and his wife, Emma, took its toll. By December he had to be released from jury duty because of anxiety, exhaustion and heart pains caused from overwork. Edgar rallied from these health problems, and in January 1925 won the first golf tournament under lights (at two a.m.) on the El Caballero golf course. *The Moon Men*, his four-part sequel to *The Moon Maid*, ran in *All-Story Weekly* from February 21 through March 14.

Munsey editor Bob Davis then talked Edgar into donating copies of his novels to the O. Henry Memorial Library. Established in Asheville, North Carolina, in 1925, the collection was dedicated to the memory of the American writer William Sydney Porter (O. Henry), who lived from 1862 to 1910. Edgar reluctantly complied to Davis' request, saying, "I might make myself ridiculous by sending them...."[1]

The Asheville Chamber of Commerce thanked Edgar and included his set of books in the Library of American Fiction. The third floor of the renovated Pack Memorial Library in downtown Asheville now houses the O. Henry Memorial Library. Edgar was also pleased that his novels, especially the Tarzan tales, were the world's most translated books in several foreign languages. As Tarzan's popularity continued growing, Edgar was surpassing authors such as John Galsworthy.

The *Smithsonian* magazine article "Tarzan the Eternal" described the Ape-Man's impact on popular culture:

> During the mid–1920s, a strange jungle fever swept much of the world. From Japan to Iceland and Latin America, thoroughly modern citizens imagined themselves as lords of the jungle swinging from branch to branch on vines. Across the United States, tribes of children took to the trees. In Germany millions were inspired by the heroics of an Ape-Man. And throughout the Soviet Union, readers in offices, streetcars and factories devoured an American book about a boy raised by African apes. In one remote village, a group of peasants stood, mouths agape, as a soldier read them the story.[2]

Edgar had to mortgage Tarzana Ranch for $200,000 to save the failing El Caballero Country Club. Overwork brought him to the edge of collapse. But he continued selling lots while attempting to launch the Rolling Hills Golf Club near L.A., planning a new home in Beverly Hills (which didn't come to fruition), continuing his daily writing schedule, and attending to the enterprises of Edgar Rice Burroughs, Inc. With his family responsibilities and the distance widening between he and Emma, it's a wonder he didn't have a nervous breakdown.

Tarzan, Jungle King of Popular Culture

While Tarzan was rising in popularity, another character appeared who would become a member of a popular culture superhero pantheon that's also part of Tarzan's 100-plus-years history. Writer Earl Derr Biggers published *The House Without a Key*, the first Charlie Chan mystery, in 1925. The Chinese-American detective was very successful in whatever medium he appeared: books, radio, movies, comic strips, comic books, TV, even an animated Hanna-Barbera production. Following Tarzan and Zorro, Charlie Chan was the third extraordinary archetype of 20th century modern media to become a founding element in the creation of the superhero genre.

Edgar's Western *The Bandit of Hell's Bend*, published as a book in June 1925 by A. C. McClurg, included a dust jacket and one plate illustrated by Modest Stein. Born in Kovno, Russia, in 1871, Modest Fedora Aronstam immigrated to the U.S. by himself at the age of 17. He lived in a Jewish ghetto in New York's Lower East Side. After a relationship with Emma Goldman and a brush with notoriety as an anarchist, Aronstam changed his name to Stein and studied art. By 1898 he was contributing pen and ink work for many newspapers including *The New York Herald*, *The New York Sun* and *The New York World*.

And by 1925, Tarzan's adventures were published in 17 languages, and Edgar's foreign royalty checks were growing to enormous proportions. Again, the Ape-Man's worldwide popularity had come to the financial rescue, and Edgar finally got the relaxation he needed. The family left early in August on a 1400-mile camping trip to and from the Grand Canyon. Edgar celebrated his 50th birthday on September 1 in Phoenix, Arizona, before they returned home.

The third novella in the Moon trilogy, *The Red Hawk*, ran from September 5 through September 19, 1925, in *Argosy All-Story Weekly*. On October 3 the novel *The Eternal Lover*, a reincarnation fantasy about the romance between a Stone Age man and a 20th-century woman, was published by A.C. McClurg. The dust jacket and frontispiece were by J. Allen St. John. Burroughs fans and scholars consider this as one of his greatest works, along with *The Land That Time Forgot*, *The Mucker*, *The Moon Maid*, *The War Chief*, *Beyond Thirty*, *I Am a Barbarian* and the best of the Mars, Venus, Pellucidar and Tarzan books.

Tarzan's popularity has often taken bizarre forms. Examples include a horse named Tarzan which belonged to the Prince of Wales (Edward, son of King George V of the United Kingdom); the Tarzan Assault Course, an English Royal Marines training program; a phylogeny software used in the study of evolutionary relatedness; a series of Tarzan drapery-upholstery fabrics sold by Interior Mall.com; and the white stallion of movie cowboy Ken Maynard.

Maynard, born Kenneth Olin Maynard in 1895, began working for circuses and carnivals at 16. As a young man he became a rodeo performer and a trick rider for Buffalo Bill's Wild West Show. By 1923 Maynard was appearing in movies and became a cowboy star. His horse Tarzan appeared in literally dozens of movies including *The Demon Rider* (1925), *Overland Stage* (1927), *Come On, Tarzan* (1932) and *Lightning Strikes West* (1940). Edgar welcomed the publicity.

On February 6, 1926, the three Moon novellas were published as the book *The Moon Maid* by A.C. McClurg; the dust jacket and frontispiece were the work of J. Allen St. John. On the 15th of that month, Edgar signed a contract with Joseph P. Kennedy's FBO and R-C Pictures for the production of a new Ape-Man film adventure, *Tarzan and the Golden Lion*. Kennedy was father of future president of the United States, John F. Kennedy. On the family front, Joan portrayed Kathie in the school play *The Student Prince* and later played a part in *Enter Madame*. Joan met her future husband, James Pierce, at a swimming party held at the still struggling El Caballero Country Club. Pierce, a former All-American center on the Indiana Hoosiers football team, later coached high school football. One of his athletes at Glendale High School was Marion M. Morrison, known later as John Wayne. Upon meeting Pierce, Edgar became convinced that he would be the perfect celluloid Tarzan.

Hulbert and Jack (John Coleman Burroughs) attended the Los Angeles Coaching School, which offered small classes with more personalized instruction. Jack, inspired by his father's career, began writing and illustrating his own stories and created science fiction serials. He even used his father's ploy of the cliffhanger ending, entertaining other students with his to-be-continued tales. Jack, with the aid of his famous father, also learned to write poetry. The Burroughs family moved again, from Los Angeles back to Tarzana. Edgar had had a cottage built on Lot 76 of his tract and he also opened an office on Avenida Oriente.

Once settled in, he got back to business, negotiating a screen test for Joan's beau James Pierce for the part of Tarzan in the upcoming movie *Tarzan and the Golden Lion*. Pierce was soon to become the fourth motion picture Tarzan.

On September 18, 1926, A.C. McClurg published the novel *The Mad King*, a Ruritanian romance set in a country called Lutha. It borrows elements from historical Balkan countries that were coerced into taking sides during the first world war. The dust jacket and frontispiece are the work of J. Allen St. John.

In December, Edgar gave his blessings to the Edgar Rice Burroughs Club. Organized by Isaac Boorstyn, an Atlanta, Georgia, 15-year-old, the fan club included girls in its ranks. Edgar and Isaac wrote to each other, Edgar including Tarzan's (his own) views on animals. Concerning coyotes he wrote, "I could shoot them from my bedroom window, but I would much rather see them than kill them."[3] He mentioned the lily ponds he had constructed on his property to attract birds, adding: "The birds seem to quickly learn that they will not be molested."[4] He also wrote, "When I was a boy and young man, I wanted to kill things as I think most boys and young men do, but as we grow older we take more pleasure in life than death."[5]

Ed also wrote to Isaac about a boy who, lost for three days in the Mount Hood area of Oregon, drew inspiration from having read the Tarzan books. Jackie Strong didn't let himself panic, built a shelter from sticks lined with grass and survived until he was found. Edgar suggested to Isaac that young Jackie be rewarded with an honorary membership in the Edgar Rice Burroughs Club. This fan club, along with Herman Newman's Tribe of Tarzan, founded in 1916, were parts of an already existing (if not mainstream) fandom trend that would eventually grow into the vast fan organizations that flourish to this day.

In February 1927 Ashton and Florence Dearholt paid Edgar a visit to discuss the possibility of producing movies based on some of the non–Tarzan novels. Florence, born in 1904, had been an actress since 1920 and played a lead role in *The Johnstown Flood* (1926), which included Carole Lombard, Clark Gable and Gary Cooper in the cast. Ashton Dearholt (born in 1894), who sometimes acted under the name Richard Holt, was also an independent producer of Westerns in which he starred. For years, Edgar had wanted to produce his own films but the deal the Dearholts were offered by Pathe Studios for *The Mucker*, *The Outlaw of Torn* and other novels was unacceptable. The studio was willing to pay only $10,000 apiece for the rights. Nevertheless, Edgar and Emma developed a very good friendship with Ashton and Florence. Florence and Joan Burroughs were particularly close and Florence's younger brother Edgar Gilbert, a great fan and collector of Burroughs' novels, became friends with Jack. On February 19, 1927, *The Outlaw of Torn*, the second story written by Edgar back in 1912, was finally published in book form by A.C. McClurg, with a J. Allen St. John dust jacket illustration. The next day, a stock company stage production of *The Whole Town's Talking*, with Joan Burroughs in the cast, opened at the Weber Little Theatre in Ogden, Utah. Edgar and Emma attended.

The War Chief, a historical novel sympathetic to the plight of Native Americans, appeared in *Argosy All-Story Weekly* from April 16 through May 14. After a savage raid on white settlers, Apache warriors take little Andy MacDuff back to their camp. The white boy is adopted by Geronimo, renamed Shoz-Dijiji (Black Bear) and grows up hunting, fighting and eventually becoming an honored war chief. Shoz-Dijiji fights back at the white men who are invading Apache country, and would rather fight and kill than live on a reservation. He also falls in love with a white woman named Wichita Billings, and she with him, not knowing that he is actually a white man (he knows but doesn't tell her). Burroughs' experiences with Native Americans during his younger days in the U.S. Cavalry helped enhance this sensible and sensitive portrait of the last days of the Apache nation. Edgar also managed to weave an interracial love story within *The War Chief*, one of his very best stories.

The May 1927 release of the Tarzan film *Tarzan and the Golden Lion* is notable for the casting of a pre–*Frankenstein* Boris Karloff. Karloff, in black body makeup, portrays African warrior Owaza. Hired to portray the Ape-Man, Joan Burroughs' boyfriend James Pierce was the "awkward" Tarzan. Despite his athleticism, he comes off as clumsy, and the action scenes suffer. Edgar disliked the film. Karloff, who received an autographed edition of the novel from Edgar, wrote to the author thanking him for the gift. The two would cross paths again years later.

In June, Joe H. Neebe of the Detroit-based Campbell-Ewald Advertising Company visited Edgar to propose a Tarzan newspaper comic strip. Neebe's idea was to form a business called Famous Books and Plays, Inc., which would market the strip to the Hearst newspapers. By the mid–1920s William Randolph Hearst owned a national chain of 28 papers. The potential profits and publicity from this new media form of the Ape-Man appealed to Edgar. He moved his office into a Spanish-style cottage at 18354 Ventura Boulevard in the middle of July. This cottage, over 85 years later, still houses the offices of Edgar Rice Burroughs, Inc.

Edgar's sixth Mars story, *The Master Mind of Mars*, was first published in its complete form in the 1927 *Amazing Stories Annual*. The cover and ten interior illustrations are the work of Frank R. Paul. Paul, born in Vienna, Austria, is credited with influencing generations of science fiction and fantasy artists, fans and even writers such as Ray Bradbury, Forrest J Ackerman and Arthur C. Clarke. In *The Mastermind of Mars*, Earthman Ulysses Paxton is transmigrated to Mars (as with John Carter), works under the famed scientist Ras Thavas, rebels and then sets things straight in a leaping, swordfighting, superhuman manner.

Edgar was still hot on the idea of creating his own town. He came up with the August 1927 publication *The Tarzana Bulletin*; a guide to the development of the proposed town of Tarzana, it outlined the construction of new stores and office buildings. The September issue included an appeal by Edgar for the protection of wildlife. On September 15, *The War Chief* was published in book form by A.C. McClurg with the dust jacket artwork of Paul Stahr. An A.C. McClurg publishers report for the same month reported that sales of Burroughs books in the United States and the United Kingdom alone were now 6,350,000 copies.

Joan Burroughs' acting career continued with roles on stage and singing parts in films. Her acceptance by the Menard Players at the Glendale Playhouse earned her $40 a week; she worked in a different play every week, while rehearsing next week's play during the off hours. Edgar continued working hard on the development of the town of Tarzana. Residents of the Tarzana Tract petitioned for their own post office. But Tarzan, Texas, on State Highway 176 in central Martin County, beat them to the draw. The name Tarzan was chosen by postal officials; such was the incredible popularity of the Ape-Man. To this day, Tarzan, Texas is a tourist spot with a ghost town, hotel and a cotton gin.

A first edition with dust jacket of *The Tarzan Twins,* a children's book published in 1927.

Tarzan, Jungle King of Popular Culture

On October 10, 1927, *The Tarzan Twins*, written by Burroughs for children and published by Volland, appeared with the dust jacket art and 42 illustrations by Douglas Grant. *Blue Book* ran the next adult tale in the Ape-Man series, *Tarzan, Lord of the Jungle*, from December 1927 through May 1928. The title is only one of the many racial, colonial issues that have hung over the Ape-Man over the years. Tarzan fan and Burroughs Bibliophiles member Robert R. Barrett asked:

> Where in the world did you ever get the idea that Burroughs' Tarzan ever ruled the African jungle—or that he did so because his noble heritage made him a better person than the natives? Burroughs used Tarzan's noble blood and birth as a springboard to explore heritage overcoming environment. Burroughs never did refer to Tarzan, in any of the 26 novels featuring him, as King of the Jungle.... Granted there was a novel titled *Tarzan, Lord of the Jungle*, but that did not refer to Tarzan ruling a portion of the African forest—but to the fact that he discovered an ancient medieval civilization lost on the Dark Continent, and they discovered that he was of noble birth—hence the title Lord.[6]

In later Tarzan novels, Burroughs does refer to the Ape-Man as the Lord of the Jungle. But what Barrett pointed out still makes sense, as Tarzan is, indeed, an English lord who is from the jungle, and not King of the Jungle, which, again, Burroughs never implied in his stories. This is just one of the many cultural issues that would eventually arise concerning Tarzan of the Apes.

On July 2, 1928, came the announcement that Joan and movie Tarzan James Pierce were engaged to be married. Despite the unpopular prohibition against alcohol, booze was not hard to find, especially for the wealthy. But Edgar decided that Joan and James' wedding should be non-alcoholic, as he feared the breakout of drunken fights. Everything went well. Joan and Pierce were married at Tarzana Ranch near the east end of the lily ponds.

Edgar plowed on with his efforts to develop the town of Tarzana. This plan advanced on July 20 at a meeting of the Tarzana Civic League. A resolution to name the community after the Ape-Man was passed, 95 percent of the members voting in favor. The next step was the Civic League's assertive application for a post office.

While this was happening, the 15-chapter movie serial *Tarzan the Mighty*, starring Frank Merrill as the Ape-Man, began running on August 13, 1928. National gymnastics champion Merrill had been a second runner-up for the title of the World's Most Perfectly Developed

Man. He is also credited with the vine-swinging technique that would be a staple of subsequent movies. Considering the difficulties of filming the literary Tarzan's mode of travel through the trees, brachiation, the vine-swinging was the best alternative. As with the other Tarzan films, comparisons to the real Ape-Man (the literary character) left this silver screen incarnation wanting.

On the cover of this July 1967 fanzine is champion gymnast Frank Merrill, who starred as the Ape-Man in two films—*Tarzan the Mighty* (1928) and *Tarzan the Tiger* (1929).

Merrill's Ape-Man, capable of defeating lions and apes in combat, has a time of it besting a villain (Al Ferguson) in Chapter 3. Then in Chapter 7, the Ape-Man does battle with said villain and some conspirators, faring better. In Chapter 10, Merrill has another struggle with the villain before he can disarm him. These inconsistencies would plague many of the later Tarzan movies. The real Ape-Man would simply have wrenched a weapon from any villain's hand and then thrown him across the room. No sweat for a superhuman. *Tarzan the Mighty* was a box office success but Edgar disliked it, partly because a character named Mary Trevor (played by Natalie Kingston) took Jane's place as the Ape-Man's romantic interest.

Joe H. Neebe's Campbell-Ewald Advertising Company was running low on funds, and Neebe pitched Edgar the idea of turning the proposed Tarzan newspaper comic strip over to a well-established syndicate. Edgar was pleased with the artwork of Harold (Hal) Foster, and the first six strips appeared in the *London Tid-Bits* with an American release pending.

According to science fiction notable Sam Moskowitz,

> In response to constant prodding from *Blue Book* for more Tarzan, Burroughs wrote on March 21, 1928, that these days he was writing Tarzan stories only at premium rates. Like A. Conan Doyle before him with Sherlock Holmes, he had begun to tire of the character and found it increasingly difficult to come up with new situations to challenge his hero. He finally succumbed to the blandishments of the editor, and on March 21, 1928, sent in *Tarzan and the Lost Tribe*, which was changed to *Tarzan and the Lost Empire*.[7]

From October 1928 through February 1929, *Tarzan and the Lost Empire* appeared in *Blue Book*. Edgar's interest in ancient Rome (going back to his school days) served him well in this tale of a remnant of Roman colonialists discovered in the wilds of Africa by the Ape-Man.

On January 7, 1929, the American release of the daily *Tarzan* newspaper comic strip made the Ape-Man one of the first syndicated adventure strip heroes. Hal Foster, its brilliant artist, was born in 1892 in Halifax, Nova Scotia. He studied at the Chicago Academy of Fine Arts and later created and drew the famous *Prince Valiant* newspaper comic strip, which still appears in hundreds of newspapers (now illustrated by Thomas Yeates). Artist Burne Hogarth, who would later brilliantly illustrate Tarzan for the newspaper comic strips, had this to say about his predecessor:

Harold "Hal" Foster became the first Tarzan comics artist with the 1929 debut of a daily Tarzan newspaper comic-strip. In 1937, Foster created the Prince Valiant comic-strip, which still runs in hundreds of American newspapers.

Foster, of course, was the initiator of the realist, true-figure tradition. He took the anatomical figure that comes out of the Renaissance and put it into the comic strip, which is an extraordinary achievement. This kind of virtuosity had never been known. Imagine doing the human figure outside of the poses that come from art schools ... imagine that one could release the mind to think of every possible position in the universe of form and content of action. This is what Foster opened up. Not in any time in the history of the world had this happened.[8]

The third Inner-World story, *Tanar of Pellucidar,* ran in the March through August issues of *Blue Book* in 1929. Jason Gridley has invented a radio frequency called the Gridley Wave, and he catches a transmission from the center of the Earth sent by that old scientist Abner Perry. The Empire of Pellucidar, a confederation of Stone Age tribes created by Perry and David Innes, is in peril from the Korsars, pirates that even the dreaded reptilian Mahars fear. As related through the adventures of a warrior named Tanar, the Korsars also have captured David Innes and imprisoned him in a dim, grungy cell.

The next Tarzan tale, *Tarzan at the Earth's Core,* is a direct sequel to *Tanar of Pellucidar.* Published in *Blue Book* from September 1929 through March 1930, it is one of the top fan favorites of the Tarzan stories. The Ape-Man, Waziri chief Muviro and Jason Gridley lead an expedition to the center of the Earth where they have amazing adventures before releasing David Innes from prison.

Back on the outer crust of the earth, Edgar, displeased with the royalties he was earning on his books, announced that in future he would self-publish; Grosset and Dunlap would handle the reprints. He traveled to New York to negotiate a deal with the Elser and Metropolitan Service to publish the book version of *Tarzan and the Lost Empire.*

Edgar's investments in a San Fernando Valley airport and an airplane engine company called Apache Motors lost him money. He wanted to expand the family home with the idea of someday moving back to the Tarzana Ranch, yet he sent a telegram to his new publishers asking for help being placed as a war correspondent in the Russo-Chinese conflict. An incredulous reply offered no assistance. Edgar's wish to take a break from work by going into a warzone is an indication of the demands a multimedia business placed on him—but, as always, he marched on, as his father or Tarzan would have.

Grosset and Dunlap's *The Illustrated Tarzan Book No. 1* showcased

300 vibrant Hal Foster illustrations from the original *Tarzan* newspaper comic strip series, which used captions rather than word balloons. *Tarzan and the Lost Empire* made its first book appearance on September 28, 1929, via Edgar's new publisher, Metropolitan. The dust jacket and interior plate were the work of A.W. Sperry. Frank Merrill starred for a second time as the Ape-Man in *Tarzan the Tiger*, with Natalie Kingston as Jane. Released in both silent and semi-sound forms, this film contains the first audio victory cry of the mangani, also known as the Tarzan yell. It sounds like a guy who pounded his thumb with a hammer. And again, the incongruity of a character that can fight wild animals but struggles with one relatively puny human strains credibility. But Tarzan fans made it a hit.

In October 1929 the publishers of Metropolitan Service informed Edgar of renewed interest in the Tribe(s) of Tarzan Club, created in 1916. By December, he and Emma were grandparents: Joan and James had a daughter, Joanne; Edgar's upcoming Pellucidar book would be dedicated to her. In January 1930 Edgar and Emma celebrated their thirtieth wedding anniversary. During February, Edgar, an avid fan of automobiles, bought a Bugle Cord for $3790. In March he suffered severe abdominal pains, and on the 18th his brother Frank Coleman Burroughs (born 1872) died. Through grief over Frank's death, and his own health problems, Edgar soldiered on with the responsibilities of running Edgar Rice Burroughs, Inc.

From April through September *A Fighting Man of Mars* was serialized in *The Blue Book* magazine. *The Blue Book* paid him $8000 for the first serial rights. This story involves Tan Hadron's quest to rescue a princess, including encounters with the crazed cannibals of U–Gor, the six-limbed white apes, giant spiders, a mad scientist and a mad ruler with a deadly weapon that can disintegrate metal. During May, Edgar, Elser (from Metropolitan Service publishers) and Joe Neebe, now with Sound Studios Company of Detroit, worked out details on the upcoming *Tarzan* radio show. On May 29, *Tanar of Pellucidar* was published as a book by Metropolitan. In June 1930 Edgar met with MGM executives about a proposed Tarzan film.

The next superhero to grab the interest of the American public was the Shadow. A combination of Dracula, Sherlock Holmes and Zorro, this mysterious night prowler began in 1930 as an announcer on Street

& Smith's radio show *Detective Story Hour*. The Shadow is an adventurer who, like Sherlock Holmes, is a detective and assumes other identities; like Dracula he has hypnotic powers to cloud human minds, learned from Tibetan mystics; he performs Houdini-like escapes and can make himself appear to be in one place while actually being in another. The Shadow was an inspiration for later characters such as Batman—an early, important figure in the modern pop cultural pantheon of 20th and 21st century superheroes which began with Tarzan, Zorro and Charlie Chan.

Tarzan continued his invasion into the pop cultural mass media. With the publication of the latest Tarzan novel *Tarzan and the Lost Empire*, Burroughs' books passed the $8,000,000 mark. Added to his previous avenues of exploitation, the Ape-Man was up to his biceps in multimedia forms. Tarzan was a multimedia superstar before the release of the first MGM feature film.

But if Edgar thought his greatest creation had reached the pinnacle of his fame and influence on American and world culture, he had a jaw-dropping surprise coming.

7

Tarzan the Invincible

The Ape-Man took on an invasion into his territory by communist agents in the *Blue Book* magazine serial *Tarzan, Guard of the Jungle*, which ran from October 1930 through April 1931. Tarzan had been missing from the jungle for quite a while, and he reappears to lead the fight against international secret agents building an empire in Abyssinia. James Bond was still decades in the future, old boy.

The Burroughs family moved back into the original Tarzana home that had become the El Caballero Club House. Edgar and Emma now owned 30 acres, which needed to be landscaped. But Edgar's health problems caused him to have a series of operations, and again it became a struggle to keep up with the financial demands of the ranch. Luckily for Edgar, the Ape-Man, after defeating the fascist invaders in the last story, continued on his media roll. *Tarzan at the Earth's Core* made its first appearance in hardback form via Metropolitan Books. The action-packed J. Allen St. John dust jacket, depicting the Ape-Man in battle, is one of the more popular illustrations inspired by the saga.

On December 11, 1930, a post office at the Tarzana community, population around 300, was officially approved by Washington. The Tarzana post office on Ventura Boulevard opened on December 16 and Tarzana, California, officially became a registered city. As with characters of ancient lore and history such as Hercules, Romulus and Alexander the Great, Tarzan of the Apes was deified in world culture by having cities named in his honor.

In February 1931 Edgar and Emma attended the college matriculation ceremony of their youngest child Jack. And that same month, in the midst of the Great Depression, Edgar Rice Burroughs became the publisher of his own works. He hired his nephew Studley Burroughs to illustrate an upcoming Edgar Rice Burroughs, Inc., book.

On March 15, 1931, Tarzan appeared as a Sunday color newspaper comic-strip illustrated by Rex Maxon. The above Maxon print is from a United Features Syndicate series of gift pictures.

7—*Tarzan the Invincible*

On March 15, *Tarzan* appeared as a Sunday color newspaper comic strip page illustrated by Rex Maxon, and later done by Hal Foster. American newspaper comic strips date back to the late 19th Century, and by 1906 the Sunday comics concept was embraced in great numbers by adults and children alike. The "funnies" pages offered educational strips, puzzles and the adventures of favorite characters including Flash Gordon, Little Orphan Annie, Prince Valiant, Tillie the Toiler and Tarzan.

During April 1931 Edgar learned at a meeting at MGM that Irving Thalberg, the studio's "boy wonder" producer, was enthusiastic about the big-budget Tarzan project. At a second meeting Edgar submitted conditions concerning his character and then referred MGM executives to Ralph Rothmund, secretary of Edgar Rice Burroughs, Inc. By the 15th, Edgar received a $20,000 check from MGM. He was also hired as a script consultant at $1000 a week for five weeks.

In May 1931 *A Fighting Man of Mars* was published as a book by Metropolitan, with dust jacket and frontispiece by Hugh Hutton. This story, seventh in the Mars series, includes another heroic female character (and ultimately a homage to his adventurous mother Evaline): Tavia, an escaped slave is a sharp, self-reliant fighter. That same month, *The Land of Hidden Men* began running in *Blue Book*. In this story, an American finds a lost city in the Cambodia jungles and shares adventures with a jungle princess and the ghosts of the Khmers.

Meanwhile, Edgar could not help notice that the advent of sound movies had changed the way motion pictures were made, especially in technical terms. Early 1930s films such as *The Champ* (starring Wallace Beery), *City Lights* (Charlie Chaplin), *Dracula* (Bela Lugosi), *Frankenstein* (Boris Karloff), *Indiscreet* (Gloria Swanson), and *The Public Enemy* (James Cagney) are examples of popular culture raised to heights greater than they would perhaps have achieved had they been silent movies; had they not been produced at a time when technology and culture were merging into a new phase of communication. The new big-budget all-sound MGM Tarzan production would appear in the wake of other rather formidable films, including, *Dr. Jekyll and Mr. Hyde* (Fredric March), *Little Caesar* (Edward G. Robinson), *Monkey Business* (the Marx Brothers) and *Waterloo Bridge* (Mae Clarke).

Tarzan's battle against communist imperialists continued in *The*

Tarzan, Jungle King of Popular Culture

Triumph of Tarzan, which appeared in *Blue Book* from October 1931 through March 1932. Joseph Stalin is a character at the beginning of the tale, not only organizing another attempt to invade Africa but ordering a hit on Tarzan of the Apes. An interesting case of censorship occurred over this story. French writer Francis Lacassin noted,

> [T]he crater people in the French version of *Tarzan Triumphant* (*Le Triomph de Tarzan*) differ from those in the English-language version. Instead of degenerate descendants of an early Christian sect inspired by the apostle Paul, they are adherents of the cult of Goota, founded in the 7th century by an adept of the prophet Emile Le Vaillant who took refuge in Africa after his master's martyr-dom. This example of religious censorship was paralleled in the American news-paper strip version, *Tarzan and the Fire Gods*, in which the crater people are descended from followers of Alexander the Great.[1]

In *The Triumph of Tarzan*, the Ape-Man, on a mission kept secret even from his closest friends, infiltrates a country that is being invaded by the communists. He hunts for the communist agent leading the invasion and, with the help of his Waziri friends, the imperialists are defeated.

Meanwhile, Edgar Rice Burroughs, Inc., published its first book, *Tarzan the Invincible* (formally *Tarzan, Guard of the Jungle*), in November 1931. The cover and frontispiece were the work of Studley Burroughs. In early 1932, Edgar Rice Burroughs, Inc., contracted with Frederick C. Dahlquist of the American Radio Features Syndicate of Los Angeles for their Tarzan serial. The format would be a 15-minute program aired six days a week. Edgar approved of the sound effects that had been created for the upcoming show.

The Signal Oil and Gas Company contracted to be the exclusive sponsor for the West Coast states, and the radio serial was transcribed on 16-inch discs so that the show could be syndicated worldwide. In an amusing sideline that illustrates Edgar's continuing interest in science and the future, he informed Dahlquist that he was considering including the interplanetary rights for the use of Tarzan. Stating that radio rights might have seemed preposterous 20 years earlier, Edgar went on to point out that his future television rights would be very lucrative.

The Ape-Man returned in the adventure *Tarzan and the City of Gold*, a six-part serial published in *Argosy* from March through April 1932. The Ape-Man manages to get himself involved in the lost city's religious and political problems, and is pitted against their god, a human hunting lion, in a race of death.

Promotional flyer for the 1932 Tarzan radio serial, produced by Edgar Rice Burroughs, Inc., and the American Radio Features Syndicate of Los Angeles. The Signal Oil and Gas Company contracted to be the exclusive sponsor for the West Coast states.

In March 1932, MGM released their epic jungle fantasy *Tarzan the Ape-Man* starring Johnny Weissmuller and Maureen O'Sullivan. Janos Weissmuller was born in an Eastern European town, Freidorf, on June 2, 1904. His family emigrated to the U.S., traveling aboard the SS *Rotterdam* as steerage passengers and arriving at New York's Ellis

Island on January 26, 1905. The family was registered as Peter, Elisabeth and Johann Weissmuller. An avid swimmer since childhood, Johnny competed on behalf of the United States in both the 1924 Paris Olympic Games and the 1928 Amsterdam Olympics. He won five Olympic gold medals, a bronze medal and 52 United States National Championships, set 67 world records, and has the distinction of never having lost a race. He retired from swimming with an unbeaten amateur record. Weissmuller said in an interview, "Swimming changed my life. I wanted to grow up and be a part of Al Capone's gang in Chicago. But sports changed all that. Sports saved my life."[2] In another interview, he said, "Your guts get so mad when you try to fight poverty and ignorance. I told myself I'm going to get out of this neighborhood, if only because he's got a quarter and I haven't."[3]

JOHNNY WEISSMULLER
[U. S. A.]
WORLD'S CHAMPION SWIMMER

Weissmuller describes how director W.S. Van Dyke gave him the part of the Ape-Man: "I came into his office when he'd been trying out others and making them do all sorts of tests. He said that when I walked into his office I had the dumbest look on my face and that was what he was looking for."[4]

Maureen O'Sullivan was born in Boyle, County Roscommon, Ireland, on May 17, 1911. Hollywood director Frank Borzage, who was on location in Ireland filming portions of *Song o' My Heart*, cast her in a part, and then she traveled to

An avid swimmer since childhood, Johnny Weissmuller competed on behalf of the United States in the 1924 Paris Olympic Games, and the 1928 Olympics in Amsterdam, winning five gold medals.

Hollywood to complete the movie. MGM's Irving Thalberg chose her to portray Jane Parker in *Tarzan the Ape-Man.*

This film version appeared during a Tarzan merchandising spurt and was a huge international hit despite the Depression. Weissmuller's un-self-conscious charisma as the Ape-Man, aided by his lack of dramatic training, took moviegoers into the world of a feral-raised human as no Tarzan movie had done before. O'Sullivan was the perfect Jane, adventurous, sensual, resourceful, helping Weissmuller as he gropes along toward becoming a human. The influence of this first Weissmuller-O'Sullivan film still reverberates through movie history over 80 years after its release.

Edgar still had ideas about creating his own movie company and expanding the merchandizing of Tarzan food, toys, the upcoming radio program and other products. *Jungle Girl* (formally *The Land of Hidden Men*), published by Edgar Rice Burroughs, Inc., in April 1932, was the first book to feature the famous logo on the spine. The dust jacket illustration and six plates were the work of Studley Burroughs. In June, Hulbert and Jack Burroughs finished school and, with hardly a breather, Hulbert went off to the ROTC and Jack to a summer art school near Big Bear. Edgar and Emma, though still having marital problems, realized that plans for renovating the Tarzana home would be very expensive, and paid $25,000 for a Malibu house with a 40-foot ocean frontage.

While Edgar was cooking up ideas for new Tarzan media adaptations, there was a surge in popularity due to the continuing blockbuster success of MGM's *Tarzan the Ape-Man* and the

Maureen O'Sullivan was the perfect Jane—adventurous, sensual, resourceful (Ralph Brown collection).

growing merchandising of Tarzan-related items. For children there was the *Tarzan of the Apes* jigsaw puzzle, depicting Weissmuller and O'Sullivan, which sold for 15 cents. For adults, the July 1932 *Blue Book* ran a "Tarzan for President" editorial spoofing politics while announcing the Ape-Man's next adventure.

Tarzan was about to become a popular culture phenomenon in Argentina. Although the name Edgar Rice Burroughs meant very little to Argentinians in 1931, the *Critica* newspaper had begun publishing the Tarzan comic strip, creating great public interest in the Ape-Man. In 1932 the publisher, TOR of Buenos Aires, was under the editorial direction of J.C. Rovira, and among the many non–Argentinian authors represented in their translations were Edgar Allan Poe, William Shakespeare, H.G. Wells, Arthur Conan Doyle, Emile Zola and Edgar Rice Burroughs. TOR began with 12 Tarzan tales translated by Natal Rufino, and they sold out quickly. Then MGM's *Tarzan the Ape-Man* was released there, stirring up more Ape-Man madness. TOR promptly reprinted the 12 Tarzan novels and they were just as promptly snapped up by the public. TOR then released 16 titles—but only one, *Tarzan Triunfante* (*Tarzan Triumphant*), was written by Burroughs. The 15 others, written by Argentine authors, were unauthorized by Edgar Rice Burroughs, Inc. This series of pirated novels, called Truchas, started with *Tarzan en el Valle de la Muerte* (Tarzan in the Valley of Death). The huge success of these books, 30 illegal titles in 1933 alone, is hard to ascertain because the TOR business was destroyed in a fire in 1969, and the quantity of pirated Tarzan stories in 1930s Argentina is unknown.

While Tarzan continued his invasion of popular culture overseas, the Librarian Emeritus of the University of California at Berkeley, J.C. Powell, informed Edgar that his works were included in the honored Circle of Authors of the Golden State collection, sealed off from the public and intended for future California historians. Edgar was deeply appreciative of the honor. Signal Oil negotiated with Edgar Rice Burroughs, Inc., for the exclusive Tarzan radio broadcasting rights for California. Radio, growing through the 1920s, had built up an impressive audience and profit margins relied heavily on musical programs. In 1930 the first radio soap opera, *Painted Dreams*, was broadcast. Two years later Tarzan was about to adapt to another media form that would literally saturate world culture.

8

Tarzanmania

Blue Book Magazine published *Tarzan and the Leopard Men* from August 1932 through January 1933. While on a mission to destroy the dreaded Leopard Society, the Ape-Man is conked on the head during a wild storm and loses his memory. But he manages to finish his job of eradicating the murderous cult of Leopard Men, thinking that he is the spirit companion of a local warrior. The literary Ape-Man took it easy after these latest exertions (including being conked over the head twice).

On Edgar's birthday, September 1, 1932, *Tarzan Triumphant* (formally *The Triumph of Tarzan*) was published in hardback form by Edgar Rice Burroughs, Inc. The dust jacket and interior illustrations are the work of Studley Burroughs.

That same month, with great crowds and fanfare, the September 10 premiere of the Tarzan radio show took place at Hollywood's prestigious Fox Pantages Theater. The master of ceremonies was comedian Eddie Lambert, producer of radio's *Nine O'Clock Reverie*. Freeman Lang, a famous Los Angeles radio personality who had been owner of station KRLO (later known as KMPC), introduced the movie and radio personalities in attendance. Edgar gave a brief speech, and Joan and James Pierce added their comments. Johnny Weissmuller belted out his Tarzan yell. The 3000 fans invited by the Signal Oil and Gas Company were delirious with delight. Radio station KNX broadcast the three-hour show for the enjoyment of Tarzan fans unable to attend. This series was one of the first radio programs transcribed on electric-transcription discs for worldwide distribution.

The *Tarzan of the Apes* radio show was broadcast nationwide on September 12, 1932. Joan Burroughs played Jane after the third episode, and former film Tarzan James Pierce later became Tarzan. Signal Oil initiated a Tarzan radio show advertising blitz, creating the Signal Tarzan Club with membership cards, prizes, photographs and other items. Baseball teams sponsored by Signal gas stations were created by Tarzan Club members. The membership of Signal's Tarzan Club grew to 100,000. Tarzan had already been in print media for 29 years, the movies for 14, and now his adventures were being broadcast right into the homes of fans. At a time when the range and influence of radio was growing fast within American culture, Tarzan was there. Tarzan's radio shows were the first to be packaged for foreign distribution.

After the Tarzan Clubs formed, the Convention of the California PTA (in Long Beach), attended by delegates from different parts of California, were treated to Signal Oil's booth, which was dedicated to the Tarzan Club. Parents and teachers flocked to the Ape-Man's booth with and without their kids. As the membership of Signal Oil's Tarzan Club continued to rise (eventually reaching a staggering 415,000 members), Edgar came up with the Tarzan Clans of America. Six years would pass before his idea became a reality.

Edgar launched a new science fiction series when *Pirates of Venus* appeared in *Argosy* magazine from September 17 through October 22, 1932. Its heroes are Earthman Carson Napier and Duare, princess of the kingdom of Vepaja. Many Burroughs scholars and fans point out that the Thorists in the story represent Edgar's ongoing concerns about communism. *Pirates of Venus* ends in the classic Burroughs cliffhanger style, leaving you wanting more.

In January 1933, two of the most important and popular superheroes from the early 20th century emerged: a masked former Texas Ranger, the Lone Ranger, and his Native American companion Tonto. Like Sherlock Holmes and the Shadow, the Lone Ranger is an educated detective who uses disguises. Like Zorro and the Shadow before him, and the Phantom (The Ghost who Walks) and Batman after, the Lone Ranger's masked appearances and mysterious activities strike fear in criminals. Tonto, whose name in his tribe means Wild One, possesses the knowledge of the outdoors, has survival skills and can track and hunt. Similar to Tarzan, he is a wild man archetype of popular culture.

The second Venus novel, *Lost on Venus*, was serialized in *Argosy* magazine from March 4 through April 15, 1933. Edgar received $5065 for the first serial rights to this tale. Duare, daughter of the king of

Vepaja, is captured by the Thorists. Earthman Carson Napier, in love with the princess, charges to her rescue. This pop cultural hero faces beast-men, monstrous animals and more in his attempts to retrieve Duare. Burroughs weaves his concerns about communism and Nazi socialism into the narrative, and goes one step further than madman Adolf Hitler: the scientifically advanced city of Havatoo (the Aryan race).

The next superhero to make a huge impact on American culture was Doc Savage, the Man of Bronze. Lester Dent, writing under the name Kenneth Robeson, wrote most of the adventures in *Doc Savage* magazine, and said that his hero was a cross between Sherlock Holmes (scientific detective), Abraham Lincoln (benefactor of humankind) and Tarzan (muscular ability, and the surname Savage). Doc and his five friends (Watsons?) pioneered a trail of science fiction, mystery and adventure and paved the way for Indiana Jones, James Bond, Batman and Superman.

When writers took Clark Savage, Jr., and transformed him into Clark Kent, the Man of Bronze became the Man of Steel. Doc's Arctic Fortress of Solitude shows up in the Superman mythos. Pulp magazine advertisements promoted Doc Savage as a Superman, five years before the Man of Steel's comic book bow. The idea of Doc's crime lab on the 86th floor of the Empire State Building was used later for Batman's Batcave laboratory; the idea of a cave or hideout, a tradition that goes back to Zorro, Dr. Fu Manchu and the Scarlet Pimpernel, has often been used in the Batman mythos. The fancy gadgets of the Dark Knight (and James Bond) have nothing on Doc's inventions. Doc's connection to Tarzan will become more important in the context of the alternative and secret histories of pop cultural archetypes to come.

An earthquake hit Southern California on March 10, 1933, causing widespread damage throughout the area. One hundred twenty lives were lost, and it is estimated that property damage amounted to $50,000,000. During the next few days, aftershocks added to the disorder and destruction. The Burroughs family's Malibu house was spared from the devastation.

An emotional quake shook Edgar with the March 17 death of his role model General Charles King, former Michigan Military Academy commandant. In April, Edgar, Emma and the boys took a trip to Death

Valley. Two months later, Edgar was accepted into the International Mark Twain Society (established in 1923) for his outstanding contribution to American literature. This latest testimony pleased him in a way that all of the movies and radio and comic strips couldn't.

By July, Edgar was driven by overwork and the pressures of his failing marriage into taking a vacation from the family. He drove his Cord to Cochise County, Arizona, to inspect a gold mine in which he had purchased a quarter interest. This was the first vacation he took without Emma and their children.

Edgar's friend Sol Lesser, a Hollywood producer, held an option on making Tarzan movies. MGM was busy with their sequel to *Tarzan the Ape-Man* but its legal department could do nothing about Lesser's deal with Edgar. By August 1933, Lesser's film *Tarzan the Fearless* was ready for release. Signal Oil produced radio spots and trailers and even arranged for parades to announce the new movie Tarzan. Tarzan Club members in cities around the country held these parades through streets leading to theaters showing Lesser's Tarzan film.

Buster Crabbe in the starring role comes off as what mercifully could be described as the "goofy" Tarzan. This is a reflection of the script and direction, not of Buster himself. Before becoming a Hollywood actor, Crabbe, raised in Hawaii, attended the University of Southern California and in 1931 became the college's first All-American swimmer. He also competed in the 1928 and 1932 Olympic Games, winning a gold medal and a bronze medal.

Reminiscing about his stint as the Ape-Man, Buster commented, "I was comfortable with stunting. From the very first, I felt it was beneath me to let somebody else double for my stunts. All the swings, for instance, in my Tarzan serial—the worst Tarzan film ever made, by the way—were mine."[1]

Tarzan the Fearless was released in August 1933 as both a feature film and a serial. A battle of Tarzans had begun, and different actors would compete against MGM's Johnny Weissmuller. So far, Weissmuller, with only one film, was still far ahead. Crabbe would go on to portray both Flash Gordon and Buck Rogers.

After his graduation from Pomona College, Hulbert Burroughs went to Jemez Springs, New Mexico, and attended the University of New Mexico school of archaeology. Edgar and Emma, despite irrecon-

In August of 1933, Sol Lesser's non–MGM movie *Tarzan the Fearless* was heralded by fan parades produced by the Signal Oil Company. Framed original poster from the serial version of the film photographed by the author (Ralph Brown collection).

cilable differences, were happy that their children had opportunities most people couldn't afford. On September 1, 1933, Edgar's 58th birthday, the first hardback edition of *Tarzan and the City of Gold* was released by Edgar Rice Burroughs, Inc. The dust jacket and five interior plates were created by J. Allen St. John.

Ashton Dearholt, sent to Guatemala to make a movie for RKO, wrote Edgar from the jungle about them collaborating on a moviemaking expedition. Edgar liked the idea, but was now too busy being elected honorary mayor of Malibu Beach.

Tarzan and the Lion Man reveals Edgar's dissatisfaction with Hollywood's treatment of his Ape-Man: A movie company, BO Productions, is sent to the wilds of Africa to film a Tarzanic epic. *Liberty* magazine presented the story in nine parts, from November 1933 through January 1934. This tale is also a science fiction story about a mad geneticist who, through recombinant DNA experiments, has created a city of educated, talking gorillas and a horrible means of attaining immortality for himself. By this time, Tarzan's popularity had soared to the extent of his becoming listed in the unabridged Merriam-Webster New International Dictionary.

Edgar and Ashton Dearholt formed Burroughs-Tarzan Enterprises and planned to produce their own Tarzan movies starting with one made in Guatemala. On his own time, and at the age of 58, Edgar took flying lessons at Clover Field, in control of a Kinner Security low-wing monoplane. He would eventually buy a Security Airster plane. Emma and the boys, after learning of Edgar's new hobby, would also become interested in flying. The first hardback edition of *Pirates of Venus*, published by Edgar Rice Burroughs, Inc., on February 15, 1934, featured a beautifully illustrated dust jacket and interior plates by J. Allen St. John.

Various pressures had been building within Edgar over the last decade or so—financial troubles, advancing age, health, a failing marriage—and it all finally got to him. He left Emma and his home, moving into the Garden of Allah, Villa 23, in West Hollywood. The Garden of Allah was home to many movie and literary figures, including F. Scott Fitzgerald. Edgar and Florence had become very close. The Burroughs children tried unsuccessfully to convince their father that a reconciliation with Emma would solve his problems. Ashton Dearholt returned from Guatemala with actress Ula Holt, and they were good friends with Edgar and Florence Dearholt despite the Dearholts' impending divorce.

Tarzan had problems again with Germany after Adolf Hitler became chancellor. On May 10, 1933, Nazi party members burned books at universities across Germany. Among the authors censored were Burroughs, Albert Einstein, H.G. Wells and Upton Sinclair. In Berlin, an estimated 40,000 people attended the largest of these bonfires, where Joseph Goebbels spoke. In March 1934, *Tarzan of the Apes* was banned by the Berlin Film Control Board as being dangerous to Nazi principles of race consciousness, and because it could excite sadistic passion in its readers.

A month later, the long-awaited sequel to MGM's *Tarzan the Ape-Man* was released. *Tarzan and His Mate*, with Johnny Weissmuller and Maureen O'Sullivan, was better than the original. The film had taken eight months to create and was an even bigger hit, especially in overseas markets where Tarzan had already been very popular. In 2003 the National Film Registry chose this film for preservation. However, there was a negative impact on the popular image of Tarzan because of the enormous success of the first two Weissmuller-O'Sullivan films. Movies were very influential during the years before television. People who had never read the original Tarzan stories were now being treated to an uneducated, vine-swinging, yodeling impersonator. Still, there is no denying the quality of the films, Weissmuller's feral charisma, O'Sullivan's gutsy charm and their sensual chemistry. Weissmuller is often considered the definitive Tarzan by movie fans.

But ironically, as MGM was helping to create an even larger sphere of super-stardom around Tarzan, it also diverted attention away from the original source, the educated, complex, unique literary character Tarzan of the Apes. As with real people who became separate, legendary persons in their lifetimes, the media was dominating the popular perception of the Ape-Man to fit the limitations of budget, imagination and talent. To mine the vast resources of the imagination of Edgar Rice Burroughs would take, say, a major movie with a budget three times the $1,300,000 spent on *Tarzan and His Mate*.

In May 1934, the radio department of Edgar Rice Burroughs, Inc., used the studio at Hollywood's Radio Recordings to record a 39-part radio serial, *Tarzan and the Diamond of Asher*. Edgar had provided

Johhny Wiessmuller as Tarzan and as himself on a 1950s promotional card. The enormous success of the first two MGM Tarzan films and the huge popularity of Weissmuller's portrayal had a negative effect on the character, who was now seen as an uneducated, vine-swinging yodeler.

the story outline and Hulbert Burroughs worked on the series sales, touring the eastern cities presenting the program to radio stations and advertisers. Jack Burroughs graduated from Pomona College with an emphasis in art. His graduate project, a miniature saber-toothed tiger, was put on display at the Los Angeles Art Museum. By August, Edgar and Emma be-

An MGM publicity card featuring Maureen O'Sullivan. Her gutsy charm aided in the sensual chemistry between her Jane and Weissmuller's Tarzan.

80

came grandparents when Michael, a son of Joan and James Pierce, was born. On September 1, Edgar's birthday, the novel *Tarzan and the Lion Man* was published by Edgar Rice Burroughs, Inc. It included a dust jacket and interior art by J. Allen St. John. Western Publishing, under their Whitman banner, published the Big Little Book *The Story of Johnny Weissmuller: Tarzan of the Screen.* Containing photos and summaries from *Tarzan the Ape-Man* and *Tarzan and his Mate*, it's now a highly collectable item. As a result of Edgar's relationship with Western Publishing and Whitman, Tarzan appeared in Big Little Books, advertisers' giveaways, puzzles, children's hardbacks and other items.

On October 20, the *Tarzan the Fearless* Big Little Book, based on the Buster Crabbe movie, was published by Whitman, perhaps reminding the little ones that Johnny Weissmuller wasn't the only game in town. Herman Brix, who had played tackle in the 1926 Rose Bowl and won a silver medal in the 1928 Olympic Games, was chosen by Burroughs-Tarzan Enterprises to star in the next non–MGM Tarzan movie, *Tarzan in Guatemala.* Not to be upstaged by the great international success of *Tarzan and His Mate*, the Burroughs-Tarzan Enterprises film expedition sailed for location shooting in Guatemala aboard the liner *Seattle,* arriving during a great storm. They managed to set things up for the filming of their Tarzan movie with their new Ape-Man. There was a Whitman Big Little Book based on the film, along with a campaign by the Tarzan Club, and Signal Oil.

With the Ape-Man on a roll again, Edgar and Florence moved to Las Vegas to play tennis, socialize and wait until Edgar could file for a divorce. From November 1934 through April 1935, the six-part serial *Swords of Mars* ran in *Blue Book.* This blending of espionage thriller and science fiction has John Carter back as the hero; the Virginian enters the city of Zodanga, infiltrating the Guild of Assassins. There are also a couple of mad scientists, a spacecraft with a synthetic brain and an action-packed trip to the Barsoomian moon Thuria (Phobos).

On December 4, Edgar filed for divorce. Though Emma received a generous settlement, Edgar went into a deep depression about the effect the breakup had on his children. That notwithstanding, Edgar and Florence announced their intention to marry.

In early 1935, Edgar viewed the rushes of his Tarzan movie, enthusiastic over Herman Brix as the Ape-Man and the scenery. But by March

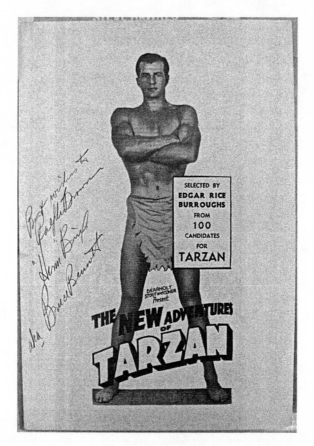

Many fans and scholars declare that Herman Brix, given the chance of better quality films, would have been the best of the movie Tarzans. He signed this item under his later name of Bruce Bennett (Ralph Brown collection).

it was revealed that there were problems, especially with the sound quality. Edgar was disappointed with what was being filmed in Guatemala.

On April 4, Edgar and Florence were married and they whizzed off on a 40-day honeymoon at the Royal Hawaiian in Honolulu. Edgar took surfing lessons. The newlyweds later settled in Beverly Hills with Florence's children Lee, six, and Caryl Lee, four; the kids adored Edgar.

Pleasure Books published *The New Adventures of Tarzan Pop-Up*, based on the upcoming Herman Brix Tarzan movie. On September 7, 1935, *Tarzan and the Leopard Men* appeared in hardback, published by Edgar Rice Burroughs, Inc., with a J. Allen St. John dust jacket (one of his best) and interior art. In *Tarzan and the Immortal Men*, which ran in *Blue Book* from October 1935 through March 1936, Tarzan and Jane discover an elixir that enables them to become immortal, thus setting up a continuity that will allow the couple to adapt seamlessly into late 20th and 21st century popular culture.

Also in October 1935, the 12-chapter serial *The New Adventures of Tarzan* was released. Brix was the first serious contender for the place Johnny Weissmuller holds as the most popular film Tarzan. Many fans and Tarzan scholars feel that Brix, given the chance in better quality films, and playing the educated Ape-Man as he did in the serial, would have been the best of the movie Tarzans. By January 1936, Edgar's movie company had serious money problems. Their release of several films, including *Drag-Net*, a suspense thriller, and *The Phantom of Santa Fe*, a Zorro-like Western, didn't turn the profits needed to sustain Burroughs-Tarzan Enterprises. But the Burroughs literary machinery plowed on. *Swords of Mars* made its first hardback appearance on February 15, 1936, with dust jacket and illustrations by J. Allen St. John.

On February 17, 1936, *The Phantom* comic strip began. Created by Lee Falk, this fabulous character originated in Falk's attraction to myths and legends and to the modern heroes Tarzan and Zorro. A mysterious jungle dweller who has fought piracy for six centuries, the Phantom was the first superhero to wear a skintight costume that became popular with later comic book heroes. Each Phantom raises his son to replace him, thus perpetuating the illusion of the centuries-old Ghost Who Walks. A very important early precursor of the superheroes now crowding the pop culture world, the Phantom is the last of the seminal 20th century superhero archetypes. The next group of heroes would consist of characters borrowing and extrapolating on elements of the original eight: Tarzan, Zorro, Charlie Chan, the Shadow, the Lone Ranger, Tonto, Doc Savage, and the Phantom. This next group of heroes would start a revolution in comic books and popular culture, and Tarzan, as always, would easily adapt.

During 1936, Whitman Publishing produced an edition of Edgar's children's story *Tarzan and the Tarzan Twins, with Jad-bal-ja, the Golden Lion*, which included 153 illustrations by Juanita Bennett. *Tarzan's Quest* (formally *Tarzan and the Immortal Men*) appeared on September 1,

1936, Edgar's sixty-first birthday, and was the last Burroughs book title with J. Allen St. John artwork. John Coleman (Jack) Burroughs would illustrate future Edgar Rice Burroughs, Inc., books.

A paranormal Tarzan story, the three-part serial *Tarzan and the Magic Men* was published in *Argosy Weekly* from September through October of 1936. Tarzan is on one of his espionage missions investigating, for Ethiopia's emperor Haile Selassie the infiltration of spies into African tribes. He is temporarily sidetracked by the activities of two sorcerers, twins who possess mind control and telepathic powers. As if these paranormal elements weren't enough, we find out that Tarzan has been investigating the extraordinary powers of witch doctors, sorcerers themselves.

No supernatural spell was needed to continue the public's adoration of Tarzan, and merchandising continued at a nonstop pace. Joseph Schneider, Inc., distributed a *Tarzan Target Game*. Whitman Publishing issued *Tarzan Ice Cream Cup* premiums for prizes. *New Tarzan Bread* promised to keep you well and strong. And there were radios, yo-yos, jewelry, toys, color-scopes and chewing gum. MGM's two films ignited cultural interest that surpassed the popular reaction to the first Tarzan movies of 1918. MGM's films, Tarzan's radio adventures and the comic strips combined with the merchandising frenzy. Added to this were the Ape-Man's pre-existing media forms (pulp magazines, books, etc.). Tarzan was incredibly popular worldwide.

As with mythological archetypes of ancient times, Tarzan, by transcending his cultural origins, became several distinct characters, depending upon the media form: feral Ape-Man of novels; stoic jungle policeman of juvenile literature; inarticulate vine-swinger of film; moody adventurer of the comic strips; stolid gentleman of the radio. In an interesting mythological similarity, Hinduism has characters that have hundreds of other manifestations. Burroughs, one of the first 20th-century artists to incorporate, was a business genius who personally took control of his career by promoting and merchandising his most successful creation. Long before Walt Disney mass-marketed Mickey Mouse, Burroughs was a pioneer of the concept that would become known as multimedia. He was warned that the different adaptations would compete against one another, saturating the market until interest in the Ape-Man waned.

9

Tarzan as Folk Hero

The November 1936 release of MGM's third Tarzan, *Tarzan Escapes*, cashed in on Tarzanmania merchandising. There was a Big Little Book of *Tarzan Escapes* which now goes for as much as $200 on the collectibles market. A two-piece, die-cut advertisement for the movie was designed as a mobile; they now go for as much as $2000. The film itself was a comedy of production problems, including the usual dangers of working with animals, plus cast, crew and director replacements. There were also censorship issues involving a climactic scene, wherein Tarzan and the African porters fight giant vampire bats. Preview audiences, especially children, were shocked at the horrific ending, which had the creatures carrying off screaming men.

When parents and media critics pressured MGM, the vampire bats were removed. The reshooting of the movie involved the insertion of scenes from the previous films and this, combined with the censorship, diluted what Tarzan fans feel could have been one of the very best movies. Nevertheless, *Tarzan Escapes* was a worldwide success and Johnny Weissmuller's Ape-Man, still inarticulate though intelligent, ruled the silver-screen jungle over both Buster Crabbe and Herman Brix, whose films were being recycled through the second-run movie houses.

Meanwhile, back in the center of the Earth, Edgar's fifth Pellucidar tale, *Seven Worlds to Conquer*, ran in *Argosy* from January 9 through February 13, 1937. It continues the adventures of Wilheim von Horst: Lost in Pellucidar after saber-tooth tigers separated members of the expedition in *Tarzan at the Earth's Core*, von Horst meets and falls in love with the maiden La-ja of Lo-har. He also has adventures involving Mammoth Men, the Gorbuses (cannibalistic albinos) and savage prehistoric animals, including a Trodon (pterodactyl) that carries him off

A production photograph from MGM's third Tarzan motion picture, *Tarzan Escapes* (1936), signed by Maureen O'Sullivan.

and leaves him poisoned and paralyzed with other living larder for its future hatchlings.

In February of the same year, the first Edgar Rice Burroughs, Inc., book with the art of John Coleman Burroughs contained both *The Oakdale Affair* and *The Rider*. Using his wife Jane Ralston and his brother-in-law James Pierce as models, Jack painted the original dust jacket illustration on a 30" × 50" canvas. He had previously worked with Bob Clampett (*Looney Tunes, Beany and Cecil*) on a proposed *John Carter of Mars* project, and would become another important artist in Tarzan-Burroughs history, proving himself as more than an artist of considerable merit.

Also in February 1937, *Argosy* published Edgar's short story *The Resurrection of Jimber Jaw*, about a Stone Age man revived by scientists and thrust into a crazy modern world. This motif later appeared in a 1958 Isaac Asimov short story, *The Ugly Little Boy*, in which a *Homo neanderthalensis* child is transported to the future. (Robert Silverberg expanded this tale into a novel in 1992.) In Philip José Farmer's literary mini-saga *Empire of the Nine*, members of a Stone Age secret society find the formula for extending their lifetimes over thousands of years. Motion pictures such as *Return of the Ape-Man* (1944), *Dinosaurus!* (1960), *Iceman* (1984), *Encino Man* (1991) and *The Man from Earth* (2007) explored this motif in different ways.

On May 2, 1937, Hal Foster's last *Tarzan* Sunday color newspaper comic strip page appeared. Foster went on to write and illustrate his own new strip, *Prince Valiant*, which became very popular and influential, and is still in hundreds of newspapers (now illustrated by Thomas Yeates). On May 9, Burne Hogarth's first *Tarzan* Sunday color newspaper page debuted. Hogarth is another important artist in Tarzan's century-long history. Born in Chicago in 1911, he grew up with an innate artistic talent and by his twelfth year was admitted into the Art Institute of Chicago. Before the *Tarzan* assignment, he was drawing for King Features Syndicate's *Pieces of Eight* newspaper pirate strip.

Hogarth was also an art educator, theoretician and the author-illustrator of a series of influential books on art anatomy. He once said of his stark, art-leaping-off-of-the-page expressionist style:

> I have never in my life done anything, from early influences on, that did not have some expressionistic drive. I recall at art school, in my early teens, the teacher would ask us to do a figure. I was always seeking to change it, to create a new variant of the pose. The instructor and I would get into discussions about it; I would say, "Well, if you didn't have to see the Mona Lisa, how would you know it's right?"[1]

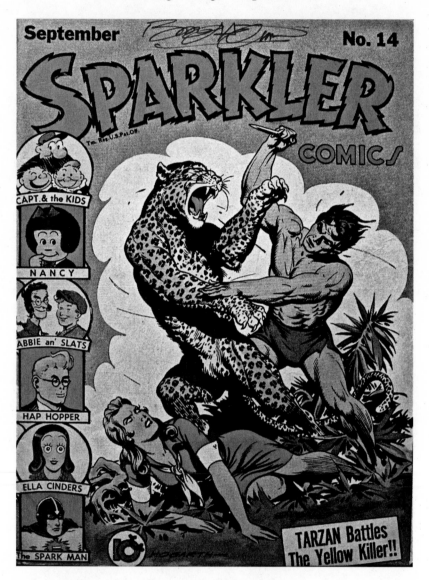

After the appearance of comic-books in the early thirties, newspaper comic-strips, including those of Burne Hogarth, were reprinted in the pages of titles such as *Sparkler* and *Tip Top*. This copy is signed by Hogarth.

Edgar's Pellucidar tale *Seven Worlds to Conquer* made its hardback book debut on September 15 with the new title *Back to the Stone Age.* John Coleman Burroughs' dust jacket and interior art are vibrant, fluid-in-motion depictions of life in Edgar's Stone Age inner-world. The wraparound dust jacket is a stunner: a hideous reptile-bird monster is carrying off an expedition member. Some of John's artistic influences were Nicolai Ivanovich Fechin (1881–1955), the Russian-American artist whose works included his famed paintings of Native Americans; landscape painter Walter Elmer Schofield (1867–1944); J. Allen St. John; and his own father, Edgar Rice Burroughs.

An interesting Tarzan meme arose because Hollywood actress Colleen Moore had a *Fairy Castle* collection at the Museum of Science and Industry in Chicago. She asked Edgar for an autograph to add to the display. Edgar and his son John Coleman Burroughs produced an illustrated miniature book titled *Tarzan, Jr.*

Part two of *Tarzan and the Magic Men, Tarzan and the Elephant Men,* ran in *Blue Book of Fiction and Adventure* magazine from November 1937 through January 1938, continuing the Ape-Man's paranormal adventures. The completion of his mission for Ethiopian emperor Haile Selassie includes Tarzan's warning to a journalist that he can never write an account of their adventures.

The next story of Carson Napier and Duare, *Carson of Venus,* was serialized in *Argosy* from January 8 through February 12, 1938. This story, written four years before American's entrance into World War II, is a satirical anti–Nazi political spy thriller in the form of a science fiction adventure. Carson Napier risks his life against man-beasts, sea monsters and an evil tyrant to rescue his beloved Duare the princess and her father the king. The Nazis appear in the form of a fascist organization, the Zani (an anagram of Nazi). They are led by the abovementioned tyrant, Mephis (with the phrase "Maltu Mephis" replacing "Heil Hitler"); Heinrich Himmler is satirized in the form of a character named Spehon, and Benito Mussolini is renamed Muso. Meanwhile, back in Hollywood, Edgar was interviewed on radio KFWB on January 23.

After Edgar's movie producer friend Sol Lesser had success with *Tarzan the Fearless,* he decided "Why not?" and did it again. Glenn Morris, a 1936 Berlin Olympics decathlon gold medal winner, was chosen to play the next Tarzan. Lesser got Edgar and Whitman Publishers to participate in his ad campaign with a *Tarzan's Revenge* Big Little Book. It contains 207 interior illustrations by Juanita Bennett.

Unfortunately, Morris's striking resemblance to Harpo Marx, the zaniest Marx Brother of them all, didn't help matters much, and the reviews of his performance as the Ape-Man were scathing. Adding insult to injury, at a Hollywood party, Johnny Weissmuller's wife Lupe Velez kicked Morris in the shins and shouted that her Johnny was the one and only Tarzan. Morris soon left Hollywood and became an insurance agent. *Tarzan's Revenge* was financially successful, but it (and the other two non–MGM films) made nowhere near the money MGM was pulling in.

Films past their first-run status still made money by circulation through second-run movie theaters. Many of these theaters thrived in urban downtown areas and played as many as three movies a day, changing programs every two or three days a week. Tarzan was now represented in four contemporary motion picture forms: Johnny Weissmuller, Herman Brix, Buster Crabbe and Glenn Morris.

Argosy Weekly ran the six-part serial *The Red Star of Tarzan* from March through April 1938. Tarzan's old friend Navy Commander Captain Paul D'Arnot enlists the talents of his friend in finding a missing member of an aristocratic family. They have adventures involving an underwater city, political upheaval and monstrous reptiles.

Back in Movieland, episodes of Burroughs-Tarzan Enterprises' four-hour *New Adventures of*

Publicity photograph for Sol Lesser's second Tarzan film, *Tarzan's Revenge* (1938). The decathlon gold medalist at the 1936 Berlin Olympics, Glenn Morris, was chosen as the next contender for the title of top Tarzan of cinema.

Tarzan serial were edited into a feature titled *Tarzan and the Green Goddess*, released in May 1938. Edgar was still frustrated over the movie versions of his Ape-Man. At age 63, he had a double hernia operation.

The June 1938 issue of DC Comics' *Action Comics* introduced one of the most important and popular archetypes in popular culture: an orphan from the planet Krypton, Kal-El, more popularly known as Superman. The name Superman was previously used in pulp magazine advertisements describing Doc Savage, the Man of Bronze. As with thousands of years of mythic archetypes transforming and combining into newer forms, many elements from the Sherlock Holmes and Tarzan sagas led to the creation of Doc Savage. The Doc Savage saga contributed to core elements of the Superman legend: the first name Clark, the Man of Bronze (Steel) sobriquet, the Arctic Fortress of Solitude. As for the choice of Clark Kent's surname: Did the real name of the Shadow, Kent Allard, come to mind?

Another influence was Tarzan. Superman's creators Jerry Siegel and Joe Shuster were great Ape-Man fans and took his unusual strength to even more improbable heights. Also, Edgar's Mars stories paved the way for the idea of going to another planet, and due to the planet's lesser gravity and other conditions, becoming a superman. The superhero genre had grown up following Tarzan's 1912 creation, and with the appearance of Superman 26 years later, a comic books renaissance would eventually embed superheroes into American culture.

On September 15, Edgar Rice Burroughs, Inc., released the first hardback edition of *Tarzan and the Forbidden City* (formally *The Red Star of Tarzan*) with dust jacket and illustrations by John Coleman Burroughs. Edgar's ninth Barsoom tale, *Synthetic Men of Mars*, appeared in *Argosy* from January 7 through February 11, 1939. This story deals with the dangers of genetic engineering and cloning, decades before our 21st century concerns. The book version of *Carson of Venus* appeared on February 15, 1939, with a striking John Coleman Burroughs dust jacket and several plates of imaginative illustrations with an ancient mythological, fairy-tale quality. By May, Edgar had produced a 32-page booklet titled *Official Guide of the Tarzan Clans of America* and revived the Tarzan Clans of America. Edgar mailed out membership circulars in an all-out promotional blitz and by June there was a Canadian branch of the Tarzan Clans.

Tarzan, Jungle King of Popular Culture

The next great 20th century superhero archetype was Batman, who first appeared in the May 1939 issue of DC Comics' *Detective Comics*. Wealthy heir Bruce Wayne trains himself to become a physical and intellectual superhuman (as with Doc Savage) and an excellent detective and devotes his life to fighting crime. Batman is a comic book version of the Shadow, who was rooted in a tough noir tradition. Batman co-creator Bob Kane cited pulp magazines, comic strips, 1930s movies and Zorro as his influences. Bill Finger got his ideas from Sherlock Holmes (detective), the Shadow (masked, caped avenger), and Doc Savage (scientist adventurer). Batman is another monumentally important archetype of modern popular culture, and the huge success of the *Batman*, *Superman* and *Wonder Woman* comic books, movies and spin-off merchandise raised the level of public awareness in the perception of popular culture; a growing awareness of popular culture as possessing attributes comparable to the classics.

In 1939, MGM went to work on *Tarzan Finds a Son!* Maureen O'Sullivan wanted to leave the series and so, in an early script, Jane was killed at the end. The backlash from fans, and Edgar's threat to sue, caused MGM to offer O'Sullivan a raise if she would stay with the series. Five-year-old Johnny Sheffield played Tarzan and Jane's adopted son, Boy. Boy had to be adopted because the Hays Code, the industry censors, wouldn't allow a child born out of wedlock. Unlike the literary saga, the MGM movie series portrayed an unmarried Tarzan and Jane.

Production photograph of Big John and Little John, signed later in life by Johnny ("John") Sheffield. Five-year-old Sheffield played Boy, the adopted son of Tarzan and Jane—adopted because the censors wouldn't allow a child born out of wedlock.

In July 1939, *The Scientists Revolt*, one of Edgar's shorter works, appeared in *Fantastic Adventures* magazine with four interior illustrations by Julian S. Krupa. Krupa, an artist and violinist, did covers and interior pages for many pulp magazines, including *Amazing Stories*, *Fantastic* and *Thrilling Wonder Stories*. The *Scientists Revolt* narrator describes how Europe had collapsed, and through a social uproar and scientific progress order is restored.

On September 1, 1939, Edgar turned 64, Germany invaded Poland, and declarations of war on Germany began World War II. Edgar hoped that the U.S. wouldn't get "dragged into Hitler's private war."[2]

The Ape-Man was still riding the Tarzanmania wave. *Tarzan Finds a Son!* (1939) was another smash hit worldwide. The addition of the adopted son began a trend of removing some of the sensuality and rougher edges from the series. This fourth MGM production was a movie for the whole family, unlike the first two films *Tarzan the Ape-Man* and *Tarzan and His Mate* which had more action and violence, and raw steaming sensuality between Weissmuller and O'Sullivan as the jungle lovers. And there was no doubt who the favorite motion picture Tarzan was: Johnny Weissmuller. Edgar's new Tarzan Clans newsletter was even headed with: *Johnny Weissmuller, Chief of Chiefs.*

Whitman Publishing's Big Little Book of *The Son of Tarzan* was released on September 21. Four days later, *Tarzan the Magnificent* was published by Edgar Rice Burroughs, Inc., with dust jacket and interior illustrations by John Coleman Burroughs. It was comprised of two separate paranormal pulp magazine tales, *Tarzan and the Magic Men* and *Tarzan and the Elephant Men*.

On October 17, 1939, Cab Calloway recorded the song "Tarzan of Harlem" on his album *Are You Hep to the Jive?* The next day, the radio program *Texaco Star Theater* had Edgar as a guest as Ken Murray unveiled his production of *The Home Life of Mr. and Mrs. Tarzan, or, The Apes of Wrath.* Edgar impressed everyone with his professionalism and the ease with which he performed.

Edgar was concerned about business, as the war in Europe had caused a slowdown of revenue. Yet Tarzan in all forms continued to prosper. Parker Brothers became the 26th company licensed to manufacturing Tarzan items. The movie series seemed as if it could go on forever. The Sunday color comic strip page by Burne Hogarth, com-

Maureen O'Sullivan, Johnny Weissmuller, and Johnny Sheffield as Jane, Tarzan and Boy. The addition of Boy in *Tarzan Finds a Son* removed some of the sensuality and rougher edges from the series.

bining a classic expressionistic look within the fantasy of Tarzan's world, was considered art. The fan clubs grew.

And so did the war in Europe.

On January 21, 1940, Edgar's brother Harry, born in 1868, died while at his daughter's home. But through health problems and personal trials Edgar continued working. *Tarzan and the Madman* was begun at this time; Jack Burroughs recorded Edgar on a Burroughs Dictaphone wax cylinder dictating part of the novel. The first hardback edition of *Synthetic Men of Mars,* with dust jacket and illustrations by John Coleman Burroughs, was released on February 15. That March, April and May, *Thrilling Adventures* serialized Edgar's western *The Terrible Tenderfoot.* In this story, Deputy Sheriff Buck Mason, accused of murder and kidnaping, comes out slugging.

The April 1940 *Blue Book* featured the short story *Tarzan and the Champion.* The heavyweight boxing champion of the world, vacationing in Africa, throws his weight around one time too many in the wrong neighborhood. Tarzan swiftly defeats the champion in a display of speed, strength and ferocity. The Americans are then kicked out and warned never to return.

Despite tension in his second marriage, Edgar put Florence, Lee, Caryl Lee, a maid and a Packard sedan on board the S. S. *Matsonia* bound for Hawaii on April 18, 1940. He followed almost a week later, arriving on the S.S. *Monterey,* and then rented a house at Kalama. Edgar and Florence were very social by nature, and though they were a couple drifting apart, they made friends with film editor Hal Thompson and his actress wife Rochelle Hudson. By May 1 Edgar was in fine form. He introduced the new Tarzan radio series, which debuted on the Hawaiian station KGU. During the broadcast, he stated that his Mars stories would also be aired soon. He joked that they would not stampede the public with an invasion scare as Orson Welles had done with his 1938 Mercury Theater adaptation of H.G. Wells' novel *The War of the Worlds.*

On May 7, Edgar drove with the family to Pearl Harbor, where they were denied entrance. When Edgar identified himself, a Marine sergeant secured authority from the captain of the yard, who assigned a corporal to show them around. Later, the captain of the naval vessel *California* invited Edgar on a tour at Pearl Harbor's famous Battleship Row. Edgar and Florence mixed well with the top military brass, who were in awe of Edgar. But the military presence in the area around Kalama was a clear reminder that for years there had existed an alleged conspiracy by Issei (first generation immigrants born in Japan) and Nisei (second generation born in Hawaii) to Japanize Hawaii. Despite Hawaii's heavy American military presence, widespread fears of an attack gripped the populace. Edgar, unconvinced, wrote to his brother George, describing Oahu as a great island-fortress.

In June 1940 *Tarzan and the Jungle Murders*, an espionage tale, appeared in *Thrilling Adventures*. Spies steal documents concerning a new weapon to be used in the war, and Tarzan and a British military commander foil their plans. As if stressing the espionage aspect of this story over the Tarzan aspect, Edgar's original title was *Murder in the Jungle*.

The September 15, 1940, release of *The Deputy Sheriff of Comanche*

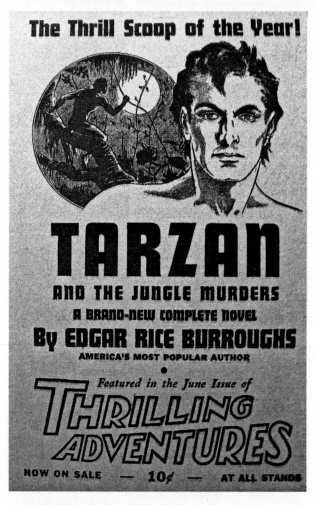

"Tarzan and the Jungle Murders," an espionage tale, appeared in the June 1940 issue of *Thrilling Adventures* magazine.

County (*The Terrible Tenderfoot*) was the last Burroughs book to appear until 1944 because of the wartime paper shortage. By early 1941 *John Carter and the Giant of Mars* (written by John Coleman Burroughs with Edgar's help) appeared in *Amazing Stories* magazine. Jack also illustrated the John Carter of Mars Sunday newspaper comic strip page and did many Big Little Book covers. Jack eventually produced over 125 illustrations for his father's works.

Edgar's next Venus story, *Slaves of the Fish Men*, premiered in the March issue of *Fantastic Adventures*: Earthman Carson Napier and Amtorian (Venusian) Duare share adventures and escapes in a land of amphibious beings led by the tyrannical King Tyros the Bloody. Also, the John Carter adventures continued with *The City of Mummies*, which appeared in the March 1941 *Amazing Stories*.

The end of Edgar and Florence's marriage was laced with her fear of the growing Japanese threat. Florence left Hawaii. Edgar suffered a slight stroke while sleeping but trudged on. In June, *Black Pirates of Barsoom* appeared in *Amazing Stories*. Edgar then checked into a hospital because of a bladder problem. Meanwhile, he was being sued for divorce by Florence. He also was planning to build a house in Tarzana. The July 1941 issue of *Fantastic Adventures* featured another story of Carson Napier and Duare on Venus, *Goddess of Fire*. John Carter was back in the August *Amazing Stories* tale *Yellow Men of Mars*.

The man just never stopped.

From August 23 through September 6, *Argosy* featured the serial *The Quest of Tarzan*. Each of the three installments had an interior illustration by Virgil Finlay, one of the master artists of pulp magazine era fantasy and science fiction. Tarzan helps a company of shipwrecked sailors, passengers and animals on a Pacific island, finds a lost Mayan outpost and is mistaken by a young Mayan woman for the god Che, Lord Forest.

In October 1941, John Carter was swashbuckling his way through the pages of *Amazing Stories* in Edgar's *Invisible Men of Mars*. Edgar had quit smoking and drinking, got himself down to about 183 pounds, and he and son Hulbert played paddle tennis in the afternoons. "Hully" wrote a letter to his brother Jack remarking on their father's physical recovery. Then it was back to Venus: The November issue of *Fantastic Adventures* presented, *The Living Dead*.

On December 7 at 7:55 a.m., Edgar and Hulbert were, as usual, on the hotel tennis court. They had a view of the coast that extended from Diamond Head to Barbers Point. They heard distant sounds of firing and saw bomb bursts over Pearl Harbor and Hickam Field. Assuming that a military practice exercise was taking place, father and son continued their game. Told by a man that the Japanese had attacked, Edgar and Hully passed this off as a rumor. A supply ship offshore near the hotel was almost hit, and the explosion rocked them to their senses.

A radio call for able-bodied men to enlist for duty prompted Edgar, Hulbert and a friend named Anton Rost to volunteer. They were sworn in, stationed at the wharf warehouse and assigned sentry duty (armed with Springfield rifles) at the Honolulu Tuna Packers Ltd., with Patrol 2, Company A, 1st Battalion. Edgar later received reassignment as a guard and then as an escort of enemy aliens (Japanese) to the Immigration Station. The march to escort an enemy-alien to the Station could sometimes be long and strenuous. Edgar felt like the first hike had almost killed him, but his indomitable will would rally one more time for the adventures to come.

Like his father, Major George Tyler Burroughs, and Tarzan of the Apes, Edgar would never give up.

10

Edgar's Epic Adventures

Edgar was summoned to General Headquarters by Brigadier General Kendall Fielder, chief of intelligence under the commanding general of the Army in Hawaii. Fielder also was responsible for security and censorship. He asked Edgar to write a daily column to be printed in local newspapers and through the press services. Fielder hoped it would boost civilian morale. At his office, Edgar composed the first column, and dashed back to General Headquarters with it in the afternoon. It was broadcast that evening over radio KSU and KGMB, Honolulu. On December 13, 1941, the newspaper *Honolulu Advertiser* began running Edgar's column, titled *Laugh It Off*. The first in his series of humorous war-related articles included praise for the Filipinos at Kewalo Basin and the Red Cross girls. The *Star-Bulletin* newspaper carried Edgar's column concurrent with the *Honolulu Advertiser* for a while, and eventually secured exclusive rights.

When Edgar brought the second column to Gen. Fielder's office, he was presented with a War Correspondent identification card and a green arm brassard with a red C. At age 66, Edgar became one of World War II's oldest war correspondents. Edgar was extremely proud of this accomplishment. Whether he thought about it or not, over the years Edgar had turned himself into a celebrity apart from Tarzan. His war correspondent status left no doubt in his mind that he could hold his own in the real world even against old age, and that more formidable foe: the mighty Ape-Man.

MGM's Tarzan series continued with Johnny Weissmuller, now 37 years old, and Maureen O'Sullivan, 30, in *Tarzan's Secret Treasure*. Released in December 1941, the film co-starred Johnny Sheffield as Boy and character actor Barry Fitzgerald as O'Doul. The Tarzan-Jane family tree house was more modernized in this entry, and the chimp could

Spanish language promotional print for MGM's 1941 production *Tarzan's Secret Treasure*, starring Johnny Weissmuller, Maureen O'Sullivan, and Johnny Sheffield.

probably run the place by herself. Budget cutbacks, caused in part by a dwindling foreign market (caused, in turn, by the war) changed the way films were made at the studio. *Tarzan's Secret Treasure* contained a good bit of stock footage from earlier Tarzan films, and also from *Trader Horn* (1931).

This fifth MGM Tarzan adventure was filmed on the MGM lot; in the Lake Sherwood area; at Iverson's Ranch in the Santa Susanna Mountains; and in Silver Springs and Ocala, Florida. The MGM lot included a mock-up of the Mutia Escarpment, the dangerous mountain that explorers ascend to reach Tarzan's country. The mock-up was at the west end of Lot 1 with the sound stages and the lake. The summit of the Escarpment was filmed on Lot 2 and in Sherwood Forest (so named, along with Lake Sherwood, because Douglas Fairbanks' 1922 *Robin Hood* had been shot at both places). The Lake Sherwood area began its real development in 1904 because of a cattleman's need for water. W.H. Matthiessen had a dam built. In 1925, William Randolph Hearst bought the property.

The history of the Iverson Ranch in the Simi Hills starts in 1880 with the homesteading of 160 acres of rock by Augustus Wagman. Eight years later she married Karl Iverson. By 1912 the California Aqueduct brought water and many people to the Los Angeles area. The Iverson family ranch began its business relationship with moviemakers that same year. Set in the northwest corner of Chatsworth, the ranch has stood in for Africa, Asia, the old American West, the South Seas, Mexico, you name it. *Tarzan's Secret Treasure*'s underwater photography took place in Florida at Wakulla Springs, with Lloyd Knechtel supervising the filming. His cameramen used a camera-bell attached to the bottom of a barge, filming a great ending showing off Weissmuller's swimming above and under the water.

With Edgar gifted with a fine imagination, there was no way that his *Laugh It Off* newspaper column could compete with what was going on his head, his Normal Bean. In January 1942 *Beyond the Farthest Star* appeared in *Blue Book*. An American airman is shot down and killed by Luftwaffe Messerschmitts during World War II. Except that he awakens on another planet (*a la* John Carter on Mars) and becomes immersed in a war that has been going on for 100 years. In his 1965 book *Edgar Rice Burroughs: Master of Adventure*, Richard Lupoff noted:

"Instead of painting war as a glorious exercise in heroic adventure, as he had in many of his earlier interplanetary tales, Burroughs pictures the Polodan hundred-year war as a bitterly cruel, murderous process, not only destructive of life and property but utterly sapping the spirit of the living."[1]

Promotional photograph from Tarzan's Secret Treasure, autographed by "John" Sheffield, Maureen O'Sullivan, and Johnny Weissmuller.

Edgar's life as an author, businessman, war correspondent and civilian guard included playing tennis to help stay in shape. His weight dropped to around 175. On January 18, 1942, Hulbert enlisted in the Army Air Corps as a photographer. This, plus the eventual end of the *Laugh It Off* column, may have spurred Edgar toward wanting a more active role in the war. After gas mask practice with a civilian organization, he was introduced to Col. Earl Bourland, an officer involved with the Businessmen's Military Training Corps (the BMTC), a civilian guard regiment of around 1200 with basic military training. Members consisted of middle-aged professional and executive types, and over 60 percent had previous military experience.

Another BMTC officer was Brigadier General Thomas H. Green, officially executive assistant to the commanding general. Under martial law, General Green occupied a position equal to that of the governor of Hawaii. Edgar was quickly promoted to second lieutenant, became the public relations officer (who else but the master?) and also the drill instructor for new recruits. He became qualified to carry a Colt .45 wherever he went. But after too many complaints, General Fielder decided that Edgar was overtraining the recruits with rigorous hikes, drills and calisthenics.

An interesting Tarzan memetic sideline of the 1940s was a Los Pachucos subculture in Los Angeles similar to the Tarzanes in Mexico City. The Tarzanes were musicians who wore their hair longish in honor of Johnny Weissmuller's Tarzan. Pachucos with their zoot suits and the others with their Tarzan hairstyles were much misunderstood by the mainstream culture of the day; in some cases people felt threatened. But Don Tosti (1923–2004), whose *Pachuco Boogie* became the first million-selling Latin record, forged his "Only for tarzanes (Pachucones)"[2] music to fit into a growing, wider audience.

The Return to Pellucidar, Edgar's next Inner-World tale, debuted in the February 1942 *Amazing Stories*. Two interior black-and-white illustrations are the work of J. Allen St. John. The March 1942 *Amazing Stories* presented *Men of the Bronze Age*, the second of a planned four novellas (beginning with the previous *The Return to Pellucidar*) which would eventually comprise a book-length work. *Tiger Girl*, the third of the four planned Pellucidar novellas, was published in *Amazing Stories* in April. In this story, David Innes is mistaken for a god and attempts to instate a democracy in a place called Tanga-tanga. Many Burroughs fans and scholars rate the resulting novel *Savage Pellucidar* (published 21 years later) as one of Edgar's most satirical and entertaining.

Edgar's prose was moving away from a somewhat verbose Victorian style, to a more terse, compact way of writing. A style of writing not unlike noir, or hard-boiled. Carefully chosen words that stimulate the imagination take the place of overabundant description dominating all you see. Dashiell Hammett and Raymond Chandler are obvious examples of crisp, tight storytelling. Many of the old Gold Medal paperback thriller writers of the 1950s and '60s, especially Donald Hamilton, are masters of the less-can-be-more story format. This type of storytelling is especially evident in two of Edgar's best and last works, *Tarzan and the Foreign Legion*, and *I Am a Barbarian*.

In April 1942, Edgar was promoted to major by the Businessmen's Military Training Corps. In July 1865, 77 years earlier, Edgar's father had been discharged from military service with the title of brevet major. Now Edgar, on his own merits, was the major. Edgar continued to stay in shape; the wartime food shortages helped get his weight down to 168.

Edgar's friend Ashton Dearholt died suddenly on April 27. As was Edgar's way, the grief he felt was shouldered and carried along with his activities. The major (Edgar) and Hawaiian Provost Marshal Major Frank Steere conducted an inspection of the island defenses: foxholes, observation posts, gun emplacements. Edgar was planning a BMTC exercise at these locations, despite falling down hard three times, and Major Steere falling twice.

In May, Edgar received a clean bill of health from his doctor and finalized his divorce from Florence. Hulbert Burroughs wrote his brother Jack and told him of their father's decision to remain in Honolulu, adding that the old man deserved his share of great times. In June, Edgar ran into Hulbert near the Niumalu Hotel where everyone was ecstatic that the U.S. Navy had utterly defeated an Imperial Japanese Navy attack on Midway Atoll. After the euphoria of the crowd died down, Edgar and Hulbert were able to catch up. Hulbert was commissioned as a second lieutenant, and Jack served in the reserves and as a war effort artist for Hollywood and Douglas Aircraft. The conversation would invariably lead to Tarzan. Edgar had tried to see last year's

Tarzan movie at the base theater a few times but the lines were always too long.

In August 1942, Edgar was lecturing to officers of an anti-aircraft artillery regiment about the advantages of working with the Businessmen's Military Training Corps in event of a real emergency. During this meeting he was introduced to two African American majors, and could see no distinction between white and black. Hulbert was posted to different Air Force bases in the South Pacific as a U.S. Army-Air Force documentary and combat photographer. At Guadalcanal, where the battle lasted 40 days, Hulbert was aboard a plane that was hit by machine guns and a shell, which didn't explode.

On the business front, Tarzan still led the way to fame and fortune for Edgar, despite a year without a new story in the saga. Stephen Slesinger was a producer of films, radio, television, a comic strip creator and an integral part in the creation of the licensing industry; he also had secured merchandising rights to Tarzan back in 1933, during the early part of Tarzanmania. The proliferation of Tarzan toys, games and many other items, and how they were presented to the public, is considered a blueprint of character merchandising, which developed in large part because of Slesinger's efforts. Tarzan also continued to be heard on radio. Rex Maxon's daily *Tarzan* comic strip, as popular as it was, came nowhere near the literal genius Hogarth's Sunday color pages. Hogarth's matchless "living art" earned him the sobriquet "The Michaelangelo of Comic Strips."

Tarzan's New York Adventure (1942) was the last of MGM's series and the Weissmuller-O'Sullivan team-ups. The original title had been *Tarzan Against the World*. In the film, Boy is kidnapped by unscrupulous circus owners, and Tarzan and Jane track them down to New York City. MGM rented the Hagenback-Wallace circus and set it up on their back lot. Charles Bickford is Buck Rand, the main villain; Virginia Grey and Paul Kelly are sweethearts who help Tarzan and Jane; Chill Wills is the older circus veteran who helps Boy escape from his captors. Elmo Lincoln, the original screen Tarzan, has a bit part as a circus roustabout (a transient circus laborer). As always, MGM animal trainer George Emerson doubled for Weissmuller when needed, and handled the sometimes unpredictable animal actors. When we see Tarzan make a 200-foot dive off the Brooklyn Bridge, it's actually a weighted dummy;

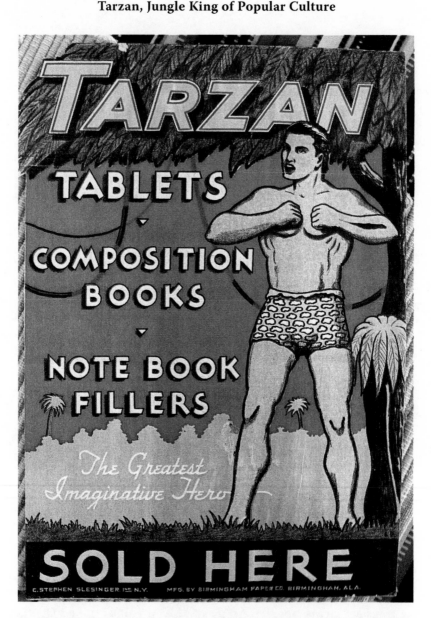

An early thirties window card, using the Ape-Man to sell school supplies. The proliferation of Tarzan merchandise and its presentation to the public was a blueprint for modern character marketing, which developed in a large part due to the efforts of Stephen Slesinger.

its fall was filmed by Jack Smith from atop a tower on the MGM back lot. This is one of the all-time Tarzan motion picture favorites.

In October, Edgar Rice Burroughs received his United Press credentials and approval from the War Department to be an accredited war correspondent. His influence and observations would now expand beyond the confines of Honolulu into a more active sphere of the war, and Edgar was more than ready to get into the thick of it. But he had

Spanish language promotional print for the 1942 MGM production of *Tarzan's New York Adventure.*

to wait for his bureau chief to give him an assignment. In December, Hulbert was promoted to first lieutenant and Edgar received his orders: travel to New Caledonia, the New Hebrides and the Fiji Islands writing articles and spot news. Edgar left in a G87 transport plane carrying 11 passengers, landing at Canton Island. Located in the South Pacific halfway between Hawaii and Fiji, this was a stopover for Navy Air Transport Service flights and a staging post for attacks on the Japanese-held Gilbert Islands.

Edgar began writing the first in a series of war diary entries which would later become *Happenings in New Caledonia and Australia.* He was next flown to New Caledonia for a short stay, before being transferred to Sydney, Australia, on December 24. Tarzan, everpresent the world over, made his appearance in the area: MGM's Australian executives gave Edgar a special screening of *Tarzan's New York Adventure.* The executives also set up print, radio and newsreel interviews. *Tarzan's New York Adventure* was the first film shown free to servicemen overseas.

The subjects of Edgar's war writings included a field artillery exercise at a Dumb Valley camp, hard traveling by horse or mule through jungle and mountain, and visits to wounded enlisted men at a military hospital. On January 30, 1943, he was ordered to return to Pearl Harbor on a damaged destroyer, the USS *Shaw,* by way of Suva in the Fiji Islands and Tutuila in the American Samoas, where he visited Pago Pago. The USS *Shaw* arrived at Pearl Harbor on March 2. Edgar wrote a 60-page account of the trip, *The Diary of a Confused Old Man, or Buck Burroughs Rides Again.*

MGM had dropped their Tarzan series, but Edgar's friend Sol Lesser was eager to continue with the terms of his ongoing contract with Edgar Rice Burroughs, Inc., to produce Tarzan movies. Now his films wouldn't have to compete for attention with releases from another production company. The State Department contacted Lesser in his position as a producer of Tarzan movies: The Ape-Man was considered a propaganda weapon due to his incredible popularity, and a motion picture depicting his fight against the Nazis would help focus attention on the message of democracy vs. fascism.

Independent film producer Sol Lesser (1890–1980) began his career in the early days of the movie business. He had worked with performers such as Bela Lugosi, Jackie Coogan and silent-screen great Lon Chaney, "The Man of a Thousand Faces." In his book *Edgar Rice Burroughs and Tarzan*, Robert W. Fenton quotes Lesser: "[The State Department] made it clear to me that there was no greater potential vehicle that could reach the minds of people with a message than that contained in a Tarzan picture."[3]

In response to the Department's request, Lesser, who was Jewish, was enthusiastic about sending his Ape-Man on a mission to fight the Axis. Tarzan and friends took on Nazi invaders in the February 1943 RKO release *Tarzan Triumphs*. The refusal of Maureen O'Sullivan to continue as Jane necessitated a plotline wherein she is temporarily in England with her family. Johnny Sheffield was on hand as Boy; Sig Rumann portrayed the gruff sergeant killed by Tarzan; Stanley Ridges personified evil as Colonel von Reichart; and Frances Gifford played Zandra, who helps Tarzan and Boy battle the Nazis. (Gifford had appeared in the 1941 serial version of Edgar's *Jungle Girl*.)

Directed with energy by William Thiele, who came to Hollywood in the 1930s from Germany, Sol Lesser's new Tarzan movie portrayed the Ape-Man as a symbol of freedom and American values, and an isolationist forced to enter the war. The "Now Tarzan make war" scene literally brought cheering audiences to their feet—the Ape-Man was enraged and ready to set things straight. *Tarzan Triumphs* also benefits from a rousing score by RKO contract composer Paul Sawtell.

For the RKO Tarzan series, the Los Angeles State and County Arboretum in Arcadia, near the San Gabriel

Promotional photograph for *Tarzan Triumphs* (1943), with Johnny Weissmuller. The U.S. State Department suggested that Tarzan could be used to focus attention on the dangers of fascism—Sol Lesser heartily agreed.

Mountains, stood in for Africa. The Arboretum includes a lagoon and lush vegetation, which added to the illusion of a tropical environment. The modern history of the site begins in 1845 with Scotsman Hugo Reid and his Tongva Native American wife, Victoria Bartolomea Comicrabit. The couple were awarded the land grant of the area, and after a series of other owners, the site fell into the hands of Elias Jackson "Lucky" Baldwin. Baldwin had become wealthy through mining investments and accumulated 63,000 acres in Southern California where Arcadia and Monrovia are located. "Lucky" founded the original Santa Anita Park racetrack and the Oakwood Hotel, and his influence helped Arcadia grow into a city. Elias Jackson "Lucky" Baldwin became Arcadia's first mayor.

Tarzan Triumphs was also filmed at Lake Sherwood and Sherwood Forest (where parts of the MGM series had been shot), and the scenes in the village of the Palandrians were staged at the RKO Encino Ranch. The Encino Ranch was 89 acres of land near the Los Angeles River and what is now the Sepulveda Basin Recreation Area. Interiors were done at RKO Studios. Released in February 1943, 14 months after the U.S. entered World War II, the film was a moneymaker. The great success of *Tarzan Triumphs*, Lesser's first post–MGM-era Tarzan film, filled him with confidence that Tarzan had resurgence appeal, which would certainly turn out to be the case. Lesser threw himself into his next Tarzan project.

Amazing Stories presented the further adventures of John Carter of Mars in the February 1943 issue. *The Skeleton Men of Jupiter* was intended as the first in a four-novella serial which would eventually appear together in book form. The Skeleton Men of the title refers to the Morgors, inhabitants of Sasoom (Jupiter), who are hell-bent on invading Barsoom. Many Burroughs fans and scholars consider the Mars series, when you strip away all of the fighting, adventures and romances, as an allegory of the quest for immortality. In the *Billion Year Spree*, British author Brian Aldiss describes Carter's transmigration to the Red Planet this way: "Wafted by mystical and Blavatskian means across the gulfs of space, John Carter finds himself on Mars."[4] The reference to Helena Blavatsky (a founder of Theosophy) is to spirit-travel, also known as out-of-body experiences. These transmigrations, linked to the "deaths" and "resurrections," seem to be the key to the mystery of life and death on Burroughs' Mars.

Back here on planet Earth, the December 1943 release of Lesser's *Tarzan's Desert Mystery* (only ten months after *Tarzan Triumphs*) continued Tarzan's feud with the Nazis. With Jane still in England, Boy (Johnny Sheffield) and Cheta the chimpanzee are the Ape-Man's family. Nancy Kelly dominates most of the scenes she's in as Connie Bryce, a traveling magician but in reality an espionage agent on the side of the Allies. Kelly is known for her Broadway stage performances, and later received an Academy Award nomination for *The Bad Seed* (1956). The action in *Tarzan's Desert Mystery* pits the Ape-Man not only against the Nazis, but a man-eating plant, prehistoric monsters (stock footage from the 1940 film *One Million B.C.*) and a giant spider. Kelly's feisty Connie battles the giant arachnid, throwing large rocks at it, before Tarzan intervenes. A Nazi is fed to the monster spider! Ben Johnson (1918–1996), the Academy Award-winning actor who began as a rodeo cowboy and stuntman, doubled for Weissmuller in the scene in which Tarzan leaps down onto the horse. *Tarzan's Desert Mystery* was filmed in Alabama Hills in Inyo County, California, and the desert action scenes staged at the Olancha sand dunes near Lone Pine, California, and in the Mojave desert. Lesser again shot his jungle sequences at the Los Angeles Arboretum, and filmed the outdoor city scenes at the RKO Encino Ranch.

Edgar wasn't able to see either of his friend's new Tarzan movies for quite a while because the lines at the theaters were always too long.

In March 1944, Edgar's new friend, Brigadier General Truman H. (Ted) Landon, commanding general of the Seventh Army Air Force Bomber Command, arranged for Edgar to receive a second war correspondent assignment. The Army flew Edgar from Honolulu on the 20th, and he arrived at Tarawa in the Gilbert Islands. Four months earlier, Tarawa was a battle site: American forces fought their way into the Japanese-controlled central Pacific region, thus creating an Allies staging post for the invasion of the Marshall Islands. After a week, Edgar was transferred to Eniwetok in the Marshalls and visited many islands and atolls. On Kwajalein Island, he was reunited with his oldest son Hulbert, still a combat arial photographer.

The 68-year-old Edgar then went on two daytime bombing missions in a B-24 Liberator bomber that targeted Japanese installations with 500-pound bombs; the "ack ack" (anti-aircraft guns) shot back at them. In a letter to his friend Donald L. Jackson, later a U.S. representative from California, Edgar wrote, "Had a swell time...."[5]

In April, Edgar was ordered to return to Honolulu and he was transported via a hospital plane. His 7000-mile mission (and personal adventure) was quickly followed by the re-instatement of his *Laugh It Off* column for *The Honolulu Star Bulletin*, *The Honolulu Advertiser* and *Hawaii: A Magazine of News and Comment*. "The Major" (Edgar) had settled back down in his cottage at the Niumalu Hotel in Lanikai, and also returned to another of his occupations, writing fiction. He had an idea for a World War II novel.

In Tarzana, after a decrease in the wartime paper restrictions, Edgar Rice Burroughs, Inc., published its first hardback in four years, *Land of Terror*, with a dust jacket and illustrations by John Coleman Burroughs. Though begun by Edgar in October 1938, this fifth tale in the Pellucidar series was never published in magazine form. As with the earlier *Tarzan the Untamed* (1919), Edgar experimented with the idea of a city of the mad; the idea of the world as an insane asylum in a quirky, humorous package of Stone Age action and adventure.

On June 30, 1944, Edgar's article "Our Japanese Problem," appearing in *Hawaii* magazine, presented a positive opinion of the loyalty maintained by the Japanese on the Islands (in opposition to his earlier, suspicious sentiments). In September, *Hawaii* published Edgar's "What Price Tolerance," in which he demanded that automatic citizenship be conferred upon alien parents of anyone who had served honorably in the armed forces.

September 1, 1944, was Edgar's sixty-ninth birthday and he celebrated with Hulbert, Brigadier General Kendall Fielder and other officer friends. (A later Venus novel would be dedicated to the general.) In October, per Edgar's wishes, John Coleman Burroughs had the ashes of his grandmother, Mary Evaline Burroughs (Edgar's adventurous mother), removed from the Pierce Brothers Crematorium where they had been in storage for over two decades. As Edgar was in Hawaii, Jack, Joan Burroughs Pierce and business secretary and family friend C.R. Rothmund arranged for Mary Evaline's ashes to be buried at the south side of a walnut tree which stands in the front yard of the Burroughs, Inc., offices in Tarzana.

On November 5, Edgar's first wife (and mother of his children)

Emma Centennia Burroughs died suddenly of a stroke. Granted leave by the military, Edgar and Hulbert took a plane to the U.S., where they were met by Joan and Jack. Edgar hadn't spent a Christmas with his family in 11 years (since his separation from Emma), and now for the first time got to meet two new grandchildren, Jack's boys Johnny, two years old, and Danton, five months old. In his Army uniform, Edgar later visited ex-wife #2 Florence, her new husband Dr. Alfred Chase, and Caryl Lee. Florence was impressed with Edgar's state of health and how well he looked in his uniform. But in late December he needed another hernia operation, which delayed his return to Hawaii. By January 1945, though, he felt well enough to sit for a portrait painting by John Coleman Burroughs.

Edgar returned to Hawaii on February 3, and Hulbert arrived ten days later. Edgar was soon reunited with an old acquaintance from the 1927 movie production *Tarzan and the Golden Lion*: Boris Karloff had been a bit and supporting actor 17 years ago, but in 1945 he was considered one of the greatest and most respected movie and stage actors. Edgar took some friends, including General Kendall Fielder, to dine with Karloff, and they later saw the great actor perform on stage in *Arsenic and Old Lace*.

An Edgar Rice Burroughs-Boris Karloff mystery concerns Boris of Karlova, a character in Edgar's novel *The Rider* (1918, but written three years earlier). William Henry Pratt changed his name to Boris Karloff around 1910. Could Edgar have seen a review or poster with Karloff's stage name, or even a stage play in the Chicago area and, intrigued by the name, used it as the basis for his character? Coincidence? University of Louisville curator (emeritus) of the Edgar Rice Burroughs Memorial Collection, George T. McWhorter told me, "The next step would be to find any of the actor's letters or diaries which mention a possible meeting of these two giants."

Other than the 1927 filming of *Tarzan and the Golden Lion*, and the above dinner and attendance of *Arsenic and Old Lace* in Hawaii, there seems to be no other "meeting of these two giants." Karloff worked in many California companies as an actor, including in Southern California during 1918. He also worked as far east as Chicago. The Burroughs family moved from Chicago to California in 1919, but they had been making trips to Southern California every year before that, staying sometimes for months on end. Stage productions were then very popular and Edgar and Emma were theatergoers; it's possible that Edgar saw Karloff in a play, or just saw the name in a review. Edgar is known for borrowing, modifying and using interesting names for his characters. Or is it all coincidence?

On December 3, 1943, Louella Parsons had announced in her Hearst newspaper column what turned out to be an exaggerated rumor: that Maureen O'Sullivan had consented to again portray Jane in Sol Lesser's upcoming *Tarzan and the Amazons*. Released in April 1945, this movie heralded the return of Jane, but in the form of 27-year-old Brenda Joyce, an actress who had made her film debut in the 1939 *The Rains Came* with Tyrone Power and Myrna Loy. In this entry, Johnny Weissmuller, almost 41, had gotten himself into shape and did some swimming and battled a rubber crocodile. Johnny Sheffield, now 14, appeared as Boy for the sixth time, and Barton MacLane played a villain. The queen of the Amazons was portrayed by Maria Ouspenskaya (1876–1949), the Russian-born actress twice nominated for Oscars. She's also notable for her role as Maleva in Universal's *The Wolf Man* (1941) and *Frankenstein Meets the Wolf Man* (1943), both starring Lon Chaney, Jr., as the Wolf Man.

On May 8, 1945, V-E Day, Edgar listened to radio reports of the surrender of Nazi Germany and the end of the Third Reich. Two weeks later, he received another war correspondent assignment, this time from the Navy, and left from Pearl Harbor on the USS *Cahaba*. Commanded by Captain Julian Burnbaum, the *Cahaba* was an oiler heading for the Carolines and other western Pacific islands to refuel American naval vessels. Edgar's United Press dispatches described fueling operations on different kinds of vessels, encountering island people mostly untouched by so-called civilization, and meeting Lt. Tyrone Power.

Kerama Retto, an atoll west of Okinawa, had been liberated at the end of March but the Japanese forces hadn't given up. Edgar accompanied a shore party there and they were shot at by a sniper. Everyone scrambled to cover, and no one was hit. While they were making their way back to the ship, a Japanese plane roared over the party. It bombed the admiral's vessel into flames, and then did an explosive kamikaze dive into another ship. Edgar had wanted to be in the thick of it and he got it. Earlier, his plane had gotten shot at during bombing raids, and now had had to avoid sniper bullets and watch a kamikaze explode into fire.

Invigorated by his adventures, Edgar returned to Hawaii on July 15, 1945. On August 15, Japan surrendered. Edgar told his son Jack in a letter that the town had turned into a madhouse, and everyone appeared to have been drunk. The surrender documents were signed aboard the battleship USS *Missouri* on September 2 (the day after Edgar's birthday), ending the war. Hulbert Burroughs was ordered back to the mainland and received his discharge papers. Edgar planned to return to Southern California but a series of angina attacks left him confined to bed for more than a month. By October 28 he was able to board a plane for the mainland.

Edgar moved into a house at 5465 Zelzah Avenue, Encino. Still weak from his over-exertions in the Pacific, he spent much of his time resting. In a letter to Thelma Terry he revealed: "Had a heart attack while out in the Philippine Sea in July and then another quite bad one in September in Honolulu."[6]

Edgar's accomplishments and adventures during World War II filled him with a pride and happiness that replaced his feelings of failure for not having lived up to his father's imposing image, rejection of his application to West Point, a medical discharge by the cavalry because of a weak heart, and having to depend on Tarzan to get him out of financial difficulties.

This time, Edgar had shown his father and Tarzan a thing or two.

11

"The Greatest Single Fictional Achievement of our Time"

By the time 1946 rolled around it had been over five years since the last new tale in the Tarzan saga. The use of Tarzan as a meme, a cultural touchstone, appeared in the stories of Tove Jansson (1914–2001), the Swedish-Finn author and comic strip creator of the Moomins (a family of trolls in the forests of Finland). Jansson was inspired by Hans Christian Andersen, Mark Twain and Edgar Rice Burroughs. She sprinkles many Tarzan references throughout her stories, and in the novel *Finn Family Moomintroll* (1948) there is a Tarzan game in a drawing room. The Ape-Man also appears in her Moomintroll comic strips; sometimes the characters read the book or play Tarzan while dressed in a loincloth.

Tarzan, with his Moomintroll appearances, continued to grow as a character of worldwide popular media, expanding as a meme, a cultural tradition out of the sphere of Edgar Rice Burroughs and his merchandising empire. But the absence of a new story in the Tarzan saga was drawing the attention of the mainstream public away from the source legend and toward alternative interpretations of Edgar's unique archetypal hero.

Meanwhile, Sol Lesser was at the helm of the next RKO Tarzan film. A huge publicity campaign included advertisements in major magazines, and during February 1946 *Tarzan and the Leopard Woman*, starring Johnny Weissmuller, was released to theaters. Brenda Joyce continued as Jane, Johnny Sheffield played the maturing Boy, and the exotic Acquanetta portrayed Lea, queen of the leopard people. Professional wrestler Abe "King Kong" Kashey has a small part as a tribe strongman who, always beaten by the Ape-Man in their friendly wrestling matches, is picked up off the ground and hurled into a crowd.

Johnny Weissmuller's co-star in the 1946 RKO production *Tarzan and the Leopard Woman* was the exotic Acquanetta, who signed this photograph.

Paul Sawtell created the tense musical score, and the leopard people's dance ritual was choreographed by Lester Horton (1906–1953). A dancer, choreographer and teacher, Horton arrived in California in 1929 and worked on many early Hollywood musicals and other films during the 1940s and early '50s, among them *Moonlight in Havana* (1942), *The Cli-*

max (1944) with Boris Karloff and *South Sea Woman* (1953) with Burt Lancaster. The filming of *Tarzan and the Leopard Woman* included the usual hazards of working with animal actors. Lesser had Cheta the chimp as a main character in his movies, and chimpanzee actors got cranky and ferocious. After six years of performing, the apes (especially the males) became dangerous and had to be retired. Compounding this problem in Lesser's latest film was the added dangers of working with leopards.

Enter Swedish-born Olga Celeste (1887–1969), a leopard trainer who worked in vaudeville leopard acts before her performances at the Luna Park Zoo in Los Angeles from 1925 to 1931. On March 3, 1928, she had played with a lioness inside a cage, a newsreel proclaiming "Wild petting parties shock Californians."[1] Celeste also worked her magic with the felines in director Howard Hawks' *Bringing Up Baby* (1938) with Katharine Hepburn and Cary Grant. There were no problems with the big cats during the filming of *Tarzan and the Leopard Woman*, despite a battle scene between leopards and Tarzan and friends. Weissmuller stabbed some stuffed leopards, and Olga Celeste, out of camera range, literally stood guard over the real animals with her whip, ready to lay down the law if necessary.

As an example of Tarzan's worldwide appeal and his influence on popular culture: Journalist Dolph Sharp wrote in 1969,

> A few years ago, when UNICEF doctors had trouble getting Indonesian children to come in for tuberculosis inoculations, they arranged to have the movie film *Tarzan and the Leopard Woman* run in the local theater. Price of admission: acceptance of an injection. From then on, it was standing room only—and no more difficulty in getting the children immunized.[2]

On September 1, 1946, Edgar celebrated his 71st birthday at Joan's, where they watched old movies on a 16mm projector. On Saturday evenings he enjoyed showing movies to his family, especially Laurel and Hardy comedies. Around this time he began a new Tarzan novel, writing 15,000 words before work was halted by his health problems: angina, arteriosclerosis and Parkinson's. Edgar Rice Burroughs, Inc., published the first hardback edition of *Escape on Venus* in October, dust jacket and illustrations by John Coleman Burroughs. The book is dedicated to Brigadier General Kendall J. Fielder, Edgar 's Intelligence Officer friend who was attached to the U.S. Army at Fort Shafter, Honolulu, during the war.

In October Edgar was interviewed by Forrest J Ackerman—"Uncle Forry" to his many fans. Ackerman, a Los Angeles literary agent and collector of science fiction, fantasy and horror memorabilia, would later edit the legendary *Famous Monsters of Filmland* magazine. Ackerman was thrilled to meet the mastermind behind the Tarzan, Mars, Venus and Pellucidar series. Ackerman noted that Edgar

> wasn't too happy with Tarzan's transformation into a screen hero. He had thought of him, he said, as a pretty grim character, and the movies made him too humorous for his liking. He has a projector, with prints of *The New Adventures of Tarzan* and others, but he hasn't seen all the Hollywood versions of his stories. Of the nine different actors who have played the part, he liked Herman Brix the best.[3]

Tarzan's evolution as a multimedia figure was a result of the popularity of newspaper comic strips. Comic books began appearing in the U.S. around 1932, with reprints from the comic strips. The comic book format we are all familiar with started in 1934. In the Michael Barrier-Martin Williams book *A Smithsonian Book of Comic-Book Comics*, it is noted, "*Famous Funnies* was sold on newsstands for a dime, and it was soon being published on a monthly schedule. It was the first true comic book in the modern sense."[4] Like the premium comic books given to customers by retail operations, *Famous Funnies* contained reprints of newspaper comic strips. *New Fun* #1, appearing in 1935, was the first comic book consisting of all new stories and artwork.

By February 1947, Dell Publishing was in its eighth year of their Four Color comic book series. Four Color served as a tryout for certain titles, many of which would become a series with their own number sequence. Dell's Four Color issue #134, *Tarzan and the Devil Ogre*, was written by Robert P. Thompson and illustrated by Jesse Marsh, another important artist in the history of the Ape-Man. Marsh (1907–1966), who had previously done animation for the Walt Disney Company, was the first artist to illustrate original Tarzan comic books. (Earlier Tarzan comic books had been reprints of the newspaper strips.) Dell's *Tarzan and the Devil Ogre* was snapped up by fans, all 450,000 copies selling out in less than a week.

In April 1947 Sol Lesser's *Tarzan and the Huntress* starred the 42-year-old Johnny Weissmuller, Brenda Joyce as Jane and 15-year-old

Johnny Sheffield (now almost six feet tall) as Boy. The storyline has the Ape-Man and company battling unscrupulous big-game hunters and trappers. The cast also includes Patricia Morison as the huntress. Morison, a stage and movie actress-singer, often portrayed femme fatales in films such as *Without Love* (1945) with Katharine Hepburn and Spencer Tracy, *Dressed to Kill* (1946) starring Basil Rathbone as Sherlock Holmes, and *Song of the Thin Man* (1947) featuring William Powell and Myrna Loy as Dashiell Hammett's detective couple Nick and Nora Charles.

Barton MacLane, who appeared as a villain in the 1945 *Tarzan and the Amazons*, is back as one of the hunters; he ends up falling into a lion trap and is eaten by a hungry, angry lion. The Los Angeles County Arboretum and Botanic Garden again stood in for Africa. Animal trainer Albert Antonucci handled the chimpanzee chores, and B. Reeves Eason directed the climactic elephant stampede that sends the villains packing. British mystery writer Leslie Charteris, creator of the Saint, helped with the script. *Tarzan and the Huntress* was a huge hit.

An upstart invention that would eventually rival motion pictures in popularity had been commercially available since the late 1920s: television. Sustained television broadcasting started in Germany in 1929; the American public became more aware of this invention because of its appearance at the 1939 World's Fair. In July 1947, Edgar bought an RCA television set. A July 3 entry in his diary states, "I watched an LA-Hollywood baseball game at Wrigley Field—the first television picture I had ever seen..."[5] Edgar liked watching baseball, wrestling and boxing.

In 1947, Macmillan published *Golden Multitudes* by Frank Luther Mott, a book chronicling the history of best sellers in the U.S. He listed American's best sellers from 1690 on, with an elite 13 titles per decade. To attain best seller status for the years 1910 to 1919, a sale of at least 900,000 copies was necessary. Alongside books such as *Pollyanna* by Eleanor H. Porter and *Penrod* by Booth Tarkington is Edgar's *Tarzan of the Apes*.

A Tarzan fan named Vern Coriell, born in Pekin, Illinois, in 1918, was the son of acrobats who toured the country performing at circuses and fairs and in vaudeville. His father also did stunt work for motion pictures and in 1928 had doubled for Lon Chaney, "The Man of a Thousand Faces," in the silent film *Laugh, Clown, Laugh*. Vern first became aware of Tarzan in the movie *Tarzan and the Golden Lion*, but it was an issue of *Blue Book* magazine that introduced him to the real, the *mythic* Tarzan and other characters and worlds created by Edgar Rice Burroughs. In 1947 Vern was on the verge of becoming a very important factor in the history of the Ape-Man. The Tarzan fan movement and fandom in general had taken on wider proportions by the 1930s. By the late 1940s, fans were able to communicate, through the fan columns in pulp magazines, with the likes of Ray Bradbury, Robert Bloch (author of *Psycho*) and Forrest J Ackerman.

Vern wrote letters and articles for the periodicals, and secured Edgar's permission and blessings to take on the task of a fan news letter. Starting as a mimeographed fanzine, *The Burroughs Bulletin*'s first issue (July 1947) contained a then recent 1946 interview with Edgar by Ackerman: "And what of the master mind behind these out-of-this-world conceptions? Edgar Rice Burroughs today is 71, and taking it easy after two heart attacks sustained while acting as a War Correspondent for the U.S. Navy at Honolulu. He is remarkably well preserved for his age, and converses intelligently and interestedly."[6]

The *Bulletin* was sent free to Burroughs fans, including the influential *Chicago Tribune* book critic Vincent Starrett. Starrett's review of Vern's brainchild prompted a deluge of requests for the publication from around the world. This was an important factor in the proliferation of pop culture fandom that now pervades our modern culture. Burroughs fans communicated with one another, groups were organized, and new fanzines appeared, including *The Amtorian, The Barsoomian, The Safari News, ERB-dom* and *ERBANIA*.

In August 1947, the second Tarzan title in Dell Publishing's Four Color comic book series, *Tarzan and the Fires of Tohr* (illustrated by Jesse Marsh), sold well. This confirmed what the company already knew: Tarzan should have his own number-sequence title.

The next tale in the Tarzan saga, *Tarzan and the Foreign Legion*, was released by Edgar Rice Burroughs, Inc., on August 22, 1947. A fan favorite, it was dedicated to Brigadier General Truman H. (Ted) Landon, commander of the Seventh Army Air Force Bomber Command during the war. John Coleman Burroughs provided a striking dust jacket and interior plates that represent his art at its best. In this World

Vol. 1 No. 1   July 1947

EDGAR RICE BURROUGHS: An Exclusive Interview
Creator of New Worlds   By: Forrest J Ackerman

Here in America I have just visited the man who has fascinated
two generations with his New Worlds of the imagination:

Pellucidar--the hollow world at the earth's core, timeless land
of prehistoric perils.
· Barsoom--What we call Mars. Fantastic planet of four-armed sword
-smen....of Green men and thoats....of creatures whose heads crawl,
crab-like, from their living bodies!
Amtor--the veiled amphibious Evening Star, Venus! Primeval
globe of dinosaures and fish-men.

EDGAR RICE BURROUGHS' books--and there are over half a hundred
of them--are available in as many languages. Several have even been
rendered into Braille for the blind, and one--notably Princino de
Margo--has been published by a progressive English firm in the arti-
ficial language, Esperanto!

And what of the master mind behind these out-of-this-world conceptions? Edgar Rice Burroughs today is 71, and taking it easy after
two heart attacks sustained while acting as a War Correspondent for
the U.S. Navy at Honolulu. He is remarkably well preserved for his
age, and converses intelligently and interestedly.

"Granddad" Burroughs, father of three and grandfather of 4, has
seen science catch up with many of his "fevered imaginings" since he
sold his first story, "Under the Moons of Mars", in 1912. "In some of
early Mars books," he chuckles, "I made the mistake of describing
'amazing airships' which traveled at the incredible speed of 200
MILES AN HOUR!"

"Under the Moons of Mars", known in book form as "A Princess of
Mars", he signed with a pseudonym: Normal Bean. This pun-name was
meant to indicate that the author was a normal being, but the play on
words was lost when the name appeared in print as Norman Bean. However, his first Mars story was such a sensational success that he revealed his true identity when he introduced Tarzan, superman of the
jungle.

When he moved to California some years ago, to the quiet little
suburb of Los Angeles originally known as Reseda, his fame overshad-
owed the town and today it is known as Tarzana!

In 1947, Vern Coriell's first issue of *The Burroughs Bulletin* was sent to
Vincent Starrett, the influential Chicago Tribune book critic. Starrett's
review of the fanzine started a deluge of requests for it from around the
world—an important moment in the history of pop culture fandom.

122

War II thriller, Colonel John Clayton (Tarzan of the Apes), an officer in the British Royal Air Force, is on a military transport plane that is shot down over Sumatra. Tarzan, a group of Americans, and others from differing cultures band together, becoming the "Foreign Legion" of the title, and fight the Japanese during the waning days of the war.

In September 1947 Rex Maxon left the *Tarzan* daily newspaper comic strip to work on western comic books; in the mid–1950s he did the interior art for Dell Publishing's *Turok, Son of Stone* #1 (two Native Americans in a lost world inhabited by dinosaurs and other pre historic life). Burne Hogarth, the artist of the *Tarzan* Sunday page, was assigned to supervise the daily strip, sometimes having to come up with artwork. The busy Hogarth had also created the Cartoonists and Illustrators School; it was renamed the School of Visual Arts in 1956, and is now one of the world's leading art schools.

Dell Publishing's *Tarzan* #1 was released as a January–February issue in 1948, with art by Jesse Marsh. Spinoff titles would eventually appear: *Tarzan's Jungle Annual, Tarzan's Jungle World, March of Comics* Tarzan titles, *Korak, Son of Tarzan*. The Dell Tarzan series cleverly mixed elements of Edgar's novels with the MGM and RKO movie versions. This blend created the best alternative (other than the literary saga itself) to the "Me Tarzan, you Jane" image promoted by motion pictures. Of the radio and newspaper comic strip versions of the character, the strips were much more dynamic, but the Ape-Man's personality (though educated) and family relationships weren't as fleshed out as in Dell Publishing's *Tarzan* series. Comic books had long ago surpassed newspaper comic strips in popularity, especially after DC Comics had unleashed Superman, Batman, Wonder Woman, the Flash and an explosion of other superheroes upon world popular culture.

The Ape-Man of the Dell comic books is educated but feral and has superhuman strength. He also is the wealthy John Clayton, Lord Greystoke. Jane's hair is black rather than blond, as in Burroughs' original stories. The use of the name Boy for the child is taken from the movies, as is the family's treehouse.

Dell comic books, with their fantastic elements from Burroughs' novels (dinosaurs, mad scientists, crocodile people, etc.) and the MGM and RKO movies, inspired many children and adults to read the original stories. Seeing the Ape-Man in comic books depicted not only as educated, but flying airplanes and helicopters and treating humans and animals in medical emergencies made readers curious about Edgar's original character.

Sol Lesser's next Tarzan movie, *Tarzan and the Mermaids* (1948), was filmed in Mexico and starred Johnny Weissmuller and Brenda Joyce as the Ape-Man and Jane, but this time there was no Boy. Sheffield had grown almost as large as Weissmuller, so Lesser decided it was time to eliminate him from the series. (Viewers learn that Boy went to England for a formal education; in a letter to his parents, he says that his athletic coach wants him to compete in the Olympics.) Monogram hired Johnny Sheffield to play the title role in their Bomba the Jungle Boy series, and he appeared in 12 Bomba films between 1949 and 1955.

For *Tarzan and the Mermaids*, Sol Lesser cast George Zucco as the high priest who tries to force a young woman to marry a villain disguised as the god Balu. Zucco is perhaps best known for his portrayal of Prof. Moriarty in *The Adventures of Sherlock Holmes* starring Basil Rathbone as Holmes and Nigel Bruce as Dr. Watson. He also appeared in many of Universal's 1940s horror films, including *The Mummy's Hand* (1940), *The Mad Ghoul* (1943) and *House of Frankenstein* (1944). Linda Christian plays Mara, the young woman in danger of being coerced into betrothal to the bogus "god" until Tarzan and Jane come to the rescue. Christian (real name: Blanca Rosa Welter) was the Mexican-born daughter of Blanca Rosa (who was of Spanish, German and French descent) and her Dutch engineer husband. Linda acted in many Mexican and Hollywood movies, and has the distinction of being the original James Bond heroine in a 1954 TV adaptation of Ian Fleming's *Casino Royale*, eight years before the first Bond feature film starring Sean Connery.

Tarzan and the Mermaids was directed by Robert Florey (1900– 1979), a French actor-director-screenwriter who came to Hollywood in 1921. Florey directed over 50 movies, including the Marx Brothers' *The Cocoanuts* (1929) and Universal's Edgar Allan Poe adaptation *Murders in the Rue Morgue* (1932) with Bela Lugosi as the insane Dr. Mirakle. Raul Angel Garcia, Weissmuller's *Tarzan and the Mermaids* stunt double, performed Tarzan's dangerous dive off the cliffs into the ocean. Russian-born Dimitri Tiomkin composed the music; his distinctive scores grace such great motion pictures such as *Mr. Smith Goes to*

Washington (1939), *Shadow of a Doubt* (1943), *High Noon* (1952) and *The Alamo* (1960).

The exterior scenes were filmed at various locations in and around Acapulco on the Pacific coast of Mexico, with the interior and under-water scenes shot at the Churubusco Studios in Mexico City. The ex-terior scenes of Balu's temple were shot at the Aztec ruins of San Juan de Teotihuacan. Weissmuller liked Mexico very much; later, with John Wayne, he became part owner of the Los Flamingos hotel in Acapulco, eventually retiring there in the 1970s.

Tarzan and the Mermaids was beset with many problems. Inclement weather held up production, and a hurricane demolished some of the sets. Lesser suffered a heart attack and had to return to Los Angeles. A carpenter fell off of a boat into the water; the action of the ocean caused two boats to crash into one another with him between, crushing the man's skull.

Despite Weissmuller's age and what some fans consider an idiotic script, the film was another blockbuster, especially overseas. This was Weissmuller's last Tar-zan film, as Lesser felt he was getting to old for the part and because of Weissmuller's insis-tence that he should receive a percentage of the gross earnings. Columbia hired Johnny to star in their Jungle Jim series, based on the newspaper comic strip char-acter created by artist Alex Ray-mond (creator of Flash Gordon, another John Carter–inspired hero) and pulp magazine writer Don Moore. Johnny starred in 16 Jungle Jim adventures, playing himself in the last three because the producers of the TV *Jungle*

Leaving behind the Tarzan franchise, Johnny Weissmuller went on to star in sixteen Jungle Jim adventures for Columbia Studios. Later, he reprised the role for the *Jungle Jim* television series. Publicity photograph in-scribed by Weissmuller.

125

Jim show (also starring Weissmuller) had secured the rights to the character.

It may be difficult for many these days to understand how popular the Tarzan films were. As a writer interviewing Johnny Weissmuller for a national magazine noted,

> At his peak as Tarzan, Weissmuller's films drew 140 million persons each. One year in the mid–1930s, 75 million loaves of Tarzan Bread were sold. Eventually, Johnny cashed in to the extent of $150,000 a picture. He got thousands of fan letters each week. At a 1946 personal appearance in Galveston, Texas, so many fans crowded onto a pier to see him that the pier collapsed 17 feet to the beach and surf, injuring 37.[7]

There were concerns over how well the Tarzan movie series would fare after Weissmuller's exit. In his Burroughs biography *Tarzan Forever* (1999), John Taliaferro put it this way: "One cannot imagine a tougher act to follow than Weissmuller's Tarzan...."[8]

On March 26, 1948, Edgar Rice Burroughs, Inc., released Edgar's penultimate novel in his Mars series, *Llana of Gathol*, comprised of four *Amazing Stories* magazine tales. The book's dust jacket and interior Illustrations are the work of John Coleman Burroughs. An ulsio (giant rat), a dead man with hypnotic powers, despot rulers and a machine that keeps all citizens catalogued for long range death (if needed) are only part of the story. This entry in the Mars epic is considered humorous by many fans and scholars, and is another example of the parody Edgar added to his stories in later life (*Savage Pellucidar* and *Tarzan and the Lion Man* being two other examples).

By 1949, a significant amount of the public were unaware of Tarzan as a literary character (a distinct archetype from other media forms) because of the huge popularity of the movies, radio shows, comic books and comic strips. Sol Lesser and director Lee Sholem reportedly interviewed about 1000 actors to find a new Ape-Man for their Tarzan series. Concerns that Weissmuller's departure would adversely affect Tarzan's movie popularity were unfounded; Tarzan himself was definitely the draw. The January 1949 release *Tarzan's Magic Fountain* stars Lex Barker as a rather bland Tarzan. Barker was a descendant of Roger Williams, founder of Rhode Island, and Sir William Henry Crichlow, who had been a governor-general of Babados, an island country in the

Concerns that Weissmuller's departure would harm Tarzan's popularity were unfounded. Tarzan, himself, was the draw. Lex Barker and Brenda Joyce as Tarzan and Jane in Sol Lesser's *Tarzan's Magic Fountain* (1949).

Lesser Antilles. Brenda Joyce continued on as Jane, but this would be her last film in the franchise.

Edgar, now confined to a wheelchair because of Parkinson's, had a serious heart attack in December 1949 and was placed in an oxygen tent. He had left instructions to be cremated; his ashes were to be buried beside his mother's under the black walnut tree in front of the Edgar Rice Burroughs, Inc., offices in Tarzana, the city he had created.

Autographed photograph of Brenda Joyce, who had already played Jane four times opposite Johnny Weissmuller before starring with Lex Barker in *Tarzan's Magic Fountain* (Ralph Brown collection).

Edgar, bravely facing the fact that the end of his life was near, said, "If there is a hereafter, I want to travel through space to visit the other planets."[9]

On March 19, 1950, he ate his breakfast and then sat up in bed to read the Sunday newspaper comic strips, keeping tabs on his greatest creation's adventures. The newspaper dropped from his hands. Tarzan was with the master of fantastic adventure during his last moments, as if saying, "Goodbye, old friend."

The housekeeper discovered Edgar's body and notified his family and his physician, Herman Seal. Two days after the death of the grandfather of American science fiction, businesses in Tarzana shut down for an hour during the funeral. Edgar was cremated at Chapel of the Pines in Los Angeles. Per his instructions, his remains were buried next to his loving, adventurous mother. A March 20, 1950, *Van Nuys News* article reported that Edgar had requested that his friends, instead of sending flowers to his services, contribute to the Crippled Children's Fund.

The *Reno Evening Gazette* (Reno, Nevada) began its report with "Edgar Rice Burroughs, whose own twist on the theory of evolution—Tarzan—brought riches that Darwin never dreamed of, is dead."[10] Irwin Porges, in his mammoth biography *Edgar Rice Burroughs. The Man Who Created Tarzan*, referring to Edgar's burial next to his mother, stated, "So in this final action Edgar's life continued. He was now part of the nature he had worshipped and sought to protect—the nature whose creatures he had always viewed as superior to man."[11]

As to the Ape-Man himself, issue #9 of Vern Coriell's *The Burroughs Bulletin* treated its readers to an "interview" with the purported real Tarzan, as if in anticipation of the later expansion of his popular culture parameters. This article appeared about 22 years (the issue is undated) before Philip José Farmer's "interview" with John Clayton, Tarzan, in the April 1972 issue of *Esquire* magazine. Tarzan in popular culture was growing toward ways that Edgar probably hadn't conceived, even with his super-imagination and brilliant marketing strategies.

Robert C. Ruark, author of the bestselling novel *Something of Value* (whose experiences inspired his book about the Kenyan Mau Mau rebellion against British rule), wrote in a syndicated newspaper column of March 28, 1950: "There is no doubt in my mind that Tarzan of the Apes was the greatest single fictional achievement of our time."[12]

12

The Burroughs Bibliophiles

Two months after Edgar's death, Sol Lesser released *Tarzan and the Slave Girl* (1950) with Lex Barker in his second foray into the cinematic adventures of the foster son of Kala the she-ape. Directed by Lee Sholem, nicknamed "Roll 'Em" Sholem by his Hollywood peers because of his ability to direct films with incredible speed and competence, the film features Vanessa Brown as Jane. Born Smylla Brynd in Vienna, Austria, to a Jewish couple, Brown had been taken by her family to France in 1937 to avoid persecution by the rising Nazi Party. After settling in the U.S., she was hired by RKO and made her film debut in *Youth Runs Wild* (1944). The cast of Lesser's newest Tarzan adventure also included Denise Darcel, whose most important Hollywood role came four years later in *Vera Cruz*, directed by Robert Aldrich and starring Burt Lancaster and Gary Cooper. *Tarzan and the Slave Girl* was filmed at the Iverson Movie Ranch, the Los Angeles County Arboretum and Botanic Garden, and the RKO's 40-acre backlot.

August 20, 1950, marked the last Burne Hogarth–illustrated *Tarzan* newspaper Sunday comic strip page. Hogarth had drawn the Sunday page for 12 years (1937 to 1945 and 1947 to 1950). A recipient of dozens of international awards, including the National Cartoonist Society Advertising and Illustration Award in 1975 and the Magazine and Book Illustration Award in 1992, he continued to educate, write, create and theorize on art until his death at age 84 in 1996.

Bob Lubbers, a comic strip and comic book artist, joined United Feature Syndicate and continued the newspaper *Tarzan* daily and Sunday strips. Born in 1922, he had studied at the Art Students League of New York and began his comic book career at age 18. Lubbers is also noted for his work on *Li'l Abner*, *The Saint* (based on Leslie Charteris's character Simon Templar) and *Long Sam*. Lubbers' comic book work includes stints with Marvel Comics and DC (using the pseudonym Bob Lewis). His Sunday Tarzan comic strips were honored at the 2009 *Tarzan!* exhibition at the Musee du quai Branly in Paris, France.

In the fall of 1950, Cyril Ralph Rothmund, general manager of Edgar Rice Burroughs, Inc., was contacted by Walter White Jr. of Commodore Productions and Artists. By December, a contract was signed allowing Commodore Productions the right to produce a half-hour Tarzan radio program. Cast as the Ape-Man, Lamont Johnson had been a radio performer for years, on shows such as *The Adventures of Frank Merriwell* and *Broadway Is My Beat*, before acting and directing on television, then films. *Tarzan* debuted on January 4, 1951, over the Los Angeles radio station KHJ; the call letters were reportedly an acronym for Kindness, Happiness and Joy. Originally owned by the *Los Angeles Times* newspaper, KHJ was later purchased by Don Lee in 1927 for his Mutual Broadcasting System. Twenty-four years later, *Tarzan* was broadcast over the entire system, sponsored by Dr. Ross Dog and Cat Food. *Tarzan* was broadcast nationwide following the 54th episode, and would hold its own in the Nielsen ratings with the likes of *Jack Benny*, *Amos 'n' Andy*, *Our Miss Brooks* and *Groucho Marx*. There was also an Australian Tarzan radio series (over 800 episodes) that was also broadcast in New Zealand and South Africa.

RKO's March 1951 release *Tarzan's Peril* was probably the best of Lex Barker's Tarzan films. Jane was played by Virginia Huston, known for her film noir and adventure movies, including the Robert Mitchum classic *Out of the Past*. Dorothy Dandridge, a singer, actress and Best Actress Oscar nominee (for *Carmen Jones*) is proud and strong as Melmendi, queen of the Ashuba. George Macready gives a riveting performance as the evil slaver and gunrunner Radijeck. Most of *Tarzan's Peril* was made in the U.S., but location shooting in Kenya made it the cinematic Tarzan's first adventure filmed partly in Africa.

Meanwhile, back in Tarzana, Cyril Ralph Rothmund took care of business at Edgar Rice Burroughs, Inc., managing the general merchandising of Tarzan items, which included toys, trading cards, coloring books and records. The radio dramatizations continued. The Dell comic book series, with its blending of the novels in the saga and the MGM and RKO movie versions, produced exciting art and imaginative stories propelled by exotic peoples, savage animals, poachers, slavers, an occasional mad scientist (including the benign Dr. Macwhirtle), giant spiders, lost civilizations, dinosaurs and other prehistoric creatures. This was during the period of photo covers of Lex Barker as Tarzan, with the interior art of Jesse Marsh, a veteran of Dell's *Gene Autry* comic book. In January 1952, the *Dell Giant* series released *Tarzan's Jungle Annual* #1, the first in a series of 100-page comic books that continued for the next six years. Dell also had three *John Carter of Mars* comic books (375, 437 and 488) in their Four Color series. Bob Lubbers continued illustrating both the daily and Sunday newspaper comic strips, with Dick Van Buren writing the stories. Whitman Publishing's children's editions of *Tarzan and the Forbidden City* and *Tarzan and the City of Gold* were abridged: Editors removed some of the violence and, in the latter case, the sexuality. Both books featured interior illustrations by Jesse Marsh; the dust jacket illustrations were the work of Don McLoughlin.

Despite the efforts of Edgar Rice Burroughs, Inc., to maintain complete control over Tarzan's media incarnations, many unauthorized Tarzan movies were made in China, Spain, India, South America, etc. There was even a Turkish rip-off that has attained cult status, 1952's *Tarzan in Istanbul* with Tamer Balci as Tarzan. *Tarzan and the Brown Prince* (1972) with Steve Hawkes as the Ape-Man is another unauthorized film that is considered a cult movie.

The Tarzan fandom movement continued to grow. Hugo Gernsback, an inventor, writer, magazine publisher and founder of the Science Fiction League, had published the addresses of fans back in the 1920s and 1930s, and these fans organized into local clubs. Tarzan-Burroughs fandom had been in existence since 1916 and now, 36 years later, *Burroughs Bulletin* publisher Vern Coriell conceived of an organization that would unite the different Tarzan-Burroughs fan-clans for communication, events and the creation of new tribes. He wanted to call it the Burroughs Bibliophiles. The several other Burroughs fan publications (*The Jasoomian, ERBANIA*, etc.) were also attracting readers in a way they perhaps weren't expecting: serious and sometimes scholarly analysis of the Tarzan saga and Edgar's other creations.

In April 1952, RKO released Sol Lesser's *Tarzan's Savage Fury*, Lex Barker's fourth film in the role. The Ape-Man gets mixed up in a Cold War conflict between England and the U.S.S.R. over national security.

Many unauthorized Tarzan movies were produced around the world—in China, Spain, India, South America, etc. A 1952 Turkish film, *Tarzan in Istanbul*, has attained cult status. Promotional print for the film from Barcelona, Spain, released under the title "Tarzan Versus the Mau-Mau."

Elements of the mystery, suspense and thriller genres were added to the plot, as Edgar had done with some of the tales in the literary saga (*Tarzan the Invincible* and *Tarzan Triumphant*, for example). Unlike the novels, wherein Tarzan is actually connected to England's intelligence services and functions as a secret agent, the Ape-Man of *Tarzan's Savage Fury* works outside of any formal organization. Jane was played

The Burroughs Bulletin and other fan publications—*ERBANIA, The Jasoomian*, etc.—attracted readers who gave serious scholarly attention to the Tarzan literary saga. The above issue of *ERBANIA*, #45, is from 1980, with cover art by Frank Reyes.

by Dorothy Hart, who had stood out in Mark Hellinger's classic noir drama *The Naked City* (1948), and then became a United Nations spokesperson. Paul Sawtell continued as Lesser's music composer. Polish-born, he had earlier scored two films featuring other important popular culture archetypes: *The Pearl of Death* and *The Scarlet Claw* (both 1944) starring Basil Rathbone and Nigel Bruce as Holmes and Dr. Watson. *Tarzan's Savage Fury* was directed by Cy Endfield, who, 12 years later, would direct the magnificent *Zulu* (1964) with Stanley Baker and Michael Caine.

By 1953, Tarzan's mainstream audience consisted of moviegoers of all ages. Television wasn't yet broadcasting feature-length films in great numbers but drive-in movie theaters recycled movies of all genres, as did the second-run movie houses and the urban downtown theaters sometimes referred to as "fleabags." The fleabags had the best triple-features for your money: three war movies; three comedies, three Westerns, three sword-and-sandal flicks, three monster movies, three Tarzan movies, etc.

Tarzan as a meme, a cultural inheritance, a world legend above restrictions of a niche, surfaced in many forms including an unlikely context: the hard-boiled, noir private detective novel. In Raymond Chandler's masterpiece *The Long Goodbye* (published in 1953), gangster Mendy Menendez sizes up Philip Marlowe, perhaps leaving a clue to the character of Chandler's iconic private detective: "Tarzan on a big red scooter," he drawled. "A tough guy."[1]

In Sol Lesser's June 1953 release, *Tarzan and the She-Devil*, Ape-Man Barker protected his elephant friends from ivory poachers Monique Van Vooren and a pre–

Sol Lesser released his fourth movie with Lex Barker, *Tarzan's Savage Fury*, in 1952. Dorothy Hart was cast as Jane (**Ralph Brown collection**).

Perry Mason Raymond Burr. This was Barker's last Tarzan, as he wanted to avoid typecasting. Seven years later he played the fiancé of Anita Ekberg in Federico Fellini's classic *La Dolce Vita* (1960), and he is ribbed during the film for his work as Tarzan.

In January 1954, John Celardo succeeded Bob Lubbers as artist on the *Tarzan* daily newspaper comic strip. Celardo, born in 1918 on Staten Island, New York, also took over the Sunday strip on February 28. Celardo had studied at the Art Students League of New York City, and drew at the famed Eisner-Iger shop (comics producers) when he was a young freelancer. His career included work on the *Tales of the Green Beret* newspaper comic strip and cartoons in Street & Smith magazines. He was also an assistant art director and artist for Fiction House, which published magazines and comic books.

The memetic growth of Tarzan as a world popular culture figure continued in an extreme form in Israel. To set the stage: The Ape-Man had been very popular there since the late 1930s, when Israeli pop culture writer Eli Eshed says, "the Zionist movement was searching for a suitable role model of a new strong Jew close to nature. Weissmuller's image appeared on Zionist propaganda posters as the face of the ideal Israeli sabra, and various teachers and youth movement guides presented Tarzan specifically as played by Weissmuller as a way to encourage children to enjoy the strenuous life of the outdoors."[2]

Following this, the first 11 Burroughs Tarzan novels were translated into Hebrew. They were so popular that during the 1940s and 1950s, the famous children's author Igal Mosinzon spoke out about the damaging effect Tarzan was having on children, and included these sentiments in books he wrote. Despite his efforts, Tarzan became more of a national obsession in Israel, especially from 1954 to 1964. It started with ten different, competitive series of original Tarzan stories, published without the knowledge of Edgar Rice Burroughs, Inc. Around 1000 of these adventures, by ten competing publishers, eventually appeared. About half of them are science fictional, with Tarzan as a secret agent dealing with aliens and monsters. He sometimes worked for the Israeli government in political hot spots. (Simultaneously he was fighting the "evil Jews" in unauthorized stories coming out of Syria and Lebanon.) In a further example of a continuity of popular culture, some of the Israeli stories involve his adventures with characters such as Dracula, Flash Gordon, Dr. Fu Manchu, Dr. Jekyll and Mr. Hyde, and Sheena, Queen of the Jungle.

Israel's Tarzan madness of the '50s and '60s was the complete opposite of the Ape-Man's standing in France. Richard Ivan Jobs' *Global Perspectives on Tarzan: From King of the Jungle to International Icon*

> traces the history of Tarzan comics in late 1940s and early 1950s France, and the ways in which these texts became the focus of moral panics about the detrimental effect of comics on French youth. In the early 1950s, Tarzan comic books written, illustrated and produced in the United States were very popular with French children and teenagers. After being targeted by the Commission for the Oversight and Control of Publications for Children and Adolescents, Tarzan comics were pulled from circulation in France. Tarzan comics, critiqued for violence, sexuality, nudity, for their Americanness and for their popularity, were not sold again in France for more than a decade because the Commission feared they would lead to moral degeneracy.[3]

About 35 minutes into the classic Hollywood movie *The Caine Mutiny*, Captain Queeg (Humphrey Bogart) receives a message on the radio: "Gwendelyn, this is Tarzan." Bogie replies, "Tarzan, this is Gwendelyn."

Another important memetic reference to Tarzan as world pop cultural legend can be found in William Brinkley's 1956 naval war novel *Don't Go Near the Water*. A Tarzan-Burroughs publicity stunt involves dressing Pacific island natives as savages to greet the visiting Edgar Rice Burroughs. But the Tulurans dress in shirts and pants like anyone else. A night of drinking and talking with the Tulurans secures their participation in the project.

Vern Coriell's *The Burroughs Bulletin* had grown to a 48-page publication by issue #12, which featured articles by Robert Ruark (*Something of Value* 1955) and science fiction great Philip José Farmer. But despite the constant expansion of the Tarzan archetype in worldwide culture, the movie franchise, though successful, was in dire need of a change from the same, tired formula. This change began inauspiciously.

In the 1955 Sol Lesser production *Tarzan's Hidden Jungle*, a new cinematic Ape-Man was introduced. Weightlifter Gordon Werschkul, working as a lifeguard in a Las Vegas hotel, caught the casting-eye of a Hollywood agent. Gordon had recently been a military policeman and an Army drill sergeant. The young, genial, muscular man was flown to Hollywood for a test as the next movie Tarzan. Gordon was given a name change to become Gordon Scott and became the eleventh actor to portray the Ape-Man in an authorized film. Though Gordon is one of the more popular cinema Tarzans, his first film wasn't very good (but it *was* successful), and his "Dean Martin hairdo" is an incongruity. Nevertheless, Scott has a natural masculine temperament and delivery that strengthens his performance, and his action scenes are vigorous and believable.

In 1957, the first color Tarzan film, *Tarzan and the Lost Safari*, starred Gordon Scott, Betta St. John and Wilfrid Hyde-White. Sol

GORDON SCOTT ("TARZAN")

R.K.O.

A new cinematic Ape-Man, Gordon Scott, was introduced to moviegoers in Sol Lesser's *Tarzan's Hidden Jungle* (1955). Promotional card signed by Scott.

Gordon Scott and Eve Brent starred as the jungle couple in *Tarzan's Fight for Life* **(1958). Photograph autographed by Scott and Brent (Ralph Brown collection).**

Lesser put more money into this movie, and even sent an expedition (headed by Miki Carter) to Africa to film wild animals and scenery with Gordon Scott as the Ape-Man romping about. There were no problems, except with a 500-pound lion that Gordon had worked with for over a month. The lion, grumpy one day, swiped out and tore open Gordon's leg, which required 32 stitches. For children, Whitman Publishing released an illustrated *Tarzan and the Lost Safari* adaptation authorized by Edgar Rice Burroughs, Inc., illustrated by Tony Sgroi, and with a wrap-around cover photo of Gordon as the Ape-Man.

The series had become unimaginative. It continued without the budgets needed to create compelling plots and exciting special effects to represent the genius of Edgar's stories. In Lesser's next Ape-Man movie, *Tarzan's Fight for Life* (1958), Gordon Scott got tangled up with a python during the filming of a fight scene, crashed to the ground and was almost crushed to death before several handlers unwound the snake. (He told a group of Burroughs fans about this back in the 1980s and had us all laughing.)

Lesser then filmed three pilot episodes of a proposed Tarzan TV series that didn't sell. Lesser had the episodes edited and released as another 1958 Ape-Man movie titled *Tarzan and the Trappers* with Gordon Scott as Tarzan and Eve Brent as Jane. Brent, who also starred as Jane in the previous *Tarzan's Fight for Life*, had her time in the Hollywood limelight. According to *AMC*, the American Movie Classics magazine, "When Brent traveled to her hometown of Fort Worth, Texas, shortly after the film's opening, she couldn't even leave her house, as stampedes of fans pawed outside for a glimpse of the latest jungle queen."[4]

Although Gordon Scott was getting better in his Ape-Man portrayals, the series itself was still plodding along. A fresh approach was needed to spark a resurgence of interest in the movies and in Tarzan himself. The Tarzanmania that swept through the 1930s and 1940s had eventually settled down after World War II, as people moved forward with their lives. Tarzan was just another character like Superman and Batman. The Tarzan-Burroughs fandom movement (the Burroughs Bibliophiles) continued growing, however, and was aided by science fiction and fantasy organizations such as the Science Correspondence Club, which united fans nationwide. Then academic debate over the merits of Burroughs' novels emerged to challenge the assertion that *Tarzan of the Apes* should be dismissed as literature. Super Tarzan fan Philip José Farmer, in his feral man anthology *Mother Was a Lovely Beast*, wrote, "This use of satire in the Tarzan books has been overlooked by most literary critics, who regard Tarzan as a two-dimensional character in a comic book-type adventure series."[5]

At the same time, the works of certain science fiction and fantasy writers were becoming accepted as literature within academic circles. *New York Times* reviewer Villiers Gerson called Theodore Sturgeon's *More*

Than Human one of 1953's best novels. Ray Bradbury's *Fahrenheit 451*, also published in 1953, was described by August Derleth of the *Chicago Sunday Tribune* as a work of brilliant imagination. Richard Matheson scored with *I Am Legend* (1954) and *The Shrinking Man* (1956). Philip José Farmer, whose first literary success was his 1952 novella *The Lovers*, earned the prestigious Hugo Award as Most Promising New Writer. One of Farmer's early inspirations was the Tarzan saga of Edgar Rice Burroughs.

The next Tarzan resurgence would aid in worldwide scholarly acceptance of popular culture as valid subjects of study. Tarzan was at the head of a 20th century pantheon of modern pop cultural super-heroes and archetypes, and those yet to come.

13

The Return of Tarzan

Before the 1960s fan madness over Muhammad Ali, James Bond and the Beatles, a '50s rock'n'roll craze fueled by Elvis Presley, Chuck Berry and others grew in mainstream popularity. Another, if unlikely, fad also took off into the public consciousness: the monster craze. Many factors, including the publication of the legendary magazine *Famous Monsters of Filmland* (edited by Forrest J Ackerman), resulted in over a decade of monster/science fiction/fantasy multimedia frenzy. As with Tarzan marketing, one could buy monster toys, books, coloring books, figures, trading cards, comic books, magazines, costumes, etc., in excess. And the classic horror and science fiction films appeared regularly on television showcases with titles such as *The Vampira Show*, *Shock!*, *Nightmare* and *Creature Features*.

Concurrent with the mainstream emergence of rock'n'roll and the monster craze was the beginning of the next Tarzan resurgence. Tarzan's media incarnations had always been popular, but especially the movies, which were telecast during the 1950s and 1960s and also shown at second-run, downtown movie theaters and drive-ins.

The resurgence began with a redefining of the movie Tarzan's personality and a break from the traditional "Me Tarzan, you Jane" stereotype. Sol Lesser, needing to slow down some, sold his contract with Edgar Rice Burroughs, Inc., to movie and TV producer Sy Weintraub. Weintraub went with Burroughs' literary character in some ways—and in some ways, not. Tarzan was educated and articulate, but his feral inclinations were toned down and his superhuman strength was missing. Gordon Scott, the "Dean Martin" Tarzan, got a haircut and, under the direction of John Guillermin, became the "grim" Tarzan in *Tarzan's Greatest Adventure* (1959), one of *the* most popular Ape-Man films. Scott's performance is a tight, concentrated portrait of a man obsessed with revenge.

In one of the most popular Tarzan films of them all, *Tarzan's Greatest Adventure* (1959), Gordon Scott played a literate, grim Ape-Man. The above oddity (signed by Scott) is a promotional card for audiences in Brussels.

For all his muscular bulk, though, the screenplay has Scott's Ape-Man having a time of it defeating villain Anthony Quayle as Slade in the action-packed finish. Nevertheless, *Tarzan's Greatest Adventure*, a fast-paced, well-directed, well-acted jungle thriller, also benefits from a tense musical score by Douglas Gamley. Many fans of this film cite Quayle's Slade, played in classic neurotic fashion, as the best Tarzan movie villain and an integral factor in the movie's success. This film was a needed change from previously adequate but uninteresting series entries. The cast also includes a young Sean Connery as a villain, three years before his portrayal of British secret agent James Bond in *Dr. No*.

The year 1959 also saw the release of another Tarzan movie, MGM's *Tarzan the Ape-Man* starring Denny Miller in a remake of their 1932 classic. Denny Miller had been a basketball star at UCLA; before being hired to play the Ape-Man, he had a small part in the major motion picture *Some Came Running* with Shirley MacLaine, Dean Martin, and Frank Sinatra. Denny said in an interview, "I later told people they named the movie after me because I was the only one who 'came running'—I came running to tell Dean Martin that somebody was in town to shoot Frank Sinatra! I had rehearsed my one line 7,480 times, and

"TARZAN'S GREATEST ADVENTURE" 59/231

In *Tarzan's Greatest Adventure*, British actor Anthony Quayle played Slade, an insecure, neurotic, obsessed villain. Many fans cite Quayle as the best villain in a Tarzan movie, and an integral ingredient of the film's success (Ralph Brown collection).

I gave it to him in rehearsal and waited and waited for his response. And he finally looked up and said, 'I got lines?' [*Laughs*] He was very relaxed!"[1]

The 1959 *Tarzan the Ape-Man* contains original music by jazz great Shorty Rogers. Denny Miller, asked by writer David Fury if he had regrets about being one of the movie Tarzans, replied, "I know there are other guys that consider the role of Tarzan ruined their career and phu-phu it, and don't sign autographs, but I've never understood that. I've really had a marvelous experience at all levels with the thing and I still do use the fact … my license plate reads 'X-TARZAN,' and I get a lot of jollies out of that."[2] Miller continued his career as an actor, author and health advocate, and he was also an avid supporter of the Burroughs Bibliophiles until his death in 2014.

144

There was also a resurgence for Vern Coriell's *The Burroughs Bulletin* despite his not having released a new issue in over a year; back issues were being passed around among fans. And in May 1960, Al Guillory Jr. and Camille "Caz" Cazedessus, Jr., released their fanzine *ERB-dom*, taking an academic approach to the Tarzan saga and other Edgar Rice Burroughs works.

Sy Weintraub shot about 60 percent of his second Tarzan movie in Africa and the rest (interior and campsite scenes) on sound stages in England. Directed by Robert Day, *Tarzan the Magnificent* (1960) continued the producer's redefining of the cinematic Ape-Man with a solid performance by Scott as a thoughtful man of action. Despite the reduction of Tarzan's feral qualities, it is one of the best Ape-Man movies, charged with fine villainous portrayals by John Carradine and Jock Mahoney. Shakespearean actor and Hollywood character star Carradine is the head of a vicious clan of outlaws. Jock Mahoney, as the old man's eldest son, is terrific as the cold, calculating Coy Banton.

Writing on *Tarzan the Magnificent* in a biography of Jock Mahoney, Tarzan fan Gene Freese states,

The film concludes with a memorable fight scene between Jock and Scott, with both men giving the nearly five-minute battle their all. The fight scene was shot mostly at Kenya's Fourteen Falls. The two men do all their own stunt work and make it one of the all-time great screen fights as they pound one another

Gordon Scott in the Sy Weintraub production *Tarzan the Magnificent* (1960), one of the most popular Tarzan films. Signed by Gordon Scott.

145

over the rocks and into the water.... [W]hen Scott tried to come on a little strong in the fake fight, Jocko surprised him with his own strength and knowledge of hand-to-hand combat.... Jocko's experience as a stunt coordinator helped immensely. By choreographing the action scenes on location and doing his own stunts, Jocko saved producer Weintraub thousands of dollars. At one point Jocko even doubled Tarzan Gordon Scott when the scene called for both men to take a diver into the water before the climatic fight. It was Jocko who executed both dives.[3]

Tarzan fans, movie critics and general filmgoers who had seen the previous *Tarzan's Greatest Adventure,* noticed that the series was picking up the pace. After their first-runs, these two Weintraub Tarzan films were shown regularly for years at drive-ins, second-run theaters, etc.

Concurrent with the growing quality of Weintraub's Tarzan movies, was another factor in the upcoming Tarzan resurgence: the still-growing fandom movement. When Pittsburgh was selected as the site of the 1960 World Science Fiction Convention, *Burroughs Bulletin* editor Vern Coriell and Clarence B. (Bob) Hyde, a computer programmer at U.S. Steel, decided that now was the time to formally organize Tarzan-Burroughs fans into a consolidated institution. Hyde, a member of the World Con Convention Committee, was able to schedule a panel for the fans.

On September 5, 1960, at 11:00 A.M., the two-hour event united Tarzan-Burroughs fans at the 18th World Science Fiction Convention. Although Coriell's job commitment prevented him from attending this important event, Hyde and other fans elected to name the group "The Burroughs Bibliophiles" (the name Coriell had come up with). Hyde was elected president; Stanleigh B. Vinson vice-president; Charles Reinsel treasurer; Robert Horvath, secretary; and Vern Coriell, editor. Vern's *The Burroughs Bulletin* was voted the group's official periodical, and his *The Gridley Wave* its monthly newsletter.

Rita Coriell, the Burroughs Bibliophiles' secretary-treasurer for 20 years, told how Vern visited her and "got out a little 5x8 card file and worked the entire weekend. I couldn't figure out what he was doing, but learned later that this little box represented the Burroughs Bibliophiles."[4] To this day, over a half-century later, this international organization hosts annual conventions in different locations. One event is a Dum-Dum, named after the drumming ritual of the mangani in the

Tarzan saga, and the other, the ECOF: Edgar Rice Burroughs Chain of Friendship.

The 1960s Tarzan resurgence suddenly took on larger mainstream proportions. In December 1961, a Downey, California, teacher banned the Tarzan novels from the school library on grounds that Tarzan and Jane were not married, and thus not a fit subject of literature for children—a decision based on knowledge of only the movie version of the Tarzan and Jane relationship. It became national news. A December 28 AP wire story countered with statements by fans, pointing out that Tarzan and Jane had been married at the end of the second novel in the saga, *The Return of Tarzan.* Tarzan fans in Santa Ana had to rise up against suppression of the books, and publications from *The Long Beach Independent* to the *Wall Street Journal* covered the controversy.

At a board meeting called by Superintendent Bruce Moore of the Downey Unified School District, they unanimously voted to keep the Tarzan books in the library. The Downey Lions Club donated $200 to the school district for the purchase of more Tarzan and Zane Grey books (Grey had come under fire because of rough language). In terms of publicity, this national media uproar couldn't have benefited Tarzan and Edgar Rice Burroughs, Inc., more than if Edgar himself had risen from the dead to conjure it up.

In 1962, the Tarzan resurgence again took on even wider media parameters. Book publishers, fans and other readers were eager to go back to the primitive, to return to the source of the now 50-year pop cultural legend. Ace Books and Ballantine Books both secured rights from Edgar Rice Burroughs, Inc., releasing paperback reprints with cover art by Frank Frazetta (Ace) and Dick Powers (Ballantine). For a time, one out of every 30 paperbacks sold in the U.S. were Tarzan novels, and other items such as comic books, games, puzzles and toys could be found by eager fans at the local drug stores, "five and dime" variety stores and department stores.

Added to the redefining of Tarzan in Sy Weintraub's first two movies, and the important sustained growth of the fandom movement, this staggering new interest took the Tarzan resurgence into a wider range of popularity than it would have attained, had the novels themselves not been at the center of the school library conflict. The American public had known Tarzan from countless media interpretations. Now, with Edgar's novels back in print and in the spotlight, the mythic Hero-Wanderer returned in a modern, pop cultural form: that of a savage, educated, inter-genre and complex Ape-Man.

Weintraub, on the heels of two very good Tarzan adventures, out-did himself by taking a production company to India for his third film, *Tarzan Goes to India* (1962). Jock Mahoney, one of the greatest all-around stuntmen in movie history, and the arch-villain in the previous film, inherited the part in the series from Gordon Scott, who had left for Europe to make other movies. Mahoney's Tarzan is more himself as he fights, leaps and swings in a grand manner befitting a pop cultural demigod. Quoting fan-writer Gene Freese:

> Despite his advancing age (42), [Mahoney] is a fine Tarzan, representing the character with uncommon grace, poise and dignity. Unlike many of his predecessors, Jocko did all of his own stunts and refused to use a foot loop when swinging from the jungle vines. He would have it no other way. He even did his own jump off the wing of a biplane into the waters of the Aswan Dam despite the fact the camera was so far away no one could tell it was him. As was his intention, he comes across as much more educated and erudite than his predecessors.[5]

Tarzan Goes to India became the biggest commercial hit in Tarzan movie history.

Also in 1962, Western Publishing ended its Dell comic books activities, creating Gold Key Comics to continue its licensed material. Gold Key's *Tarzan* retained Dell's number sequence; its first issue was #132. The disparate aspects and interpretations of Tarzan's cultural popularity were exemplified twice that year: In writer Donald Hamilton's Matt Helm thriller *Murderers' Row*, Helm gets into a fight with the muscle-bound Nick aboard a boat and notes, "It was kind of like playing tag with Tarzan of the Apes."[6] And on an episode of Jack Benny's popular TV series, Jack plays Tarzan and Carol Burnett a howling Jane. Both of these examples acted as 20th-century carrying units for the Tarzan cultural idea.

The Tarzan fans were also very busy. In September 1962, the Burroughs Bibliophiles hosted an event at Chicago's Pick-Congress Hotel as part of the 20th World Science Fiction Convention. It included the Bibliophiles' first important guest, Ellen M. St. John, widow of Burroughs book illustrator J. Allen St. John. More was to come. Before becoming a science fiction, mystery and popular culture writer, Richard A. Lupoff, working for IBM, moonlighted as Edgar Rice Burroughs editor at Canaveral Press. Lupoff writes of his introduction to Tarzan:

> I entered this scene in the early 1960s. My Beloved Spouse and I were little past the newlywed stage, and I came home one evening to find her reading a somewhat battered red-covered novel. I asked what it was, and she told me it was *Tarzan of the Apes.* I'll confess that I sneered. Pat had recently received her degree in English literature, and I expected her to be reading Thomas Hardy or

"TARZAN GOES TO INDIA"
A Banner Production—An M-G-M Release

62/296

After playing the villain in *Tarzan the Magnificent*, stuntman Jock Mahoney went on to star as Tarzan himself in *Tarzan Goes to India* (1962). This movie became the biggest hit in the history of Tarzan films.

Tarzan, Jungle King of Popular Culture

Edith Wharton. To me Tarzan was an overage and overweight Johnny Weiss-muller yodeling through a series of low-budget potboilers, or some crudely drawn comic books by a fellow named Jesse Marsh. But Pat insisted that *Tarzan of the Apes* was a much better book than I thought. She convinced me to read it, and she was absolutely right, and I was hooked.[7]

Between the years 1962 and 1964, and under Lupoff's editorship, 24 Burroughs titles were released in hardback form by Canaveral Press with dazzling dust jackets and interior illustrations by artists Mahlon Blaine, J. Allen St. John, Roy G. Krenkel, Larry Ivie, John Coleman Burroughs, Reed Crandall and the incomparable Frank Frazetta. Legendary science fiction and fantasy artist Frazetta, born in Brooklyn, had attended the Brooklyn Academy of Fine Arts at the age of eight, and worked

his way up as a comic book artist. He was commissioned by Canaveral Press to illustrate a new hardback edition of *Tarzan at the Earth's Core* and the first edition of *Tarzan and the Castaways* (never before published in hardback form). That Frazetta, well known among comic book aficionados, also illustrated hardback books and covers for the Ace Burroughs paperbacks drew a certain amount of comic fandom toward the Tarzan novels.

In 1963, the Burroughs Bibliophiles' Dum-Dum was held at the 21st World Science Fiction Convention in Washington, D.C. Their guests of honor were science fiction and fantasy figures L. Sprague de Camp and

Jock Mahoney inscribed the above photograph of himself as the Ape-Man. *Tarzan's Three Challenges* (1963) grossed more than the previous all-time biggest Tarzan film, which had also starred Mahoney.

Sam Moskowitz, both honored with Golden Lion Awards. Richard Lupoff, whose fanzine *Xero* received a Hugo for best fanzine of 1963, joined in the panel discussions.

Sy Weintraub's next Ape-Man epic, *Tarzan's Three Challenges* (1963) with Jock Mahoney, was filmed in Thailand near Bangkok, and close to the Chiang Mai province. Stunning scenes of Thailand's culture, art and architecture support the well-done action sequences. An evil warlord (played with gusto by Woody Strode) threatens to depose, with violence if need be, a child spiritual leader. Tarzan is summoned by the elder monks to combat the near-invincible warlord. About midway during filming, Jock Mahoney contracted dengue fever, amoebic dysentery, tertiary malaria and pneumonia. "Any one of these diseases would have knocked a normal man off his feet," Gene Freese reported in his Mahoney biography. He went on:

> Within a ten-day period Jocko dropped over 40 pounds of muscle in the oppressive humidity. He couldn't eat and hold down anything of substance. He couldn't sleep more than a few winks at a time. Somehow, he miraculously continued to film against medical advice in an effort to get the picture completed. The pneumonia became interstitial in his lungs, which could have turned into a death sentence. In the final days of filming he was passing out from weakness dozens of times a day and there were crew members standing by to catch him should he collapse in front of the cameras. Between takes he was in an oxygen tank or wrapped in ice.[8]

Woody Strode claimed that Jocko's life was saved by feeding him antibiotics like candy. It took about a year for Jocko to regain his weight. Despite Mahoney's obvious weight loss in the film, it is one of *the* best Tarzan movies, and did better business at the box office than the previous all-time money maker *Tarzan Goes to India*, also starring Jock Mahoney as Tarzan.

In May 1963 a story by Tarzan fan William Gilmour, *Tarzan and the Lightning Man*, became a 20-page booklet supplementing Vern Coriell's *The Burroughs Bulletin* #14. This limited "first edition" of 600 copies "for free distribution to members and friends of the Burroughs Bibliophiles" was published by House of Greystoke, a creation of superfan Coriell. In November 1963, the remarkable collectability of Burroughs' first editions and even reprints prompted *The Antiquarian Bookman*, a trade journal for booksellers, to do an issue on this phenomenon. The *Editor's Corner* begins: "In the past 15 years AB has had many notable special issues, including the first trade recognition of science and fantasy fiction, magic, Horatio Alger, the 500th anniversary of the Gutenberg Bible, etc.—but none has aroused as much advance interest as the present special issue on Edgar Rice Burroughs."[9] An October 21, 1963, *Wall Street Journal* article by Edmund Fuller is simply titled "Return of Tarzan."

Gold Key launched their *Korak, Son of Tarzan* comic book series in January 1964. In issues 1 through 45, the art is the work of Russ Manning, Warren Tufts, Dan Spiegle and others. Manning, who had studied at the Los Angeles County Art Institute, worked for Western Publishing illustrating many Dell comic books. In June 1964, Canaveral Press released the first edition of *Tarzan and the Madman*, written by Edgar in 1940 but never published. The dust jacket and interior illustrations are by Reed Crandall (of DC's *Blackhawk* fame). Some fans of Philip José Farmer's Wold Newton Family/Universe concept (extrapolating, merging and restructuring of pop cultural archetypes) see this Tarzan tale as a veiled, fictionalized version of a real event: An Ape-Man double is sent by a behind-the-scenes power to help further their hegemony over the world; in this case, by impersonating a god (what else, in a Tarzan tale?) and enslaving the African-Portuguese populace.

The year 1964 was a great one for the author. Johnny Weissmuller made a multi-city tour selling swimming pools. My friend Bob Rutledge and I met Big John at the Montgomery Ward department store in Oakland, California. He wore his Jungle Jim safari outfit (without the hat), sported stylish sunglasses, posed for photos and signed items in a brisk but friendly manner. The most popular Tarzan of the movies also did TV commercials. One was filmed at Africa, U.S.A., a jungle and animal compound in Soledad Canyon near Los Angeles. Big John was given a new Buick with a faux-leopard-skin top as partial payment for his work.

While Weissmuller was selling his swimming pools, the Tarzan resurgence took an interesting turn with the unauthorized publication of five all-new Tarzan novels by "Barton Werper." Gold Star Books (a Charlton Comics arm) hired Peter and Peggy Scott to grind out these sometimes plagiarized but sometimes interesting science fiction adventures of the Ape-Man. In *Tarzan and the Silver Globe* (1964), the Ape-Man, the Waziri and a group of mangani battle extraterrestrial monsters. *Tarzan and the Cave City* (1964) is ripped off from Burroughs'

In 1964, Johnny Weissmuller went on a cross-country tour selling swimming pools.

Tarzan the Magnificent, with a magical emerald called the Light of the Night standing in for Edgar's Gonfal diamond. *Tarzan and the Snake People* (1964) mixes colonial intervention and snake humanoids. *Tarzan and the Abominable Snowmen* (1965) is just what it sounds like, with a banished Egyptian culture thrown in. *Tarzan and the Winged Invaders* (1965) is a bit more interesting: Tarzan, Jane and some mangani battle time-traveling mutants from the future.

Edgar Rice Burroughs, Inc., stepped in, suing to have the books removed from circulation. Any remaining copies were to be destroyed.

Nevertheless, it was becoming evident that the fans wanted more Tarzan in forms other than movies, comic strips and comic books. Edgar's original novels, published by Canaveral Press, Ace Books and Ballantine, were still tremendously popular due to fallout from the Downy library debacle. But the diehard Tarzan fans, and much of the general public, wanted more literary adventures.

Also, steps in the direction of an academic acceptance of Edgar's works as literature advanced. For example, a 1965 college textbook, *Literature for Composition* by James R. Kreuzer and Mrs. Lee Cogan, reprinted the first 18 paragraphs from *Tarzan of the Apes*. The Tarzan excerpt was accompanied by passages from the works of Jonathan Swift, James Thurber, H.G. Wells and other literary luminaries. R. Kreuzer, dean of Queens College of the City University of New York, stated, "The idea for this particular section is to demonstrate to English classes how a writer (Swift, Wells, Burroughs) gains credibility with the material on hand."[10]

Canaveral Press editor and Tarzan fan Richard A. Lupoff took a grand stride in the direction of academic acceptance of Tarzan with an excellent study of the Burroughs canon, *Edgar Rice Burroughs: Master of Adventure* (1965). And as Burroughs had, by science fictional means, made Tarzan immortal (*Tarzan's Quest*, 1936), the field was open for his classic, Burroughsian adventures to continue. Tarzan, the archetype who had become self-perpetuating and independent from Edgar Rice Burroughs 47 years earlier, had now, in the unauthorized "Barton Werper" tales, inspired a glimpse, a glimmer of the obvious potential of himself as a continuing science fiction and fantasy literary hero.

Russ Manning became the artist of Gold Key Comics' *Tarzan of the Apes* comic book series in November 1965, taking over from the ailing Jesse Marsh. The scripts were still written by Gaylord Du Bois. Manning, formerly a student at the Los Angeles County Art Institute, began his collaboration with Western Publishers in the early '50s, including his work on *Brothers of the Spear*, a backup serial which ran through the *Tarzan* comic books. Writing on Manning in *The Burroughs Bulletin* periodical (new series), Robert R. Barrett made this very good assertion, from another fan's point of view: "While given little attention by many readers of the Burroughs books, there were a number of stories dealing with Tarzan of the Apes which were every bit as entertaining as the original. They appeared in the comics section of a limited number of newspapers in the United States. The author of these newspaper strips stories was Russ Manning."[11]

Manning would later create the comic book *Magnus, Robot Fighter*, basing the superhero title character on Tarzan: The robot 1A raises the human Magnus as the mangani did with the infant Tarzan.

Although there hadn't been a new Tarzan movie in two years, the Weissmuller films were popular on television and the more recent films, Lex Barker through Jock Mahoney, ran in second-run theater circuits, sometimes shown as all-Tarzan programs or mixed with other genres. Sy Weintraub's *Tarzan's Greatest Adventure*, *Tarzan the Magnificent*, *Tarzan Goes to India* and *Tarzan's Three Challenges* were especially popular, and attracted the interest of people who had been passing on the movies. In some cases, the movies attracted them enough into wanting to also read the books.

In 1965, Canaveral Press published another first hardback edition of a tale in the Tarzan saga: Edgar's *Tarzan and the Castaways*, with a great dust jacket and interior illustrations by Frank Frazetta. This book is comprised of three tales originally published in pulp magazine form during the late 1930s and early 1940s: *The Quest of Tarzan*, *Tarzan and the Champion* and *Tarzan and the Jungle Murders*.

As if four recently unpublished-in-book-form Tarzan tales weren't enough to satisfy the fans, another non–Burroughs Tarzan novel appeared in paperback. Edgar Rice Burroughs, Inc., authorized the publication of Ballantine's *Tarzan and the Valley of Gold* (1966) by famed science fiction writer and Hugo Award winner Fritz Leiber. Endorsed as "Tarzan 25" on the front cover, Leiber's excellent novel is officially considered part of the Tarzan Saga, bringing the Ape-Man into the present (the 1960s). In Leiber's tale, Tarzan's connections to the British Intelligence services resurface, and he carries a letter of authority from Queen Elizabeth for his assignment: eliminating an insane international criminal. Tarzan's motives, as with his psychology and emotions, are mixed; his mission is for his country (to remove a supercriminal) but his heart is with the primitive people of a lost Brazilian culture he helps protect from the encroachment of civilization.

The difference between Lord Greystoke and Tarzan becomes apparent to new friends when John Clayton becomes the Ape-Man:

frightening, his face hardening. He's told, "You don't look like the same man at all."[12] On Bill and Sue-On Hillman's *ERBzine* website "Doc Hermes" states, "*Tarzan and the Valley of Gold* is well-crafted and thought out, thoroughly entertaining and deserving of more attention than it has gotten."[13]

In 1966, *Tarzan and the Valley of Gold* was also the title of Sy Weintraub's newest Ape-Man movie. The new Tarzan, Mike Henry, was formerly a professional football player for the Pittsburgh Steelers and the Los Angeles Rams. His Tarzan has too much of a drawl, and he comes off as a sort of "Texas Tarzan." Henry also sports a hairstyle that is right out of a salon and kept in place by a layer of hair spray. He wears the latest in sartorial perfection. The plot is somewhat the same as Fritz Leiber's novel of the same name, but the movie's locale is Mexico, and

In 1966, Sy Weintraub released *Tarzan and the Valley of Gold* starring ex-football player Mike Henry. Photograph signed by Henry (Ralph Brown collection).

Tarzan's secret agent status is not apparent. Many movie fans, not realizing that the literary Tarzan was already a secret agent, derisively dubbed Mike Henry (drawl and all) "the James Bond Tarzan." It's a good example of a pop cultural "representation" clashing with itself.

This adventure, shot in Mexico, included sequences on the grounds of the ancient holy city of Teotihuacan. Playwright-director Salvador Novo learned of this and wrote a newspaper article declaring that the production had degraded a national monument. The National Institute of Anthropology and History refused the movie company's request for more time to film at the site. Producer Sy Weintraub had to turn over 15,000 feet of his movie for review by the Director of Cinematography, a government agency that regulates motion picture production in Mexico. The footage was declared unobjectionable and the film was returned.

An AP wire-service article by James Bacon reported on Tarzan's cinematic resurgence:

> Down here [Acapulco] swinging through the trees is the first star in movie history who has a chance of grossing a billion dollars at the box office. Is it Charlie Chaplin? Elizabeth Taylor? John Wayne? Aye-eeeee! No! It's Tarzan. Producer Sy Weintraub, who owns the Tarzan gold mine, discloses that Tarzan movies have grossed more than $750 million.... Tarzan is the most durable and commercial of movie stars. No Tarzan picture ever came close to losing money. All have shown the kind of profit that makes bankers swoon.[14]

Working with animals as performers had always been a challenge to Tarzan films producer. During the Mexican filming of the first season of Sy Weintraub's upcoming *Tarzan* TV series, an elephant grabbed a trainer and stomped him to death. A UPI dispatch reported that the elephant "was frightened by barking dogs as it was unloaded from a ramp...."[15]

Ron Ely, hired to play the Ape-Man after Mike Henry's defection from the role, said that the elephant "went berserk. Injured five. Killed two people and the trainer. Tore the trainer apart. Pulled his arms out, ripped him apart. It happened close to a military academy, and the people from the military academy dropped the elephant just as I got there."[16]

Weinbraub, trudging on, advertised his Ron Ely TV show by staging a Tarzan reunion in Mexico City on September 1, 1966, the 91st birthday of Edgar Rice Burroughs. Held at the Churubusco Studios where

Weintraub was shooting the series, the reunion was attended by Ely, Johnny Weissmuller, Jock Mahoney and James Pierce. Jack Rutledge's AP story on the gathering mentions Ely's injuries while performing his own stunts, for example, a separated shoulder and broken ribs. This, combined with the deaths of the elephant trainer and others, helped build interest in the upcoming TV series.

Another important Tarzan meme arose during the late '60s, in a bizarre form, in the classic British film *Morgan: A Suitable Case for Treatment*. David Warner is Morgan, a Tarzan obsessed lunatic trying to win back the affections of his ex-wife (Vanessa Redgrave). Morgan hangs out at the gorilla cages at the zoo and fantasizes about being both King Kong and Tarzan. We get a glimpse of his fantasies via clips from *King Kong* (1933) and some with Johnny Weissmuller in *Tarzan and the Mermaids*. Morgan dons a gorilla suit, crashes his ex-wife's

The first Tarzan TV series appeared on NBC in 1966. The show was popular and notable for the quality of its guest stars, and Ron Ely's willingness to do all of his own stunts. Photograph signed by Ron Ely.

wedding, kidnaps her (like the impulsive Kong) and is sent to a treatment facility—a zoo, to him. Former swimming champion and ex-movie Tarzan Johnny Weissmuller was surprised when the producers of *Morgan* asked him to plug the movie by participating in a U.S. tour of the film. The 62-year-old Johnny agreed.

Tarzan's 1960s popularity also owed much to the fan movement and the creation of the Burroughs Bibliophiles. On September 3, 1966, Camille Cazedessus's publication *ERB-dom* won the Hugo Award for Best Fanzine at the Cleveland Worldcon (World Science Fiction Convention).

True magazine's September 1966 issue included an Arthur Whitman article on Sy Weintraub, his Tarzan movies and his coming NBC-TV series with Ron Ely as the first television Ape-Man. Titled "He Put Tarzan in a Tux," the article described changes in Tarzan over the years:

> Developments like these may seem strange to former Tarzan buffs who bade farewell to the Ape-Man when they stopped going to the movies every Saturday afternoon. The fact is that the changes are well in the spirit of the jungle toff's historic mission to make bales of money for his keepers. To keep the money machine producing, Weintraub and his predecessors have wrung an endless series of alterations in his character. These, in turn, have kept Tarzan ever green for so long that he stands in fiction's highest treetop today, unchallengeably the most durable pop literature creation in American history.[17]

Tarzan's first TV series debuted in September 1966. It got much press because Ron Ely had insisted on doing his own stunts. In the first season Ely suffered 17 different injuries, including being singed by fire, bitten by a lion, falling from vines, falling down a hill, etc. *Tarzan* featured many talented guest stars, including, Julie Harris, Maurice Evans, Diana Ross and the Supremes, Jock Mahoney, Helen Hayes, George Kennedy, Barbara Bouchet, Sam Jaffe, Nancy Malone, Chill Wills, Sally Kellerman, James Whitmore, Ethel Merman and Jack Elam. A well-researched and detailed article in *TeleVision Chronicles* magazine pointed out:

> Despite a history of unflattering portrayals of black characters in Tarzan movies, the series would become a showcase for the finest black actors of their generation (or of any generation, in many cases)—James Earl Jones, William Marshall, Nichelle Nichols, Robert Do Qui, Yaphet Kotto, Woody Strode, Geoffrey Holder and Lloyd Haynes, among others—in well-written, respectful portrayals.[18]

Nevertheless, Ely found himself being vilified by black personalities such as Bobby Seal, one of the founders of the Black Panthers. Ely is quoted as saying, "Guys like that, and I think even Muhammed Ali, made some comments ... and it stunned me that there was a public reaction to me as a result of playing Tarzan in regards to any kind of a racial issue.... To my knowledge, we never did anything that touched on that, and I think I would have been aware of it. We could have done it inadvertently."[19]

In 1967, the Brazilian-made *Tarzan and the Great River* pitted Mike Henry's "Tex" Tarzan against an evil cult enslaving indigenous villagers of the Amazon. During filming, a fed-up chimpanzee viciously bit Henry on the chin. It took 18 stitches to close the wound. Henry's bite got infected and he lay in a three-day coma. Then he came down with a fever and had to recuperate for three weeks. A lion bit an actor playing one of the villains.

While the current movie Tarzan was having a rough time, ex–Tarzan Johnny Weissmuller was enjoying his retirement from the celluloid jungle. In a *Films in Review* article, writer Rudy Behlmer reported,

> In 1967, while in Hollywood filming an automobile commercial, Weissmuller told Don Page of the *Los Angeles Times*: "I miss the old Hollywood crowd that used to meet at Lakeside Country Club; W.C. Fields, Babe (Oliver) Hardy, Errol Flynn, Jack Oakie, Bob Hope, Guy Kibbee. When I lived in a court in Toluca Lake, sometimes I'd come home at 3 a.m., stand on my balcony, and give the Tarzan yell. Every light in Burbank would go on. They finally kicked me out.[20]

While Tarzan was busy in movies and TV, the Tarzan-Burroughs Fandom movement was attracting adherents from the ranks of comic fans at the 25th World Science Fiction Convention (Worldcon), held in New York City in 1967. The Burroughs Bibliophiles' Dum-Dum honored Harold Foster and Frank Frazetta. These two iconic artists represented two different generational interpretations of Tarzan, also based on the artists' individual techniques and understanding of the Tarzan meme. Foster's Ape-Man (1929 through 1937) was in the style of stately paintings of classical heroes—legendary—even mythic. Frazetta's Ape-Man (the 1960s) was more blood, sweat and thunder, Tarzan the Terrible in need of a scrubbing-down.

Edgar Rice Burroughs, Inc., was now managed by Hulbert Burroughs and Robert M. Hodes. Besides the recent Tarzan book publications of Canaveral Press, the company also had authorized them to release some of Edgar's other titles, including *The Mucker* with a J. Allen St. John dust jacket and illustrations; *Tales of Three Planets*, art by Roy G. Krenkel; and *I Am a Barbarian*, illustrated by Jeffrey Jones.

In 1968, Backbeat Records' album *Willie Mae—Big Mama Thornton—She's Back* for (BLP-68) by blues singer Big Mama Thornton (aka Willie Mae Thornton) included the song "Tarzan and the Signified Monkey," written by E. Peace Jr. (Lion Publishing Co.). This Tarzan blues song was also released as a 45 RPM by Peacock Records. The Signifying Monkey is a trickster archetype of African and African-American folklore derived from Yoruba mythology.

The year 1968 marked a half-century of Tarzan in the movies. His next, filmed in Brazil, was Sy Weintraub's *Tarzan and the Jungle Boy*, the last of the three Mike Henry movies Weinbraub had made in less than a year and then shelved while his previous four films continued to play second-run. After the making of this movie, Henry declared that he had had enough of being Tarzan, enough of the extended filming schedules, and enough of the injuries and animal bites. In his book *Kings of the Jungle*, David Fury states, "Although Henry looked like he was in the most superb physical condition of his life in the film, it was obviously his mental health that had taken the most serious beating in his strenuous portrayals of Tarzan."[21]

While the cinematic Tarzan continued taking a beat-

In the late sixties, while Ron Ely was the television Tarzan, Mike Henry was the big-screen Tarzan. Spanish language promotional poster for *Tarzan and the Great River* (1967).

ing, his comic book and comic strip counterparts were attracting more attention. Iconic comics artist Russ Manning was guest of honor at the Burroughs Bibliophiles' 1968 Dum-Dum, hosted by the 26th World Science Fiction Convention at the Claremont Hotel in Oakland, California. By 1969, Manning had taken over the *Tarzan* daily newspaper comic strip (that job lasted until 1972), and he stayed with the Sunday page until 1979. Manning created some of the most striking and imaginative adventures in comics literature history.

A bizarre twist on the Tarzan archetype was a 1969 Top 10 record by country and novelty singer-songwriter Ray Stevens, the energetic "Gitarzan," the guitar man whose jungle band is "all you can stand."[22]

Back in the celluloid jungle, producer Sy Weintraub had had enough of the problems of making Tarzan movies. Though his television show was popular, he decided not to shoot another season of episodes. Also, the inferior quality of the Mike Henry films, compared with his first four, indicated that it was time to invest the money made off of the Ape-Man. Weintraub would go on to produce two Sherlock Holmes TV movies, *The Sign of Four* and *The Hound of the Baskervilles*, starring Ian Richardson as Holmes.

The decline in quality of Weintraub's last three Tarzan films helped turn attention away from the movies and onto the novels and comics adaptations. The Ape-Man continued to be self-perpetuating, adapting to the times and culture as always, but in yet another direction. Organized fandom would be a very important element in this other direction. Fandom itself had built up a more than respectable reputation, as did the recognition of pop culture favorites as worthy subjects of academic study.

Fandom got a huge mainstream boost because of a television show that had been cancelled after its 1969 season. *Star Trek*, created by Gene Roddenberry, became a cult phenomenon when disgruntled fans began letter-writing campaigns, produced a plethora of fanzines, and hosted the first Star Trek Fan Convention at New York's Hotel Pennsylvania in January 1972. Roddenberry and legendary science fiction writer Isaac Asimov were guests. The organizers expected around 500 fans to attend. Over 3000 showed up.

Tarzan and Star Trek helped to make the mainstream aware of fandom while academic studies of pop culture continued to emerge in lofty scholarly circles.

Academics not put off by the pulp fiction stigma of Burroughs' writings were discovering the intellectual components of the Tarzan novels. Edgar once proclaimed that fiction should be relegated for entertainment purposes only. Yet he layered the Tarzan saga with opposing views on controversial matters such as religion, culture, politics, war, the destruction of our environment and the excesses of the wealthy and privileged classes. The "post-movies" phase of the continuing Tarzan revival served to make other forms of the Ape-Man popular, including the original stories over the movies which had prevailed for almost 50 years. As Tarzan became literary again, interest in the original archetype would be reflected in novels, comic books, graphic novels, games and other intriguing, popular culture forms to come.

14

Ape-Man at the Popular Culture Crossroads of the Future

The emergence of two unusual types of fiction as definite, popular culture genres was pioneered by author Philip José Farmer. The idea of the reforming of Victorian and 20th-century archetypes, creating their secret lives and adventures, had gotten its popular breakthrough with author John Kendrick Bangs. His 1897 novel *The Pursuit of the House-Boat* had Sherlock Holmes going up against Captain Kidd. The cast of characters in John Myers Myers' *Silverlock* (1949) includes Robin Hood, the Mad Hatter, Beowulf and Daniel Boone. Noted Sherlock Holmes scholar W.S. Baring-Gould wrote a fictional biography, *Sherlock Holmes of Baker Street: A Life of the World's First Consulting Detective* (1962), based on the "sacred writings" and considered very influential. Northcote Parkinson followed suit in 1970 with his fictional biography of Horatio Hornblower, the Royal Navy officer in a series of novels by C.S. Forester.

These examples are precursors of two types of fiction that became late 20th and 21st century genres: crossover, and the secret "real lives" of fictitious characters. These genres were transformed into modern popular culture by Tarzan super-fan Philip José Farmer (1918–2009), the science fiction and fantasy writer who created the Riverworld series, World of Tiers series, Empire of the Nine mini-saga, and novels in which he reformed the stories of Victorian and pulp-era heroes. Farmer was also a great pioneer of the mainstream awareness of the idea of popular culture as a subject of academic study.

Farmer took giant strides with his vision, building ancient myth upon modern popular culture toward a genealogical family tree that includes many fictional characters and historical figures. Farmer's 1969 novel *A*

Feast Unknown, a reworking of the pulp, erotica and science fiction genres, includes many elements that would become part of the Wold Newton Family/Universe concept. The book was first published in paperback by Essex House as a porn novel, as it is graphically sexual and violent.

The first line of the foreword sets the tone: "I was conceived and born in 1888. Jack the Ripper was my father."[1] What a hook! Lord

In Philip José Farmer's 1969 novel *A Feast Unknown,* Grandrith and Caliban are half-brothers upon which two writers based their fictional characters—Tarzan of the Apes, and Doc Savage the Man of Bronze.

Grandrith and Doc Caliban are half-brothers, the "real" persons upon which two writers based their fictional characters, Tarzan and Doc Savage, respectively. Grandrith, the first person narrator, explains, "The events that led to the Grandriths being stranded on the West African coast are familiar to the readers of my 'biographer.' The reality was somewhat different, but the result was much as depicted in the romances based on my life."[2]

Grandrith and Caliban, though well into their seventies, seem to be men of around 30. They owe their extended life spans to an elixir provided by a mysterious organization known as the Nine. The Nine are a group of men and women from the Pleistocene era 30,000 years ago who had survived after discovering the elixir for slowing the aging process. They are behind-the-scenes manipulators, controllers of world affairs. The ancient myth of Romulus and Remus emerges in the form of the two half-brothers, Lord Grandrith and Doc Caliban, who are at first tricked by the Nine into wanting to kill one another.

Upon learning that their father had been a victim of the elixir of youth, which caused bizarre side effects (turning him into Jack the Ripper), the two superhumans join forces against the Nine:

> It would not be long before The Nine knew that the three of us had gone, however. Doc was hidden under some blankets and luggage. As soon as Hawthorpe failed to report in as scheduled, the Nine would investigate, and they would know that Caliban was still alive and with us. Then, the hunt would be on. Hunter, beware the prey.[3]

Farmer's next two Empire of the Nine novels were released in 1970 by Ace Books as one of their Ace Double series. One side is the Tarzan story *Lord of the Trees*, taking up after the events of *A Feast Unknown*; the flip side is *The Mad Goblin*, Doc Savage's. Lord Grandrith, the Ape-Man, escapes an assassination attempt by the Nine and makes his way to the place of his birth:

> I had known what to expect. The last time I'd been here, in 1947, the ravages of 59 years had almost completed the destruction. It was only sentiment that had brought me back here. I may be infra-human in many of my attitudes, but I am still human enough to feel some sentiment toward my birthplace.[4]

In *The Mad Goblin*, Doc Caliban and his friends fight off an assassination attempt on their lives. Doc's reaction is more human than his half-brother's:

Doc Caliban smelled the sting of explosives and the rich undercurrent of blood. There had been a time when he had savored those odors, even though he had not liked killing. Only once in his life, when he had gone mad from the side effects of the immortality elixir, had he enjoyed killing. Now he could not tolerate the odors associated with death once the immediate need for being in their neighborhood was over.[5]

These two titans, one feral and uninhibited, the other metropolitan and neurotic, battle the Nine's minions. Lord Grandrith is really put to the test when he must contend with the educated anthropoid of the species that had raised him: "I did not know how he had gotten here, but the Nine had to have something to do with it. He had gotten into contact with them, and they had decided to use him against me instead of killing him. They needed somebody who was stronger than I and knew all the techniques of hand and foot fighting. And who, in an arena where gunpowder and metal were forbidden, would be like a lion loose. A lion with the mind of a man."[6]

During a fog-shrouded battle at Stonehenge (the arena) between the forces of the Nine and the rebels, Grandrith fights off the anthropoid and finds the nearest monolith; "I wanted to stay in one spot, where he could not approach me from the rear, and wait for him. Even my breathing would have to be silent; I controlled the urge to suck in deep breaths."[7]

Looking down near his feet, the Ape-Man sees the arm of one of his dead comrades, wrenched out and cast away by the anthropoid. He picks the arm up by the wrist wielding it as a weapon. Out of the mists the creature charges. "I swung the arm as hard as I could before me, and it slapped his dark shoving forward face."[8]

Blinded and stunned, the anthropoid is set upon by the Ape-Man: "I came up with my left fist with all my force into his belly, exactly against the wound I had given him on that mountain road in Africa. He bent forward, clutching at his belly, and I slammed my right fist behind his left ear. He sagged forward and went down on his knees, and I hit the back side of that huge massively muscled neck with the edge of my palm. If he had been a man, he would have died. But he was only half-stunned...."[9]

Ferocious but careful, Grandrith finishes off the fallen creature; "I approached him from behind. He did not move. Then I knelt down, again with difficulty, and closed my one good hand around his throat.

167

I began to squeeze. His eyes opened. His tongue came out. He rolled his head slightly, but his arms did not move. And then that enormous chest quit rising and falling."[10] At the end of the Empire of the Nine trilogy, only five of the Nine are alive, and Tarzan and Doc Savage have crippled their organization.

Another Tarzan pastiche by Farmer, *Lord Tyger*, was published by Doubleday in a dust-jacketed hard cover (art by Seymour Chwast) in 1970. In it, a crazed millionaire creates a series of environments and events in order to develop his own Tarzan, Ras Tyger. This novel is seen by many in the Wold Newton Family/Universe context as fictionalizing the "reality" behind doubles of fabled persons (Tarzan, Doc Savage, etc.) used as agents of organizations such as the Nine. Thus, in *Lord Tyger*, the millionaire's disillusion at the failure of his creation is seen as a Tarzan clone that didn't work.

In just two years and four novels, Farmer created two genres out of a movement pioneered by authors such as John Kendrick Bangs, John Myers Myers, William S. Baring-Gould and Northcote Parkinson: the crossover genre and the "real lives" of fictional characters. The weaving of existing characters from fiction and reality into stories of alternative lives, secret lives, temporal distortions and timeline crossings would boost the means of keeping characters from popular culture, Tarzan in particular, alive through the ages.

Farmer was guest of honor at the Burroughs Bibliophiles' 1970 Dum-Dum at the Detroit Triple Fan Fair Convention. He won the coveted Golden Lion Award and was the banquet speaker on the topic of Tarzan's Coat of Arms.

Some two-part episodes of Sy Weintraub's *Tarzan* TV series were edited into movies for the overseas market and smaller movie venues in the U.S. *Tarzan's Jungle Rebellion* (1967) and *Tarzan and the Four O'Clock War* (1968) were the first released. Two years later came *Tarzan's Deadly Silence*, and again, *Tarzan's Jungle Rebellion*. By this time, Ron Ely had gone on to other roles (including Doc Savage in George Pal's film *Doc Savage: The Man of Bronze*) and also became a mystery writer.

Edgar Rice Burroughs, Inc., kept busy with merchandising. Doubleday published a series of Edgar's Mars books for their Science Fiction Book Club with dust jackets and illustrations by Frank Frazetta and

Richard Corben. Ace Books released a paperback of Burroughs' *The Wizard of Venus* and the unpublished *Pirate Blood* in one volume, illustrated by Roy G. Krenkel. For some fans and scholars, *Pirate Blood* has a rather infamous reputation as a novel that probably would have been toned down by Burroughs. As Tarzan archivist Ralph Brown has pointed out, the so-called heroes of the story are like hardened noir characters, too inured to the murders and other atrocities around them. Bruce Bozarth, on his ERBLIST.com website, said: "Burroughs wrote about seamy characters in semi-heroic molds rather infrequently. *The Efficiency Expert*, *The Girl from Hollywood* and *Pirate Blood* fall into this category."[11]

To cap the first year of the new decade, an amusing Tarzan meme was released by the British rock band The Kinks. They had a transatlantic hit with their song "Apeman," which reveals frustration with the modern world—overpopulation, inflation, starvation, nuclear threats.[12]

In 1970, Edgar Rice Burroughs, Inc., was busy with their merchandising. Another couple of shelves the author photographed, representing the variety of items in the Archives.

Tarzan, Jungle King of Popular Culture

In 1971 Russ Manning was still illustrating the *Tarzan* daily and Sunday newspaper comic strips. Manning merged ideas from adventure and science fiction stories into his Tarzan tales, creating new characters and creatures that fit into the Tarzan canon. Another amusing Tarzan meme emerged in the April *National Lampoon* magazine: a satire titled "Tarzan of the Cows" with cover art by Frank Frazetta. The Gold Key *Tarzan of the Apes* comic book title (the number sequence which had begun with Dell Comics in 1948) came out with its 200th issue in June. That same month, Gold Key's *Korak Son of Tarzan* #42 hit the stands.

Twenty-three years after his last Tarzan film portrayal, Johnny Weissmuller, the movies' most famous and popular Tarzan, attended the British Commonwealth Games in Edinburgh and was presented to Queen Elizabeth. Big John also became an honored recipient of the American Patriot Award. He was then guest of honor at the September 1971 Dum-Dum at the 29th World Science Fiction Convention in Boston. The Burroughs Bibliophiles presented Johnny with the Golden Lion Award, and he was the guest speaker.

The year 1972 was a busy one for Tarzan. Back in Tarzana, Edgar Rice Burroughs, Inc., arranged for DC Comics to take up the Tarzan comic book series from Gold Key, continuing with Gold Key's issue-number sequence (previously the numbering sequence from Dell Comics). DC also acquired the *Korak Son of Tarzan* title, continuing Gold Key's numbering sequence beginning with #46, and also produced *Weird Worlds*, featuring John Carter of Mars, and the Pellucidar stories.

DC's first issue of the Tarzan title, #207, featured the art of the legendary comic book artist Joe Kubert, who would work on the series for the next three years. Kubert, born in Poland, attended Manhattan's High School of Music and Art, which led to his work with a comic book "packagers" company, Harry Chesler's Studio. Joe Kubert drew his way up through the ranks. From the 1940s through the 1960s, his work in comic books and newspaper comic strips included *Catman Comics* #8, 1942; helping to produce the first 3-D comic books in the 1950s; and the *Sgt. Rock* and *Hawkman* DC titles. Kubert had grown up as a Tarzan fan, and stated, "Tarzan was one of the reasons I became a cartoonist in the first place, having read the strips as a kid and being really taken by the way Foster had handled it. I recall the strip vividly.

I looked forward to it every Sunday. What I tried to do was to capture the same kind of excitement it generated in me. It was like revisiting my childhood."[13] At a time when Tarzan movies were not being produced, Joe Kubert's comics adaptation attracted the popular attention of cultural critics and social anthropologists analyzing the Tarzan meme.

The literary Tarzan was on another of his rolls when new reprints of the Tarzan books were released worldwide in 16 languages; Bob Hodes, general manager of Edgar Rice Burroughs, Inc., told the *Daytona Beach Morning Journal* that the foreign sales of books and other merchandising items would add several million dollars in royalty payments for the heirs of Edgar Rice Burroughs. He added that Tarzan was going stronger than ever, and the overall 1972 income would become the highest in Tarzan history.[14]

In an issue of *Mainliner* magazine, a United Airlines travel periodical, author Col. Barney Oldfield states,

[T]hat pen-and-ink, handwritten creation of 1912 by Edgar Rice Burroughs for *All-Story* magazine has never since been a loser. It matters not whether the appraisal is made on the basis of hand-to-hand combat with man or beast, durability through the interim generations without the help of a single vitamin pill, or as a moneymaker.... [I]n 1973 alone, income attributed to his adventures and the use of his name exceeded $15,000,000. The lifetime total has long since passed $100,000,000, and he has given employment one way or another to half a million people in more than 100 countries.... [T]he *Bible* and Shakespeare and the Prophet Muhammad had much longer runs to pick up their admiring and worshipful audiences, so it's little short of incredible that in 64 years more than 600,000,000 hardcover books, comic books and magazines have been sold in 50 countries. Tarzan alone has appeared in 28 languages, with more to come. In half the nations of the present world—advanced, developing, emerging—it is truly said that only two things are known and readily identifiable in them all— Tarzan and Coca-Cola![15]

In the Herbert Ross film *Play It Again, Sam* with Woody Allen, Diane Keaton, and Tony Roberts, there's a scene where Woody Allen is in his office talking on the phone. Among some books piled on his desk is Gabe Essoe's *Tarzan of the Movies*.

In 1972, George T. McWhorter became the Rare Books curator of the University of Louisville Ekstrom Library in Louisville, Kentucky. This appointment would eventually have an impact on Tarzan and Burroughs fandom, and also the scholarly acceptance of Burroughs, Tarzan and popular culture in general. McWhorter was born in Washington, D.C., in 1931; his mother fired his imagination by introducing the boy to Burroughs' Tarzan books. George became a professional musician, his early training as a choirboy at Washington's National Cathedral preparing him for studies at the Curtis Institute of Music. He earned degrees in voice from the Eastman School of Music and the University of Michigan. A singer for six seasons with the New York City Center Opera, McWhorter also appeared frequently with the Radio Music City Hall and the New York Pro Musica.

He had a second career, that of a librarian, because of his love of books. He worked for three years in the Department of Rare Books at the University of Michigan Library in Ann Arbor and earned a Master of Arts in Library Science degree. After he became the Ekstrom Library's Rare Books Curator, McWhorter, partly inspired by a line in William Cullen Bryant's poem "Thanatopsis" ("And each one as before will chase his favorite phantom"[16]), he continued collecting books. He concentrated on the works of artist Arthur Rackham (1867–1939), amassing all of his works and 18 original paintings. Then he donated the collection to the University of Louisville library and went off on another hunt. McWhorter also continued adding to his Burroughs accumulation, including various items other than books. He would become a very important figure in the scholarship on Burroughs, whom he once described as America's greatest undiscovered national treasure.

Philip José Farmer continued his reworking of the Tarzan meme with the 1972 novel *Time's Last Gift*, in which a group of scientists from 2070 time-travel (in a vehicle called the H.G. Wells) to 12,000 BC. The novel's title refers to the fact that mankind will never again be able to travel to this particular point in time. It is gradually revealed that there is something strange, perhaps non-human about the team's medical doctor, John Gribardsun. His animal magnetism is so powerful that he is obeyed whether one wishes to or not. It turns out that Gribardsun, who adapts too easily to prehistoric life for the other members' comfort, is actually Tarzan of the Apes! When the team returns to their own time future, the immortal Gribardsun stays behind to personally experience the past, which includes becoming his own grandfather. In the context of Farmer's Wold-Newton Family/Universe, Tarzan stays in the past living through history for 14,000 years because Jane has been seriously injured, is in cryogenic suspension, and the Ape-Man plans to catch up with her just before she recovers.

Back in our timeline, Tarzan fandom was also very busy during 1972. At the September Dum-Dum, hosted by the 30th World Science Fiction Convention in Los Angeles, the Burroughs Bibliophiles had as guests artists Burne Hogarth and Russ Manning, ex–Tarzan Bruce Bennett (Herman Brix), James and Joan Burroughs Pierce and Edgar's grandson Danton Burroughs. The Golden Lion Awards went to Hogarth and Bennett. The Burroughs Bibliophiles also produced a new series of publications under the House of Greystoke imprint, including Sunday newspaper comic strip folios featuring the art of Hogarth, Hal Foster and Rex Maxon.

Philip José Farmer swung back into the fray with the fictional biography *Tarzan Alive: A Definitive Biography of Lord Greystoke* (1972). Besides allegedly being the biography of a real person, this book introduced the Wold-Newton Family/Universe concept in detail. The basis of Farmer's modern pop cultural pantheon is a meteor, which crashed to earth in 1795 at Wold Newton, Yorkshire, England. In Farmer's extrapolation of this event, the radioactive meteor caused genetic mutations in a group of investigators. The progeny of the radiation-exposed people at Wold Newton are "actual" persons who have been fictionalized into pop-cultural characters. These mutations include archetypes such as Tarzan, Sherlock Holmes, Doc Savage, Fu Manchu, the Shadow and many others.

In Chapter 23 of *Tarzan Alive*, Farmer describes Tarzan in the context of probability theory: "Tarzan had a force about him that moved him into the superhuman. This force twisted the paramagnetic lines of the fields of probability."[17] He adds, "Born on the cusp of Sagittarius and Scorpio, he had a double insurance for coincidence and favorable situations occurring in his neighborhood. Where he was, they seeded, sprouted, and bloomed."[18]

In his *Esquire* magazine "interview" with the Ape-Man, Farmer says, "Burroughs portrays you as free of racial prejudice."

Tarzan replies: "Like Mark Twain, I have only one prejudice. That is against the human race."

Farmer: "Let me not pursue *that* further."[19]

Tarzan, Jungle King of Popular Culture

Farmer's creation of the Wold-Newton family has Sherlock Holmes, Tarzan and Doc Savage as cornerstones, and is the culmination of thousands of years of myth and legend, and one of the most important inspirations of today's huge interest in popular culture and superheroes.

Besides Farmer's exhaustive reworking of the Tarzan legend, other writers inspired by Burroughs emerged. Between 1972 and 1978, Lin Carter wrote an adventure series set on the Jovian moon Callisto. British writer Michael Moorcock grew up as a Burroughs fan, at the

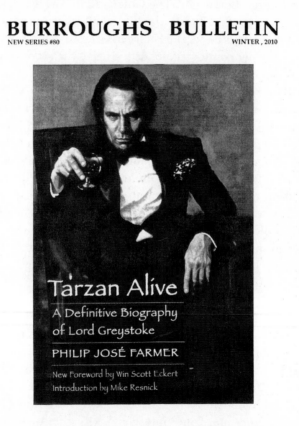

BURROUGHS BULLETIN
NEW SERIES #80   WINTER , 2010

Tárzan Alive
A Definitive Biography
of Lord Greystoke
PHILIP JOSÉ FARMER
New Foreword by Win Scott Eckert
Introduction by Mike Resnick

Tarzan as a pop culture folk-hero reached a wider mainstream audience in 1972 with Philip José Farmer's fictional biography, *Tarzan Alive: A Definitive Biography of Lord Greystoke*. Above, the fan produced *Burroughs Bulletin*, Second Series #80, 2010, celebrated the book and its revival thirty-eight years later.

age of 16 became editor of the fanzine *Tarzan Adventures*, and went on to write fantasy adventures in the Burroughs vein. Another longtime Tarzan fan, writer-journalist Mike Sirota wrote two series, the Reglathium stories and the Boranga saga, inspired by the grandfather of American science fiction. Professor of philosophy John Norman's Gor series was influenced by Edgar's John Carter novels.

In September 1973, Philip José Farmer appeared as the Burroughs Bibliophiles' banquet speaker at the Toronto, Ontario, Dum-Dum. (Ex-Tarzan Buster Crabbe, the guest of honor, was presented with the Golden Lion Award.) Farmer next edited 1974's *Mother Was A Lovely Beast*, a Feral Man Anthology in which he included stories of children raised by animals, a story of Tarzan in a future mechanized world (*Relic* by Mack Reynolds) and his own essay on feral-human mythology. The most interesting part of the book is the *Extracts from the Memoirs of Lord Greystoke*. Tarzan's life among the mangani is examined, including their social habits, language and sex practices. The "memoirs" also reveal Tarzan's subterfuge in inserting himself into civilization without revealing his true identity, his immortality or his source of wealth.

Legendary comic book artist Joe Kubert was presented with the Golden Lion Award at the 1974 Dum-Dum in Washington, D.C., hosted by the 32nd World Science Fiction Convention; he was also the banquet speaker. That same year, Kubert won the National Cartoonists Society Award for best comic book cartoonist. He would go on to found the Joe Kubert School of Cartoon and Graphic Art, located in Dover, New Jersey. The school's first graduating class included Thomas Yeates (the comic book, graphic novel and newspaper comic strip artist known for his work on *Tarzan, Prince Valiant, Conan the Barbarian, Zorro*, etc.), Rick Veitch (mainstream, alternative, and underground comic book artist) and Stephen R. Basset (*Swamp Thing*).

Philip José Farmer's *The Adventure of the Peerless Peer* (1974) teams Tarzan, Sherlock Holmes and Dr. Watson. The title page, with its John H. Watson byline, and the following notice is an example of the scope of Farmer's Wold-Newton Family creation: "Edited by Philip José Farmer. American Agent for the Estates of Dr. Watson, Lord Greystoke, David Copperfield, Martin Eden, and Don Quixote."[20] Don Quixote?

In this very humorous book, Holmes and Watson are called out of retirement to serve the British government during World War I. Their mission is to find a stolen secret formula, a mutated bacillus that when placed on sauerkraut grows at an amazing rate. The idea is to drop vials of the bacillus on Germany, thus rendering the nation sauerkraut-less and in too much of an uproar to continue the war. Stranded in the jungle during their adventures, Holmes and Watson are confronted by the Ape-Man.

Here is Watson's description of Tarzan: "He seemed to be a giant, though actually he was only about three inches taller than Holmes. His bones were large, extraordinarily so, and though he was muscular, the muscles were not the knots of the professional strong man. Where a wrestler or weight lifter recalls a gorilla, he resembled a leopard."[21] Watson adds, "[T]his man radiates a frightening ferality, a savagery more savage than any possessed by the most primitive of men."[22]

Tarzan has been searching for the Germans he believes had killed Jane (in Burroughs's novel *Tarzan the Untamed*), and the three join forces. Holmes finds the stolen formula. Watson falls in love with a woman of yet another lost world, and Tarzan goes off back to his search for Jane. By 1974, the concept of Tarzan as modern popular culture legend had been growing for 62 years. This growth had branched out into Farmer's Empire of the Nine and Wold-Newton works. *The Wind Whales of Ishmael* is Farmer's futuristic sequel to Herman Melville's iconic novel *Moby Dick*. In *The Other Log of Phileas Fogg,* Jules Verne's character is a humanoid alien on a quest (which includes the events of *Around the World in Eighty Days*) for a teleportation device. *A Barnstormer in Oz* is set in L. Frank Baum's Oz, where the Scarecrow still rules the Emerald City, there's a New Wicked Witch, and Oz turns out to be a parallel universe.

Farmer, a pioneer of the crossover and the "real lives" of media archetypes genres, inspired a trend in comics, graphic novels, movies, video games and Internet fansites of mixing characters from pop culture and history into new stories, meet-ups, alternative histories, secret histories and inter-dimensional adventures. His creation of the Wold-Newton family, and Tarzan's prominence among them, were also great inspirational boosts for the serious study of superheroes, which nowadays is taught in college classes.

15

Into the Future

When historian-teacher-writer Irwin Porges agreed to write a Burroughs biography, he had not yet seen the contents of the Burroughs family warehouse. It contained all of the documents, letters, etc., which Porges would have to review. "My first view of the warehouse piled to the ceiling with cases of documents and records came as a shock. Before me was a biographer's dream—or nightmare."[1] Porges' wife Cele, a researcher, spent three years searching through boxes of documents. Brigham Young University Press published Porges's *Edgar Rice Burroughs: The Man Who Created Tarzan* in 1975. This scholarly book was a big boost to the attention Tarzan was gaining as a significant subject of scholarly consideration.

The Tarzan fans held their 1975 Dum-Dum in Los Angeles with a Tarzan and Jane reunion; the guests included Johnny Weissmuller, Joyce Mackenzie, Jock Mahoney, Eve Brent, Denny Miller, Buster Crabbe, James Pierce and Louise Lorraine. Also celebrated was Edgar Rice Burroughs' 100th birthday. Robert M. Hodes, president of Edgar Rice Burroughs, Inc., announced that the worldwide amount of Tarzan products sold under their licensing of the character was up to around $50 million a year, ten times what it was in the early '70s. Hodes pointed out that income comes in not only from movies and television programs, but in the approximately two million dollars a year from the Tarzan-Burroughs novels, the millions of comic books published in different languages, Tarzan comic strips in 250 newspapers, advertising endorsements and royalties from the manufacturers of Tarzan items.

The Ape-Man returned to television in 1976 when Filmation began an animated series of adventures for CBS beginning with *Tarzan Lord of the Jungle*. Many viewers raised with the "Me Tarzan, you Jane" movie schtick were confused by his education. His familiar sidekick is little

N'kima the monkey, as in the literary saga, not Cheta as in old movies. The episodes used words from the mangani language, and in many ways present the true Tarzan of Edgar Rice Burroughs. The same year that Filmation's animated Tarzan TV series began, the Tarzan fans held their Dum-Dum at the Mid America Con in Kansas City, Missouri. The Golden Lion Award was presented to Jock Mahoney whose two Ape-Man movies, *Tarzan Goes to India* and *Tarzan's Three Challenges*, were the biggest moneymakers in the film franchise.

By 1977, Marvel Comics had secured the rights to produce Tarzan comic books in their own inimitable style, releasing *Tarzan, Lord of the Jungle* with the art of John Buscema. Tarzan fan Tom Roberts, writing in *The Burroughs Bulletin* periodical (new series), reported, "Although, as John would say, it may not have been the pinnacle of his career, it did produce some fine work ... and it allowed fans to compare different views and interpretations of ERB's most publicized character."[2]

George T. McWhorter decided to build an Edgar Rice Burroughs book memorial in the name of his mother at the University of Louisville. He collected all 70 first editions of the Burroughs books. He bought most of the private collection of Camille Cazedessus, a major fandom figure of the 1960s, as well as a 10,000-volume pulp magazine collection from the University of California, Los Angeles library. George later acquired all of the Rex Maxon, Harold (Hal) Foster and Burne Hogarth Sunday newspaper Tarzan pages.

Another major factor in the creation of the University of Louisville's Burroughs Memorial Collection was George's acquisition of items from the archives of Burroughs Bibliophiles founder Vern Coriell. Danton Burroughs was a great help in the project; in an issue of *Fantasy Review*, McWhorter wrote,

> Danton is hard working, dedicated, and a staunch supporter of the fans ... which makes him a unique ally in the business of building a Burroughs archive in the city of Louisville, Kentucky. Already he has sent priceless memorabilia such as the author's earliest school books (heavily annotated and drooled upon), a pen used during the author's early writing career, over sixty personally autographed and humorously illustrated presentation copies of books to his wife and children; some correspondence, a checkbook, and other primary source materials for future research.[3]

The Burroughs Memorial Collection includes first editions, reprints in 35 languages, pulp magazines, comic strips, comic books, a newspaper and periodical file, toys, games, movies, photographs, art, movie posters and other memorabilia.

But feminist, racial and political criticism of Tarzan and Edgar himself had been building over the years. In Pramod K. Nayar's incisive book on Frantz Fanon (the author of 1961's *The Wretched of the Earth*), he writes,

> Fanon argues that every society develops mechanisms for what he calls "collective catharsis," where there must exist an outlet through which the forces of rage and aggression must be released. The games children play, argues Fanon, are modes of such catharsis where excessive energies, frustrations and anger can be harmlessly expelled. Fanon lists the Tarzan stories, Mickey Mouse and adventure sagas as modes of "collective catharsis." Now this is where the colonial situation adds to the black child's burgeoning neurosis. The black child growing up in racialized, colonial situations has just "discovered" the myth of African inferiority in these fantasmatic narratives. Tarzan becomes his hero, and the child begins identifying with the *white* explorers because even black children associate themselves, indeed identify themselves with the explorer, the white adventurer.[4]

In 1959, Lorraine Hansberry's Broadway play *A Raisin in the Sun* starred the great Sidney Poitier and Ruby Dee. The character of Beneatha, played by Diana Sands, showing frustration in Act I Scene II, says, "All anyone seems to know about when it come to Africa is Tarzan." Later in the same scene, Mama (Claudia McNeil) parrots her daughter's sentiments when she tells Beneatha's Nigerian boyfriend, "I think it's so sad the way our American Negroes don't know nothing about Africa 'cept Tarzan and all that."[5]

During the 1960s, many blacks saw Tarzan as a symbol of white superiority. TV broadcasts of Tarzan movies depicted Africans as ignorant savages and seemed to underscore the racism faced by African-Americans. Yet in the original Tarzan novels, Tarzan had been adopted into a tribe of Africans, the Waziri, whom Burroughs characterized as an ideal people who lived a primeval existence and conducted themselves with dignity, pride and intelligence. Tarzan is not portrayed as a racist or colonialist—though he does rule over his domain like a fierce demigod. His eminence among humankind stems not from any racial characteristics, but from his feral upbringing by the mangani, which shaped him into a superhuman—a superhero whose only prejudice is against corruptions of the so-called civilized world.

Elaborating on this, Francis Lacassin, the French author of 1971's

Tarzan, Jungle King of Popular Culture

Tarzan, ou le Chevalier Crispe (*Tarzan, or the Constricted Knight*), wrote, "Years before the term was invented, Tarzan declared himself an enemy of the consumer society. He cannot be considered the first hippie—that title belongs to Christ—but he was among the first to feel the sickness of civilization which gave birth to that movement of passive resistance."[6]

Despite how people like Lacassin and the author of this book see Tarzan, many people still don't, and never will, agree. bell hooks, the African-American feminist author of *Reel to Real: Race, Sex and Class at the Movies*, observes,

> As a child growing up in the segregated South, I would often overhear grown black men expressing their disgust with the Tarzan narratives and with the loving devotion the "primitive" black male gave the white male hero. This television show reminded its viewers that even in black nations, on alien soil, the white male colonizer had superior skills and knowledge that were immediately recognized and appreciated by the natives, who were eager to subordinate themselves to the white man. The "bad" black natives who refused to worship white masculinity were often in the roles of kings and queens. Of course, their leadership was corrupted by greed and lust for power, which they exercised with great cruelty and terrorism. Tarzan, the great white father, used his omnipotence to displace these "evil" rulers and protect the "good" docile natives.[7]

In *The Poetics of Imperialism: Translation and Colonization from The Tempest to Tarzan,* by Prof. Eric Cheyfitz, Chapter 1 is titled "Tarzan of the Apes: U.S. Foreign Policy in the Twentieth Century." Cheyfitz maintains, "[T]he cultural function of Tarzan is radically to reduce or homogenize domestic political complexities by displacing them onto a foreign scene, whose own political complexities are thereby radically homogenized in the vision of the romance."[8]

Despite any negative impressions of the Ape-Man brought on by Tarzan detractors who see him as racist (a symbol of white narcissism), a male chauvinist and colonialist, by 1980 heavyweights Carl Sagan, Jane Goodall, Arthur C. Clarke and Ray Bradbury were also outspoken in their recognition of Edgar Rice Burroughs' genius.

In 1981, MGM released a second *Tarzan the Ape-Man* remake, with Bo Derek and Miles O'Keeffe as the jungle lovers and Richard Harris as Jane's father, James Parker. The furor over Derek's topless scenes made the film more popular than it would have been otherwise.

In March 1983, United Features Syndicate's Sunday *Tarzan* newspaper comic strip was taken over by artist Gray Morrow and writer Don Kraar. Kraar said that UFS

> were concerned that the strip shouldn't have any controversial political content. Furthermore, since the largest market is overseas, they were concerned that we not indulge in racial or ethnic stereotypes that might offend our foreign readers. I'd pointed out that the Tarzan stories had their roots in Darwin's theory of natural selection, and in the European colonial movement ... "the white man's burden," if you will. And, too, they were concerned that we not do anything to offend Christian fundamentalists or Third World nations."[9]

Piercing through the jungle air, Tarzan's famous call signals a warning to his foes – and promises rescue for Jane – in MGM's "Tarzan, the Ape Man" a new version of the classic 1932 film. MILES O'KEEFFE as Tarzan, and BO DEREK as Jane, star in this romantic adventure directed by John Derek and produced by Bo Derek from a screenplay by Tom Rowe and Gary Goddard. A United Artists Release.

Miles O'Keeffe as the Ape-Man in the 1981 MGM second remake of *Tarzan the Ape Man*. The furor over Bo Derek's topless scenes made the film more popular than it otherwise would have been.

CHRISTOPHER LAMBERT in
"GREYSTOKE: THE LEGEND OF TARZAN, LORD OF THE APES"

Christopher Lambert in the ambitious *Greystoke: The Legend of Tarzan, Lord of the Apes* (1984).

Asked what references he used for Tarzan, Morrow said, "I don't use much reference. I have a file, of course. I get a lot of mail from the Burroughs fan club, and I got them to provide photographs of themselves to insert as background characters. They get a big kick out of it."[10]

The 1984 film *Greystoke, the Legend of Tarzan, Lord of the Apes* is an ambitious, sometimes enthralling take on the legend. As portrayed by Christopher Lambert, the Ape-Man struggles to adapt to being human, often bewildered but never deceived. In a magazine article, director Hugh Hudson stated, "The whole basis of the movie is that Tarzan can penetrate the darkness of our society, because he sees it more clearly and simply than we do. He's used to fighting. He's top dog—or ape, as it were—because he's smarter and stronger. The true form of natural dominance is merit; civilization has caused it to become inheritance."[11] In the same article, Lambert talked about filming the movie in the wilds of Africa:

> We arrived toward the end of the wet season. The rain forest is an area of dense, steaming oppression and power. Vegetation is so thick, only splashes of light touch the jungle floor. We'd been advised to watch what we touched and where we walked, and were given the usual battery of yellow fever, cholera, tetanus, typhoid and hepatitis shots. But, there are still mosquitos and tsetse flies, eight kinds of poisonous snakes and an almost infinite variety of deadly spiders to avoid. I imagined what life was for Tarzan from the moment he was born. He was on a thin edge between life and death.[12]

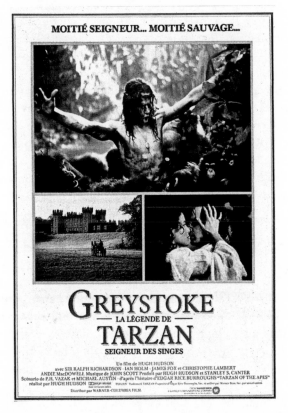

French lobby card for *Greystoke: The Legend of Tarzan, Lord of the Apes*.

Director Hudson, commenting on the test preview of the film, said,

Some of the reactions were strong because of the film's violent nature. We wanted to see how the apes would be accepted. There has never been any recall at all of any moment in which the audience didn't believe they were watching apes. I was staggered by the reaction. The audience would get frightened by them and then upset when the apes were wounded. People complained that there were too many violent things done to them, thinking the apes are real.[13]

[Making the movie] taught me a lot of things about myself and about human beings, which is also an understanding of oneself.... [I]t is about two journeys of self-discovery, the ape-king's and D'Arnot's. It's about the search for meaning. It's about coming to terms with Evil. It's about ecology, our use and abuse of the earth. It's about the struggle to create tools and weapons. It's about body language, cultural differences. It's about the ape behind the man and the man behind the ape. Not least, it's about the Fatal Impact, colonialism.[14]

The third Tarzan movie of the 1980s took a contemporary turn: The 1989 TV production *Tarzan in Manhattan* starred Joe Lara as Tarzan, Kim Crosby as a cab-driving Jane and Tony Curtis as Jane's father. The less said about this film, the better.

The 75th anniversary of the hardback book publication of *Tarzan of the Apes* was held at the Adventurers' Club in Chicago on October 21, 1989. Presentations by fans Clarence B. Hyde, George T. McWhorter and Bill Ross addressed the subject of 75 Years of the "Right Type," and the keynote address was given by Philip José Farmer.

The Burroughs Bibliophiles floundered temporarily after Vern Coriell's death in 1987. But the organization was revised in 1990 by George T. McWhorter. In Louisville, the first guests of honor were comics publisher Russ Cochran, ex–Tarzan Denny Miller, science fiction historian Sam Moskowitz and artist Burne Hogarth. Hogarth was presented with the Golden Lion Award.

The 1991 *Tarzan* syndicated TV series with Wolf Larson in the role ran for three years, and had Tarzan promoting environmental conservation. Larson stated that the series didn't intend to "beat people over the head with environmental issues.... It's an entertaining show that tries to bring interesting facts about the destruction of the rain forest, the slaughtering of elephants for ivory, and about polluting water...."[15]

But the image of "Me Tarzan, you Jane" Ape-Man persisted. And TV budget constraints limited the number of fantastic elements from the literary saga that could be included. Thus, the inter-genre aspect of Tarzan, a 79-year-old archetype adaptable to changes in science and culture, was discarded in favor of the "jungle man" approach.

This began to change around 1992. Henning Kure, a native of Denmark, had become editor of a new Tarzan comic book to be published by Semic International and distributed by Malibu Comics. A subsidiary of the Bonnier Group, an old Swedish family publishing business, Semic, through the efforts of Henning Kure, had made several offers to obtain the rights to produce Tarzan comics. Tarzan fan Duane Spurlock, who interviewed Kure for *The Burroughs Bulletin* periodical (new series) #13, noted, "Henning is immersed in Tarzan lore from years of reading and studying Burroughs and editing reprints of Tarzan comics for European markets. Henning's great love for Burroughs' creation is evident in the way he talks about Tarzan. Through the new comic book, he plans to share that enthusiasm with comics readers in the United States, Britain and Europe."[16] Kure said, "I'm not a Burroughs fan. I'm a Tarzan fan ... a fan of the one, true, original Tarzan character only."[17]

Semic International's *Tarzan the Warrior*, a graphic-novel serial from Malibu Comics, is a good example of the reshaping of a 20th century pop cultural archetype for an oncoming 21st century public. This is not to say that Tarzan was altered to accommodate contemporary standards or changes in culture. A thread throughout this book indicates that Tarzan of the Apes, as created by Burroughs in the literary saga, is a science fiction adventurer, secret agent, detective, paranormal investigator and a colonel in the Royal Air Force during World War II. Tarzan is also immortal, adapting with changing times while retaining his fundamentally mangani identity.

Tarzan the Warrior encourages the idea of Bigfoot being a North American species of the mangani, has Tarzan and Jane battling shapeshifting aliens, and many other fantastic plot elements. Another Malibu Comics graphic novel, the three-part *Tarzan: Love, Lies and the Lost City* brings the Ape-Man back to Opar.

One of the best Tarzan comic book adaptations, Eisner Award-winner Thomas Yeates' *Tarzan: The Beckoning* (1992), takes the archetype toward a 21st century context but maintains his fundamental character. This Malibu Comics graphic novel serial depicts Tarzan and Jane's fight to protect nature. Complementing Yeates' excellent artwork is his imaginative, provocative story. Interviewed for *The Burroughs Bulletin* periodical (new series), Yeates stated,

> I've always drawn for as long as I can remember, starting with crayons. I never felt I had more ability than anybody else; it was just something I stuck with until I figured it out. It's true that I began to add more detail to my drawings, because I seemed to remember more details than the other kids. My early Tarzan drawings were based on the old Weissmuller movies I saw on afternoon TV, long before I'd ever heard of Edgar Rice Burroughs.[18]

Semic International editor Henning Kure attended the Burroughs Bibliophiles' 1992 Dum-Dum in Louisville. He told Duane Spurlock, "Actually, *Tarzan Alive!* [by Philip José Farmer] was the culmination of what was going on in the fanzines at the time. I read most of the articles in *ERB-dom*, and a lot of my ideas for the present comics were founded

back then, on the basis of fan-generated ideas. I miss that kind of fandom...."[19]

The yearly ECOF Gathering, held in Denver, Colorado, the weekend of June 25–28, 1992, was attended by Burne Hogarth, Sam Moskowitz, Richard A. Lupoff and many others. This tenth annual Edgar Rice Burroughs Chain of Friendship event was hosted by John Fuller McGuigan, Jr., superfan and editor of the fanzine, *Tarzine*. McGuigan had compiled an amazing collection of books (the Dream Collection) which included the Tarzan-Burroughs books, and presented them for the enjoyment of the other fans, including Dan-

In the early 1990s, artist Thomas Yeates—pictured here at Comic-Con International San Diego 2012—took Tarzan toward a 21st century context while maintaining the Ape-Man's fundamental character. Yeates has become a major Tarzan/Burroughs artist and member of the Burroughs Bibliophiles (photograph by Bruce Guthrie).

ton Burroughs. John's collection included all of the Burroughs titles in first edition with dust jacket, and most of the books were signed by Edgar.

More chapters of the Burroughs Bibliophiles appeared. The Michigan chapter was organized by artist Brian Bohnett and called the Mad Kings, after Burroughs' novel *The Mad King*. In Atlanta, the Burroughs Bookies sprang up. Writer-actor Scott Tracy Griffin organized a Southern California chapter, the Los Angeles SubERBs.

In 1995, Dark Horse Comics published an unfinished Burroughs Tarzan novel after it had been completed by Joe R. Lansdale. *Tarzan: The Lost Adventure* was released pulp magazine-style in four parts; issues one and two had covers by Arthur Suydam. Thomas Yeates, Michael Kaluta, Charles Vess and Gary Gianni did interior graphics. A hardback first edition (with a foreword by George T. McWhorter) followed; it's considered an official volume of the Tarzan saga by Edgar Rice Burroughs, Inc., along with *Tarzan and the Valley of Gold* by Fritz Leiber and *The Dark Heart of Time* by Philip José Farmer. In *Tarzan: The Lost Adventure*, an insect-monster from Pellucidar is one of the dangers the Ape-Man faces before eventually entering a portal to the inner-world.

The 1995 Dum-Dum had as guest of honor the incomparable Maureen O'Sullivan. Maureen was flattered to receive the attention of so many fans, over 50 years after she had last portrayed Jane in MGM's *Tarzan's New York Adventure*. As David Fury pointed out,

> Of course for Maureen, the Tarzan pictures were only a part of her film work for Metro-Goldwyn-Mayer during this Golden Era of motion pictures. While working in the MGM stable of stars in the 1930s, Maureen was Mr. Mayer's favorite second leading lady in several classic films like *The Thin Man* (1934), *The Barretts of Wimpole Street* (1934), *David Copperfield* (1935), *Anna Karenina* (1935), *A Day at the Races* (1937), *A Yank at Oxford* (1938) and *Pride and Prejudice* (1940), as well as claiming the female lead in many of their "B" productions. Maureen's six Tarzan films were "A" pictures, and of course *Tarzan the Ape-Man* and *Tarzan and His Mate* are on a stratospheric level of their own as legendary classic adventures.[20]

The Golden Lion Award of the Burroughs Bibliophiles went to Joe Jusko for his brilliant paintings of Tarzan and other Burroughs characters, which were released as the *Art of Edgar Rice Burroughs* trading cards.

Tarzan, Jungle King of Popular Culture

Dark Horse Comics secured rights to the Tarzan character; over the next few years, they contributed an important volume of Tarzan lore. Tarzan's friend Mogambi has his say in Dark Horse's *Tarzan: Mogambi*, a single issue written by Darko Macan and illustrated by Bret Blevins. Mogambi warns Tarzan against becoming a representative of colonialism, while recognizing the Ape-Man's surprise at this notion, and the sincerity of friendship.

Dark Horse Comics also released a mini-series written by Bruce Jones and illustrated by Bret Blevins: *Tarzan and John Carter of Mars*, which places the Ape-Man within the world of Edgar's Martian series. Strengthening and imbedding the idea of Tarzan as a science fiction hero, Dark Horse released the mini-serial *Tarzan vs. Predator at the Earth's Core* in 1996. Walter Simonson wrote the story and Lee Weeks did the art. *Tarzan vs. Predator at the Earth's Core* is the merging of what amounts to a pop cultural myth (Tarzan) and an upcoming legend (Predator). From ancient literature into modern times, there has been a continuous motif of a pantheon of heroes and villains interacting, battling one another, and sometimes joining forces for a cause.

In the TV movie *Tarzan: The Epic Adventures—Tarzan's Return* with Joe Lara, a crystal amulet is a portal to an outer world. *Tarzan: The Epic Adventures* became a TV mini-series, and also the title of a 1996 R.A. Salvatore novel based on the series. The Ape-Man as literary saga easily adapts to societal and technological advances, and in the midst of yet another revolution in science and industry Tarzan's pop cultural status grew with technology: Tarzan user interface gaming, online games and stories stressing science fiction plots, have the Ape-Man becoming part of the future.

But, as the mini-series' supervising producer Michael McGreevey said in an interview,

> The one area that brings out drama in Tarzan is this area of aloneness. In a roundabout way, even though we're doing an action-adventure series with a ton of action, we're also doing very personal stories, centered around Tarzan's conflict over his duality and his attempt to deal with his aloneness and feelings of isolation. Joe brings a true understanding of that to the role.[21]

Dark Horse Comics began its *Tarzan* title in July 1996, and the science fictional and fantastic elements continued. So did academic studies of Tarzan as literature, with publishers Signet and Penguin including

Joe Lara, stars as Tarzan® in "TARZAN: THE EPIC ADVENTURES," a first-run action/fantasy hour set to premiere in the Fall of '96 from Keller Siegel Entertainment.

Tarzan® Trademark TARZAN owned by Edgar Rice Burroughs, Inc. and used by permission.

In a 1996 television movie, *Tarzan: The Epic Adventures—Tarzan's Return*, Joe Lara played the Ape-Man. This TV movie became a mini-series, and also a novel by R. A. Salvatore. Photograph signed by Joe Lara.

Tarzan of the Apes in their classics catalogues. Joe Jusko's robust paintings of Tarzan and company, previously released as trading cards, appeared as an art book, *Joe Jusko's Art of Edgar Rice Burroughs*. A crater on Mars was named Edgar Rice Burroughs Crater through the efforts of Carl Sagan and the Planetary Society. Primatologist Jane Goodall has stated that reading the Tarzan series had a major influence on her childhood. She fulfilled her childhood dream of living among the great apes as did Tarzan.

On August 16, 1996, Binti Jua, a western lowland gorilla at Chicago's Brookfield Zoo, rescued a three-year-old boy who climbed a railing and fell 18 feet into the exhibit. Binti, with her 17-month-old baby Koola clinging to her back, protected the human child from other gorillas, cradling him, and then brought him to the keeper's door. Binti gently held the boy until someone came to take him. The Burroughs Bibliophiles honored Binti in a ceremony with the Kala Award. (Kala is the she-ape who rescued infant John Clayton and raised him as Tarzan.)

Dark Horse Comics released a three-part adaptation of Burroughs' classic tale *The Return of Tarzan*; it was written and illustrated by Thomas Yeates, who studied and honed his talent under artist and teacher Joe Kubert. In it, the Ape-Man was back to being the stark demigod of Burroughs' imagination. Edgar often referred to his archetypal hero as having a body more like Apollo than Hercules. Yeates' depiction of the rescue of Jane Porter from a sacrificial altar is a stunner of primal energy as Tarzan battles his way through the Oparians, laying waste to them like Samson slaughtering Philistines.

Dark Horse's 1997 *Tarzan: Legion of Hate*, set during World War II, was written by Allan Gross, drawn by Christopher Schenck and inked by George Freeman. Gross stated,

> I recalled that the Zulis' mind-control emerald had been left behind in Burroughs' original story [*Tarzan the Magnificent*] and that Tarzan had buried it.... I would use this as a plot point, imagining that it had fallen into the hands of a renegade Nazi.... In the midst of a wild, battle-filled story, I couldn't help exploring the myriad racial relationships going on at the time as a backdrop for the adventure.... This was a touchy subject and I did my best not to stereotype.... In the end, it was clear that power corrupts equally and skin shade had very little to do with anything. When the Nazis have finally been defeated and order restored, Mugambi leaves Tarzan with a haunting prophecy of a changing world. Tarzan, who treated men equally, was forced to accept that perceptions can be as powerful as actions. Through no fault of his own, he could be seen as a symbol of racism, with being racist. As with many of my stories, I tried to weave in a magic moment from the original book to reinforce my story. In this case, I used a flashback to the youthful Tarzan seeing his own reflection in the pond and realizing that he looked different from all the young Great Apes."[22]

Movie Tarzan Gordon Scott, guest of honor at the 1997 Dum-Dum, was presented with the Golden Lion Award for his portrayals. Scott told the author of this book that back in the 1950s he had approached the producers of the movies with the idea of putting more ape into his Ape-Man (grunting, growling, etc.) but this was rejected. It would be decades before the movie Tarzan would be presented in this manner, in *Greystoke: The Legend of Tarzan, Lord of the Apes.*

Along with the science fictional presentations of the Ape-Man in comic books, graphic novels and the late 1990s TV incarnation, there were popular culture crossovers. The year 1997 also saw the release of Dark Horse Comics' two-part graphic novel *Tarzan: Le Monstre*. Both parts sported a cover illustration by Bernie Wrightson; the story was by Lovern Kindzierski and it was illustrated by Stan Manoukian and Vince Roucher. It fills in gaps in the Ape-Man's early adult life (before he and Jane are reunited in the novel *The Return of Tarzan*): John Clayton (Tarzan) and his friend Paul D'Arnot of the Imperial French Navy are dining at the Moulin Rouge in Paris. They are introduced to Pablo Ruiz Picasso, who says he is working on a type of art he calls Cubism. Clayton and D'Arnot then get involved in an adventure involving the Phantom of the Opera. The *Monstre* of the title refers not to the Phantom but to John Clayton, whose conversion from a seemingly normal human into the ferocious Tarzan terrifies the Opera Phantom, who is almost killed by the Ape-Man. The story ends with Christine Daae willingly continuing her training by the Phantom. Tarzan learns another lesson in compassion and forgiveness, but realizes that he is an outsider because of what is in his heart.

The popular culture crossovers continued the same year with the release of Dark Horse Comics' *Tarzan* numbers 13 and 14: *Tarzan: The Modern Prometheus*. The author of this intriguing two-part story is Lovern Kindzierski, and the stark, sometimes gothic artwork by Stan Manoukian and Vince Roucher; the covers of both issues, a moody, gothic pose in #13 and a stylistic, "Universal Pictures" pose in #14, are the work of Michael Wm. Kaluta. Again, Tarzan is in a great metropolitan city, New York of 1909. He meets Sherlock Holmes creator Arthur Conan Doyle and scientist Nikola Tesla. Operating as three detectives, they embark upon a mystery adventure concerning a mad monk and an old book of unimaginable power. The book is the diary of Victor Frankenstein; his Monster is determined to stop others from creating life from the dead. The Monster laments the fact that he can find no place of peace on the face of this planet. Tarzan arranges for the Monster to live in Pellucidar, where he can fit in.

Tarzan: Tooth and Nail, another Dark Horse Comics two-part crossover, has Tarzan, still in 1909 New York, still in his detective mode, investigating the Strange Case of Dr. Jekyll and Mr. Hyde. The last crossover of 1997 was the four-part Dark Horse *Tarzan versus the Moon Men*, a grand science fiction adventure with Tarzan, Korak, Muviro and the Waziri battling the Moon Men from Burroughs' novel *The Moon Maid*.

The 1990s Tarzan revival also included TV documentaries. *Tarzan: The Legacy of Edgar Rice Burroughs* was an episode of A&E's *Biography* series hosted by Peter Graves. *Moi, Tarzan*, a French documentary, included commentary by George T. McWhorter, and Philip José Farmer. American Movie Classics showed *Investigating Tarzan* during its four-day, 32-film Tarzan festival. In *In Search of Tarzan* (1998), Ray Bradbury, Maureen O'Sullivan, Gordon Scott and Bo Derek spoke on the subject.

Tarzan/Carson of Venus, a graphic novel serial released by Dark Horse Comics in 1998, teamed the Ape-Man with another Burroughs science fiction character, Carson Napier. That same year, the movie *Tarzan and the Lost City* starring Casper Van Dien included fantasy elements: The Waziri shaman Mugambi, portrayed by South African playwright-actor Winston Ntshona, sends a telepathic message to Tarzan, is a shapeshifter, saves Tarzan's life, and is integral to the efforts of the Waziri and the Ape-Man in their battle against evil mercenaries. Tarzan continued appearing in different genres, persisting in his (then) 86-year trend of adapting to the multimedia, pop-cultural environment.

In 1999, Philip José Farmer fulfilled a lifelong dream of publishing a non-pastiche Tarzan novel, one that would fit into the Burroughs canon. *The Dark Heart of Time*, sanctioned by Edgar Rice Burroughs, Inc., takes place in the interim between *Tarzan the Untamed* and *Tarzan the Terrible*, while the Ape-Man is tracking Jane's progress after her escape from the German army.

The last year of the 1990s also saw the Ape-Man included within the Disney pantheon with the release of their beautifully crafted animated blockbuster *Tarzan*. The film's supervising-animator Glen Keane had taken the first step by reading some tales in the saga. Then, as reported in *Disney Magazine*:

> Continuing to search for the character's ideal physical and mental attributes, Keane and his son Max traveled to Africa in 1996 for a first-hand look at the animals and jungle environment that would play such an important role in the film. Spending time with a family of mountain gorillas in Uganda provided the insights that Keane needed to understand Tarzan's feelings for his adoptive family and the complexity of his dilemma.[23]

15—Into the Future

Keane characterized the Ape-Man of the books as incredible, a genius at adaptation, and able to move like any animal from a leopard to a gibbon or a snake. The Disney *Tarzan*'s success helped fuel the Tarzan resurgence that had begun in the early 1990s with the metamorphosis of the media Ape-Man from "jungle man" to an inter-genre archetype, as in the original stories.

On July 9, 1999, the Historical Society of Oak Park and River Forest in Illinois opened their Edgar Rice Burroughs Museum. (Edgar and his family had been residents of Oak Park from 1911 through 1918.) The museum is housed on the second floor in a many-roomed mansion built before the turn of the 20th century. The ERB museum was the brainchild of Tarzan fan Jerry Spannraft, with fans Bill Ross and Mitch Harrison also lending their talents and passion to help the museum become a reality. A replica of Johnny Weissmuller's Tarzan knife was used to cut the ribbon officially opening the museum.

The popular culture crossovers continued with the September 1999 Dark Horse Comics stand-alone graphic novel serial *Batman/Tarzan: Claws of the Cat-Woman*, written by Ron Marz and illustrated by Igor Kordey. The ancient motif of two heroes (one of them wild or feral) who take a journey and battle villains and monsters dates back to the *Epic of Gilgamesh*. Here we have Batman as the Gilgamesh and Tarzan as our wild man Enkidu.

At the 1999 Dum-Dum, one of the panel discussions was titled *Tarzan on Mars*. Organized by Tarzan fan Scott Tracy Griffin of the LA SubERBs, this 38th annual Tarzan convention took place at the Warner Center Marriott in Woodland Hills, California. This event had the greatest turnout in the Burroughs Bibliophiles' history. Super-fan, writer and memorabilia collector Forrest J Ackerman was the guest of honor. Other guests included Thomas Yeates; Alex Nino (Disney illustrator and DC comics' Korak artist), and Dave Stevens (creator of the Rocketeer).

In 2000, Johnny Sheffield was given the Golden Lion Award at the Dum-Dum for his portrayals as Tarzan and Jane's adopted son in the MGM and RKO series. The next year, Dark Horse Comics published a weird teaming (and alternative history) of Tarzan and Superman. The Walt Disney Company continued their Tarzan blitz with the 39-episode animated TV series *The Legend of Tarzan* (2001) and the movies

The Dum Dum 1999 ushered in Tarzan's next century with one of the panel discussions titled, "Tarzan on Mars."

Tarzan and Jane (2002) and *Tarzan II* (2005). The deservedly short-lived 2003 WB Television Network *Tarzan* with Travis Fimmel and Sarah Wayne Callies again has Tarzan in New York, with Jane as a police detective (quite a step up from her stint as a cab driver in the 1989 *Tarzan in Manhattan*).

The Tarzan crossovers took a bizarre turn in 2004 with the publication of the novel *Tarzan Presley* by Nigel Cox. Tarzan grows up in the wild and later becomes the "king of rock and roll," baby. Go figure. Tarzan super-fan John Martin reported in his fanzine that Edgar Rice Burroughs, Inc., had filed suit to stop further publication of the book. Martin read the novel and states,

15—Into the Future

In ERB's *Tarzan of the Apes*, the young child goes from a foundling who was sus-ceptible to an early death in a multitude of ways, but who advanced in skill and education, mostly on his own, to the heights of the noblest man, even willing to sacrifice his own desires for the happiness of the woman he loved. Tarzan Presley simply survives the jungle, becomes a rock star, and then dies. End of story![24]

With music and lyrics by Phil Collins, a Broadway musical adap-tation of Disney's 1999 Tarzan movie premiered on May 10, 2006, at the Richard Rodgers Theatre. The cast included Josh Strickland as Tarzan and Jenn Gambatese, a veteran of the shows *All Shook Up* and *Hairspray*, as Jane Porter. Bob Crowley directed and created the scenic designs. Film director James Cameron has stated that Burroughs' works inspired much of the world of Pandora in his 2009 blockbuster film *Avatar*; the humanoid Na'vi are cinema cousins of the furry, tailed Waz-don in the novel *Tarzan the Terrible*.

Also that year, *Tarzan!*, an exhibition at the Musee du quai Branly in Paris, examined the Ape-Man's popularity and influence. Anthro-pologist and curator Roger Boulay insisted that Tarzan novels, films and comics became an indicator of changing cultural and political stan-dards in France, and censored and uncensored versions of the comic strip were published. The exhibit, compiled from the collections of several French museums, presents the character of the Ape-Man as an eco-warrior fighting to protect nature.

In June 2009, Tarzan became part of a Licensing International Expo at the Mandalay Bay Convention Center in Las Vegas. A Tarzan booth set into motion a Tarzan natural food line, with the Tarzan Jungle Cafe handing out samples of energy drinks, trail mix and granola. The event, sponsored by the International Licensing Industry Merchandisers' Association, was also attended by Fortune 500 firms, Hollywood movie studios, and artists and designers.

When George T. McWhorter stepped down from the editorship of *The Burroughs Bulletin* periodical and the *Gridley Wave* newsletter, Colonel Henry G. Franke III (retired) took on the mantle of editor, working tirelessly with the Burroughs Bibliophiles to help promote and preserve the legacy of the original pop cultural 20th century superhero. The Burroughs Bibliophiles organization, founded on September 4, 1960, turned 50 in 2010, and their periodical's fall issue included a brief history of the various Bibliophiles chapters.

Tarzan, Jungle King of Popular Culture

When a new species of chameleon was discovered in a small area of forest on the island of Madagascar, scientists named it Calumma tarzan. Deforestation has drastically affected this part of the central eastern highlands, which is known to the locals as the Tarzan Forest; it is near a village once called Tarzan-ville. Philip-Sebastian Gehring, study leader of the scientists, explains that in addition to this, they agreed that naming the new chameleon species after Tarzan could promote the conservation of the forest and spread awareness of the plight of animals in danger of becoming extinct because of human actions.

In another example of the continuity of popular culture, Tarzan novels aimed at a young adult audience have been written by Andy Briggs as reboot stories:

> My pitch was driven solely on rebooting Tarzan. I sometimes see criticism over this, yet the TV shows and movies do it all the time. My agenda was to bring the character to life for a whole new generation of readers. That meant it was pointless to continue a series of books that they would probably not read ... Tarzan was a *contemporary* novel when it was written—why couldn't it continue to be so? There is also the, admittedly terrible, fact that children these days *tend* not to read period novels. Of course there are exceptions, but, particularly with Tarzan, the world has moved on.[25]

A touring version of the Disney Theatrical Group's *Tarzan: The Stage Musical* began in 2012, with high school and college drama departments and regional theater groups performing the show. *Burroughs Bulletin* editor Henry Franke III, writing in the *Gridley Wave* monthly newsletter, reported that some theater groups select *Tarzan* because of the messages they believe this play underscores: acceptance of others, the importance of family, embracing diversity, and realizing one's self-worth; "*Tarzan* is family entertainment and learning all in one."[26]

The Tarzan revival that began in the early 1990s also benefited from the continued growth in popularity of artists such as Thomas Yeates and Joe Jusko, who brought originality and a sense of wonder to their illustrations of the works of Edgar Rice Burroughs and other subjects. Yeates conceived a "Tarzan and Jane in the future" concept that Alan Gordon wrote into a compelling, entertaining and thought-provoking serial for *Dark Horse Presents* numbers 8, 9 and 10: *The Once and Future Tarzan*. Yeates's concept presents a 300-year-old Tarzan as he is, an inter-genre archetype perfectly suited for the popular culture of the millennium and beyond. *The Once and Future Tarzan* was released in its entirety by Dark Horse Comics as a graphic novel in late 2012, and the epic scope of the story opens the doors to a wider perception of the ongoing Tarzan pop-cultural, modern legend.

Worldwide celebrations of Tarzan's first century included the March 2012 ECOF (Edgar Rice Burroughs Chain of Friends). Hosted by Edgar Rice Burroughs, Inc., the conference focused on Tarzan and John Carter and the release of the Disney film *John Carter*, a great Hollywood tribute to the grandfather of American science fiction.

The growth in popularity of artists Joe Jusko (second from left) and Thomas Yeates (second from right) aided in a 1990s Tarzan revival. Joining Joe and Thomas during a Tarzan Centennial panel at the 2012 Comic-Con International San Diego, are Tarzan/Burroughs writer and scholar, Scott Tracy Griffin (left); Robin Maxwell, historical novelist and author of *Jane: The Woman Who Loved Tarzan* (center); and James Sullos, president of Edgar Rice Burroughs, Inc. (right) (photograph by author).

Yeates and Jusko participated in many programs during the July 2012 Comic-Con International San Diego, including a Tarzan centennial panel with Ron Ely, writer Mark Evanier and David Lemmo, the author of this book. Yeates and Jusko won the coveted Inkpot Award in another program.

During a second Tarzan centennial celebration (the Dum-Dum) in August 2012 in Woodland Hills, California, the Tarzan-Edgar Rice Burroughs U.S. postage stamp was unveiled. Its appearance was due to years of hard work by George T. McWhorter. The Dum-Dum guest of honor was Dr. Jane Goodall, who graced the event with the unique wisdom attained by her experiences ... experiences the Tarzan fans only dream of. As Yeates told me, "She's on a different plane of existence from the rest of us." As a young girl reading Edgar's Tarzan books, she wanted to be the Ape-Man's Jane and live among the apes. Goodall pursued her dreams and became one of the most important scientists in history.

"What the chimps have taught me over the years," Goodall once said, "is they're so like us. They've blurred the line between humans and animals."[27]

Author, editor and Burroughs fan-scholar Richard A. Lupoff had this to say about the 2012 Tarzan Centennial Dum-Dum:

> Speakers were fascinating and informative. The program also included a Tarzan yell contest that was great fun, there were tours of the ERB Inc. offices, a heart-pounding dedication of the Edgar Rice Burroughs postage stamp, and a huckster room filled with lovingly produced reference works and collectible Burroughsiana. An actual Martian flying boat looked so damned realistic, my Beloved Spouse had to grab my shirt-tail to keep me from climbing into it and heading off into the wild black yonder.... Our special guest, primatologist Jane Goodall, was available to meet-and-greet, and could bound from hilarious to inspirational at will. I'll be personal: I got to share my banquet meal with former Tarzan Ron Ely and with Johnny Weissmuller's granddaughter. The only adjective that I can think of is, thrilling. Jeez, here I am well into my eighth decade, the author of 60-odd books, and suddenly—there I was, a wide-eyed fan again![28]

The 2012 Dum-Dum and ECOF were both corporate, professionally produced events hosted by Edgar Rice Burroughs, Inc.; fans also held their own celebrations. There was a Tarzan: Lord of the Louisiana Jungle Festival in Morgan City, Louisiana, on April 13 and 14, 2012, with Denny Miller in attendance. Among the many activities was the premiere of the documentary *Tarzan: Lord of the Louisiana Jungle* by author-illustrator Al Bohl and his daughter Allison. Its subject is the first Tarzan movie, made in 1918, which was partially shot in the swamps of the Atchafalaya River Basin outside Morgan City.

Another fan-generated celebration began with Ralph Brown, an important Tarzan collector and organizer within the Burroughs Bibliophiles. Ralph had proposed to me the idea of creating a Northern California chapter of the Burroughs Bibliophiles. He further intrigued me with the idea of having a Tarzan centennial event created by "just the fans." Author, historian and library technician Tom Tolley was also involved. The result of our efforts was the 2011 formation of the Northern California Mangani. Included in its ranks are writer-editors Richard and Patricia Lupoff, pioneers in the history of fandom, continuing their direct participation as fans of modern popular culture. Eisner Award and Inkpot Award–winning artist Thomas Yeates is a more than active member, also lending his musical talents to the organization.

Thanks to Tolley's tireless efforts, the Northern California Mangani held a Tarzan Centennial Celebration at the Sacramento Central Library. Tarzan memorabilia was displayed in glass cases for a month and a half and there was a two-day event in the West Meeting Room in August 2012. Thomas Yeates, John Pappas, Paula Pappas, Rachael Wenban and I began each day's programs with a musical performance of the 1960s Kinks song "Apeman." The Northern California Mangani have since expanded to include fans in Oregon and Washington, and are now known as the North Coast Mangani.

The next Tarzan movie was released to theaters in Russia during October 2013. The animated *Tarzan*, in 3D and 2D, produced by Constantin Film (a German company), has Tarzan and Jane battling a mercenary army bent on finding a meteorite that is a source of continuing energy. Ecological concerns are in the forefront of this film, as befits Tarzan's pop cultural commitment to our environment, diversity and the humane treatment of animals. The movie was released in the U.S. in 2014.

During the 2014 Comic-Con International San Diego, the IDW Library of American Comics' first volume of the Russ Manning Tarzan comics series, edited and designed by Dean Mullaney, was awarded the Eisner Award in the category of Best Archival Collection/Project-

Strips. This award, which recognizes quality achievements in the world of comics, has often been dubbed the comics' equivalent of the Academy Awards; it was named after the legendary Will Eisner, one of the earliest artists to work in comic books. Eisner had presented the concept of graphic novels to the public with his 1978 *A Contract with God and Other Tenement Stories*; his artist-author credit on this Baronet Books publication reads, "A Graphic Novel by Will Eisner." Dean Mullaney, editor of four volumes of *Tarzan: The Complete Russ Manning Newspaper Strips*, is a recipient of seven Eisner Awards.

As of this writing, Warner Bros. Pictures' 2016 *The Legend of Tarzan*, a $180 million production, will star Alexander Skarsgard (HBO's Nordic vampire in *True Blood*) as Tarzan, Margo (*Wolf of Wall Street*) Robbie as Jane, Christoph Waltz (a two-time Oscar winner), Samuel L. Jackson, John Hurt and West African actor Djimon Hounsou. The film is directed and produced by David Yates (a veteran of Harry Potter films) and co-produced by Tarzan fan Mike Richardson, founder of Dark Horse Comics. Actor Christoph Waltz, who portrays the villain Captain Leon Rom, has compared this new Tarzan film to the James Bond franchise in that Ian Fleming's Bond novels are now not specifically followed. Waltz claims that the Tarzan in Yates' movie is different from the Ape-Man of the other films and, as in the case with Bond, the plot of the movie is not based on a Burroughs book. Tarzan fans avidly await the release of *The Legend of Tarzan*, hoping for a quality rendering of the first superhero of 20th-century popular culture.

In a unique take on fandom phenomena, Tarzan fan Charles E. Early, writing about what the Internet is doing to our brains, states, "There is growing evidence that the modern media-saturated environment is changing the way people think and process information, which is in some ways detrimental to both attention span and understanding." Drawing on personal experience, he has his own take on this:

> I want to mention what I believe to be an especially significant benefit that comes from reading a master like Burroughs. The compelling nature of the stories holds the reader—especially the young reader—in a way that subtly conditions the attention span and teaches the kind of perseverance essential for grasping complex concepts. For example, I recently reread *Tarzan of the Apes* after nearly 60 years, and was quite surprised at the level of the vocabulary. Burroughs used words that caused me to stumble even now—words I couldn't have possibly understood as a ten-year-old. But the story was so riveting back then

that I kept at it in spite of the challenges, and thereby learned some important things about the nature of reading, as well as a more positive attitude toward books and concentrated effort.[29]

On the subject of fandom itself, Shari Caudron, writer and award winning columnist, spent three years of her life researching fandom phenomena for her book *Who Are You People?* Among her findings:

[A]t least a third of Americans suffer from celebrity worship syndrome, and many of the rest of us are at risk of developing the condition. After all, we live in a paparazzied, *People* magazine culture, wherein Madonna and Elvis receive far more Google hits than Darwin and Einstein.... As conventional wisdom has it, fanatics are either impressionable fools or dangerous stalkers. But in among all the articles about the psychosis of celebrity worship, I also uncovered some contradictory reports that claimed celebrity worship is actually a beneficial, biologically driven behavior that can help with social bonding.[30]

Ron Ely had this to say on fandom:

I used to hate being around the fans—I avoided it like the plague. I enjoyed the anonymity. That's why I pretty well dropped off the face of the Earth for quite a long time. But getting back out into the public again has been one of the most rewarding experiences that I can imagine. Those fans are diehard. They hang on, they don't let go. They believe in Doc [Savage] and Tarzan—they believe in them in a way that makes you want to know more about them."[31]

Again quoting writer Shari Caudron:

When born-again Christians and leather-leashed Goths come together at the same party, when middle-aged women and gum-snapping teenagers gossip online about the same celebrities, when retired auto workers and international money managers play the same board games, well, to me, that can't help but breed the kind of understanding, acceptance and community that's always been the promise, if not reality, of America.[32]

Where Tarzan fits in all this should not be underestimated. The Ape-Man entered popular culture just before the print medium began losing ground to radio, movies and comics, and the Ape-Man became the first multimedia superstar and seminal superhero of 20th-century America. Just as importantly, he went on to become a worldwide pop cultural icon, a hero sticking up for our environment and the planet on which we exist. Tarzan has also been described as sexist, racist, violent and colonialist. But French sociologist and anthropologist Roger Boulay also believes that Tarzan is an ecological superhero, and that he is a descendent of Jean-Jacques Rousseau, whom Edgar Rice Bur-

"These fans are diehard.... They believe in Doc (Savage) and Tarzan—they believe in them in a way that makes you want to know more about them." Ron Ely (left), the 1960s TV Tarzan, and the author hanging out at the A1-Comics booth after the Tarzan Centennial panel at the Comic-Con International San Diego, 2012.

roughs had studied. Rousseau believed that humans, by separating themselves too far from the natural condition, had given away a unique part of their true self and strengths.

In relation to Tarzan and Rousseau, American pop culture's takeover of global mass-marketed media promotes a character like Tarzan (in his varying forms) abroad to the point of transcendence—a sort of pop cultural imperialism, if you wish to look at it that way. Either way, through a series of novels, many motion pictures and TV episodes, comics and other units of media transmission, Tarzan became the seminal, and one of the most relevant archetypes of modern world popular culture. A hero whose century-long series of adventures reveal the characteristics of various times, places and diverse people.

Chapter Notes

Chapter 1

1. Burroughs, George Tyler, Letter dated June 27, 1861, official Edgar Rice Burroughs, Inc., ERBzine website, Issue 0943, third paragraph.
2. Porges, Irwin, *Edgar Rice Burroughs: The Man Who Created Tarzan*, Brigham Young University Press, 1975, first edition, second printing, 9.
3. Taliaferro, John, *Tarzan Forever: The Life of Edgar Rice Burroughs, Creator of Tarzan*, Scribner, 1999, first edition, 32.
4. Porges, Irwin, *Edgar Rice Burroughs: The Man Who Created Tarzan*, Brigham Young University Press, 1975, first edition, second printing, 30.
5. Burroughs, Edgar Rice, "How I Wrote the Tarzan Stories," *The New York World* (Sunday supplement), October 27, 1929, 28.
6. Aldiss, Brian, *Billion Year Spree: The True History of Science Fiction*, Doubleday & Co., 1973, first edition, 160.

Chapter 3

1. Fenton, Robert W., *Edgar Rice Burroughs and Tarzan*, McFarland & Co., 2003, 51.
2. Dumaux, Sally A., *King Baggot: A Biography and Filmography of the First King of the Movies*, McFarland & Co., 2010.

Chapter 4

1. Porges, Irwin, *Edgar Rice Burroughs: The Man Who Created Tarzan*, Brigham Young University Press, first edition, second printing, 1975, 57–60.
2. Clayton, Aaron, *Global Perspectives on Tarzan: From King of the Jungle to International Icon*, edited by Annette Wannamaker, and Michelle Ann Abate, Routledge, 2012, 187.

Chapter 5

1. Burroughs, Edgar Rice, Letter to Bert Weston, Official Edgar Rice Burroughs, Inc., *ERBzine* website; *Edgar Rice Burroughs: Bio Timeline 1910–1919*, March 14 entry.
2. American Jewish Congress, Letter to Edgar Rice Burroughs, Official Edgar Rice Burroughs, Inc., *ERBzine* website; *Archive Updates: The ERB Bio Timeline*. May 10, 1919, entry.
3. Burroughs, Edgar Rice, Letter to American Jewish Congress, Official Edgar Rice Burroughs, Inc., *ERBzine* website; *Archive Updates: The ERB Bio Timeline*, May 21, 1919, entry.
4. Mayne, Ernie, *Tarzan of the Apes*, 78 RPM recording, catalog #3491 matrix Win 6772.
5. Lord Passmore of Ghenzi, *The Burroughs Bulletin* periodical, New Series #5, January 1991, 22.
6. *New York Tribune*, Official Edgar Rice Burroughs, Inc., *ERBzine* website; Volume 1568, *Tarzan On Broadway 1921*, Reviews: "'Tarzan' Puts One in Readiness for a Laugh," September 8, 1921.
7. Fury, David, *Kings of the Jungle: An Illustrated Reference to "Tarzan" on Screen and Television*, McFarland & Company, 1994, 35.
8. Porges, Irwin, *Edgar Rice Burroughs: The Man Who Created Tarzan*, Brigham Young University Press, 1975, first edition, second printing, 359.
9. Porges, Irwin, *Edgar Rice Burroughs: The Man Who Created Tarzan*, Brigham Young University Press, 1975, first edition, second printing, 359–361.

Chapter 6

1. Porges, Irwin, *Edgar Rice Burroughs: The Man Who Created Tarzan*, Brigham

Young University Press, 1975, first edition, second printing, 456.

2. Watson, Bruce, "Tarzan the Eternal," *Smithsonian*, March 2001, 64.

3. Porges, Irwin, *Edgar Rice Burroughs: The Man Who Created Tarzan*, Brigham Young University Press, 1975, first edition, second printing, 454.

4. *Ibid.*, 454.

5. *Ibid.*, 454.

6. Barrett, Robert R., Article in *The Gridley Wave* newsletter of the Burroughs Bibliophiles #132, September 1993, (reprinted from *Comics Buyer's Guide #1010*), 1.

7. Moskowitz, Sam, "Edgar Rice Burroughs and Blue Book," in *The Burroughs Bulletin*, New Series #15, July 1993, 15.

8. Hogarth, Burne, Interview in *Crimmer's: The Harvard Journal of Pictorial Fiction*, Winter, 1975, 20.

Chapter 7

1. ERB-dom #74; 1973 review of Lacassin's treatise by Paul Spencer.

2. Haydock, Ron, "Johnny Weissmuller: King of the Jungle," interview in *Filmfax* magazine, April 1989, 61.

3. Weissmuller, Johnny. "Tarzan Today," *Saga* magazine, January, 1965, 80.

4. Haydock, Ron, *Johnny Weissmuller: King of the Jungle*, interview in *Filmfax* magazine, April 1989, 62.

Chapter 8

1. Crabbe, Buster. "Man in Motion: An Interview with Buster Crabbe," *Films in Review* magazine, July/Aug 1996, 38.

Chapter 9

1. Hogarth, Burne, Interview in *Crimmer's: The Harvard Journal of Pictorial Fiction*, by T. Durwood, Winter, 1975, 21.

2. Burroughs, Edgar Rice. Official Edgar Rice Burroughs, Inc., *ERBzine* website; *Edgar Rice Burroughs: Bio Timeline 1930–1939*. September 2, 1939, entry.

Chapter 10

1. Lupoff, Richard A., *Edgar Rice Burroughs: Master of Adventure*. Canaveral Press, 1965, 139.

2. Tosti, Don, et. al. *Only for tarzanes (Pchucones)*. CD, Arhoolie label, 2002.

3. Fenton, Robert W., *Edgar Rice Burroughs and Tarzan*, McFarland & Co., 2003, 140.

4. Aldiss, Brian, *Billion Year Spree*, Doubleday & Company, 1973, First Edition, 160.

5. Porges, Irwin, *Edgar Rice Burroughs: The Man Who Created Tarzan*, Brigham Young University Press, 1975, first edition, second printing. Letter to Donald Jackson, 640.

6. Burroughs, Edgar Rice, Letter to Thelma Terry, Official Edgar Rice Burroughs, Inc., *ERBzine* website; Issue 1524, *Lost Words of ERB Series*; *Post World War II Letters*; January 9, 1946.

Chapter 11

1. Newsreel, "Wild Petting Parties Shock Californians," *Pathe News*. Monochrome, 2 minutes and 5 seconds. Los Angeles, California, March 3, 1928.

2. Sharp, Dolph, "Me Tarzan—You Jane," *The Reader's Digest*, September, 1969, 111.

3. Ackerman, Forrest J., "A Visit with Edgar Rice Burroughs," *Edgar Rice Burroughs' Fantastic Worlds*, edited by James Van Hise, 177.

4. Barrier, Michael, and Martin Williams, *A Smithsonian Book of Comic-Book Comics*, Smithsonian Institute Press, 1981, 10.

5. Porges, Irwin, *Edgar Rice Burroughs: The Man Who Created Tarzan*, Brigham Young University Press, 1975, first edition, second printing, 694.

6. Ackerman, Forrest J., "Edgar Rice Burroughs: Creator of New Worlds," *The Burroughs Bulletin*, Original Series, Vol. 1, No. 1; July 1947, 1. Also, Official Edgar Rice Burroughs, Inc., *ERBzine* website; Vern Coriell's Burroughs Bulletins Original Series Part 1 Volumes 1–25.

7. Libby, Bill, "Tarzan Today," *Saga* magazine, January 1965, 80.

8. Taliaferro, John, *Tarzan Forever: The Life of Edgar Rice Burroughs, Creator of Tarzan*, Scribner, 1999, first edition, 362.

9. Porges, Irwin, *Edgar Rice Burroughs: The Man Who Created Tarzan*, Brigham Young University Press, 1975, first edition, second printing, 699.

10. Official Edgar Rice Burroughs, Inc., *ERBzine* website; volume 1195; "Edgar Rice Burroughs, Tarzan Creator Taken By Death,"

Reno Evening Gazette, Tuesday, March 21, 1950.

11. Porges, Irwin, *Edgar Rice Burroughs: The Man Who Created Tarzan*, Brigham Young University Press, 1975, first edition, second printing, 699.

12. Fenton, Robert W., *Edgar Rice Burroughs and Tarzan*, McFarland & Co., 2003, 182.

Chapter 12

1. Chandler, Raymond, *Raymond Chandler: Later Novels and Writings*, The Library of America, 1995, sixth printing, 482.

2. Eshed, Eli, "Tarzan in Israel," *The Burroughs Bulletin*, New Series #84, page 35.

3. Wannamaker, Annette, and Michelle Ann Abate, *Global Perspectives on Tarzan: From King of the Jungle to International Icon*, Routledge Research in Cultural and Media Studies (Book 7), 2012, 7.

4. Potter, Alicia, "Hollywood and Vine," *AMC* magazine, June 1997, 6.

5. Farmer, Philip José, *Mother Was A Lovely Beast*, Chilton Book Company, 1974, first edition, x.

Chapter 13

1. Miller, Denny, interview in *Films of the Golden Age* magazine, #28, Spring 2002, 76.

2. Miller, Denny, interviewed by David Fury in *The Burroughs Bulletin*, New Series #17, January 1994, 29.

3. Freese, Gene, *Jock Mahoney: The Life and Times of a Hollywood Stuntman*, McFarland & Co., 2014, 104 and 105.

4. Coriell, Rita, "The Coriell Years of Burroughs Fandom," *The Burroughs Bibliophiles*, New Series #12, October 1992, 32.

5. Freese, Gene, *Jock Mahoney: The Life and Times of a Hollywood Stuntman*, McFarland & Co., 2014, 111.

6. Hamilton, Donald, *Murderers' Row*, Gold Medal, 1964 reprint, 138. Also, Titan Books, 2013, 217.

7. Lupoff, Richard A., "The Long road To Barsoom," *The Burroughs Bulletin* periodical, New Series #90, 2013, 4.

8. Freese, Gene, *Jock Mahoney: The Life and Times of a Hollywood Stuntman*, McFarland & Co., 2014, 119.

9. *The Antiquarian Bookman*, November 25, 1963; *Editor's Corner*, 1.

10. Fenton, Robert W, *The Big Swingers*, Prentice–Hall, Inc., 1967, 224.

11. Barrett, Robert R., "Tarzan's Third Great Comic Strip Artist: Russell G. Manning (1929–1981)," *The Burroughs Bulletin*, New Series #13, January 1993, 11.

12. Leiber, Fritz, *Tarzan and the Valley of Gold*, Ballantine Books, 1966, 141.

13. Hermes, Doc, Official Edgar Rice Burroughs, Inc., *ERBzine* website; volume 0210; book review of *Tarzan and the Valley of Gold*, last paragraph.

14. Bacon, James, "Tarzan: He Has Gone Sophisticated; 14th Person Now In Role," *Ocala Star-Banner*, May 3, 1965, 12.

15. "TV Elephant Kills Trainer," *Lodi News Sentinel*, July 30, 1966, 2.

16. Ely, Ron, Interview by Bill Groves in *TeleVision Chronicles* magazine, #8, January, 1997, 75.

17. Whitman, Arthur, "He Put Tarzan in a Tux," *True* magazine, September 1966, 76.

18. Groves, Bill, "Tarzan," *TeleVision Chronicles* magazine, #8, January 1997, 51.

19. Ely, Ron, Interview by Bill Groves in *TeleVision Chronicles* magazine, #8, January 1997, 76.

20. Behlmer, Rudy, "Johnny Weissmuller: Olympics to Tarzan," *Films in Review*, July/Aug 1996, 32.

21. Fury, David, *Kings of the Jungle*, McFarland & Company, 1994, 202.

22. Stevens, Ray, *Gitarzan*, CD, Varese Sarabande label, 1996, Track 6.

Chapter 14

1. Farmer, Philip José, *A Feast Unknown*, Playboy Press Paperbacks, 1980, 9.

2. *Ibid.*, 15.

3. *Ibid.*, 280–281.

4. Farmer, Philip José, *Lord of the Trees* and *The Mad Goblin*, Ace Books (Ace Double), 1970, 9.

5. *Ibid.*, 232.

6. *Ibid.*, 118.

7. *Ibid.*, 119.

8. *Ibid.*, 119.

9. *Ibid.*, 119.

10. *Ibid.*, 120.

11. Bozarth, Bruce, ERBLIST.com, Section; *ERB Summary Project*; Unrelated novels; *Pirate Blood*, Introduction, second paragraph.

12. The Kinks, *Lola versus Powerman*

and the Money-Go-Round, Part One. CD, Reprise/Wea, track 12.

13. Tom Stewart, "Tarzan, Tarzan and Tarzan: The Lord of the Jungle's Long, Strange Journey," *BACKISSUE* magazine, #1, 2003, 77.

14. Hodes, Bob, Official Edgar Rice Burroughs, Inc., *ERBzine* website; erbzine.com/mag7/0701.html.jj

15. Oldfield, Col. Barney, "They're Still Going Ape Over Tarzan," *Mainliner* magazine, Vol. 18, #9, September 1974, 36 and 37.

16. Bryant, William Cullen, "Thanatopsis," *Yale Book of American Verse*, Yale University Press, 1912, edited by Thomas Raynesford Lounsbury, lines 62–64.

17. Farmer, Philip José, *Tarzan Alive*, Doubleday & Company, 1972, 188–189.

18. *Ibid.*, 189.

19. Farmer, Philip José, "Tarzan Lives," *Esquire*, April 1972, 130.

20. Farmer, Philip José, *The Adventure of the Peerless Peer*, Dell Books, 1976 reprint. Title page.

21. *Ibid.*, 68.

22. *Ibid.*, 69.

Chapter 15

1. Porges, Irwinm, *Edgar Rice Burroughs: The Man Who Created Tarzan*, Brigham Young University Press, 1975, first edition, second printing, xii.

2. Roberts, Tom, "Tarzan … The Marvel Way!" *The Burroughs Bulletin*, New Series #15, July 1993, 26.

3. McWhorter, George T., "Edgar Rice Burroughs … Dead or Alive?" *Fantasy Review*, #82, 1985, 8.

4. Nayar, Pramod K., *Frantz Fanon*, Routledge, 2013, first edition, 49.

5. Hansberry, Lorraine, *A Raisin in the Sun*, Vintage Books, 2004, 57 and 64.

6. ERB-dom #74; 1973 review of Lacassin's treatise by Paul Spencer. 252

7. hooks, bell, "Reel to Real: Race, Sex and Class at the Movies," Routledge Classics, 2009, 109–110.

8. Cheyfitz, Eric, *The Poetics of Imperialism: Translation and Colonization from The Tempest to Tarzan*, University of Pennsylvania Press, Expanded Edition, 1997, 15.

9. Kraar, Don, Interview in *The Burroughs Bulletin*, New Series #1, January, 1990, 11.

10. Morrow, Gray, "Tarzan of the Funny Pages," *Scarlet Street* magazine, #18, 1995, 77.

11. Hudson, Hugh, "Greystoke: On Cinematic Safari with Tarzan Lord of the Apes," *Prevue* magazine, #56, 1984, 65.

12. *Ibid.*, 67.

13. Hudson, Hugh, Interview in *Starlog* magazine, #81, April 1984, 23.

14. Hudson, Hugh, "Greystoke: The Legend of Tarzan Lord of the Apes," by Jessie Horsting, *Fantastic Films* #39, 1984, 17.

15. Larson, Wolf, "The New Tarzan," *Starlog* #172, November 1991, 41.

16. Spurlock, Duane, "Where Have All The Fans Gone?" Interview in *The Burroughs Bulletin*, New Series, #13, January 1993, 23.

17. Kure, Henning, *The Burroughs Bulletin*, New Series #7, July 1991, 22.

18. Yeates, Thomas, Interview With Tarzan Artist Tom Yeates, by Ken Webber, *The Burroughs Bulletin*, New Series #7, July 1991, 14.

19. Kure, Henning, Interviewed by Duane Spurlock, *The Burroughs Bulletin*, New Series #13, January 1993, 24.

20. Fury, David, "Maureen O'Sullivan: A Jewel of a Jane," *The Burroughs Bulletin*, New Series #15, July 1993, 7.

21. Garmon, Ronald Dale, and Jessie Lilley, "Tarzan Swings Again!" *Scarlet Street* #23, 1996, 35.

22. Gross, Allan, "Opportunities and Magic Moments: Reminiscences of a Tarzan Comic Book and Newspaper Writer," *The Burroughs Bulletin*, New Series #86, 13.

23. Green, Howard, "Xtreme Tarzan," *Disney Magazine*, Summer, 1999, 35–36.

24. Martin, John, *Edgardemain Jr.*, #2, October 2015.

25. Briggs, Andy, Interview in *The Burroughs Bulletin*, New Series #86, Spring 2011, 5.

26. Franke, Henry, III, *The Gridley Wave* newsletter, #374, November 2013, 1.

27. Goodall, Jane, *The San Diego Union-Tribune*, December 17, 1997, A-25.

28. Lupoff, Richard A., "The Long Road To Barsoom," *The Burroughs Bulletin*, New Series #90, 2013, 8.

29. Early, Charles E., "Master of Virtual Reality: Burroughs' Psychological Impact on the Reader," *The Burroughs Bulletin*, New Series #91, Summer 2014, 11.

30. Caudron, Shari, *WHO ARE YOU*

PEOPLE? A Personal Journey into the Heart of Fanatical Passion in America, Barricade Books, 2006, Second Printing, 148–149.

31. Ely, Ron, *The Gridley Wave* newsletter, #360, September 2012, 2.

32. Caudron, Shari, *WHO ARE YOU PEOPLE? A Personal Journey into the Heart of Fanatical Passion in America*, Barricade Books, 2006, Second Printing, 271.

Bibliography

Books

Ackerman, Forrest J. *Forrest J Ackerman's World of Science Fiction*. Los Angeles: General Publishing Group, 1997.

Aldiss, Brian. *Billion Year Spree: The True History of Science Fiction*. Schocken Books, 1975.

Benet, William Rose. *The Reader's Encyclopedia*. New York: Thomas Y. Crowell, Second Edition, 1965.

Bergen, James A., Jr. *Price and Reference Guide to Books Written by Edgar Rice Burroughs*. Beaverton, OR: The Golden Lion, 1991.

Burroughs, Edgar Rice. The Tarzan Saga, 25 volumes (counting Tarzan Twins), with three authorized additions by Fritz Leiber, Joe Lansdale (who finished an ERB ms.) and Philip José Farmer.

Burroughs, Edgar Rice. Unpublished Autobiography. Quoted extensively on ERBzine, in books, etc., Edgar Rice Burroughs, Inc.

Campbell, Joseph. *Historical Atlas of World Mythology*, five volumes. New York: Perennial Library, 1988.

Campbell, Joseph, with Bill Moyers. *The Power of Myth*. Edited by Betty Sue Flowers. New York: Doubleday, 1988.

Caudron, Shari. *WHO ARE YOU PEOPLE? A Personal Journey into the Heart of Fanatical Passion in America*. Fort Lee, NJ: Barricade Books 2006, second printing.

Chapman, Edgar L. *The Magic Labyrinth of Philip José Farmer*. San Bernardino, CA: Borgo Press, 2007.

Cheyfitz, Eric. *The Poetics of Imperialism: Translation and Colonization from the Tempest to Tarzan*. University of Pennsylvania Press, expanded edition, 1997.

Cochran, Russ. *The Edgar Rice Burroughs Library of Illustration*, three volumes. West Plains, MO: self-published, 1976, 1977, 1984. Limited to 2000 copies.

DeForest, Tim. *Storytelling in the Pulps, Comics, and Radio*. Jefferson, NC: McFarland, 2004.

Erardi, Glenn. *Collecting Edgar Rice Burroughs*. Atglen, PA: Schiffer Publishing, 2000.

_____. *Guide to Tarzan Collectibles*. Atglen, PA: Schiffer Publishing, 1998.

Essoe, Gabe. *Tarzan of the Movies*. New York: The Citadel Press, 1968.

Farmer, Philip José. *Mother Was a Lovely Beast*. Radnor, PA: Chilton Book Co., 1974.

_____. *Tarzan Alive*. Garden City, NJ: Doubleday & Co., 1972.

_____. *The Adventure of the Peerless Peer*. Boulder, CO: The Aspen Press, 1974, first edition.

_____. *The Empire of the Nine*. London: Sphere Books, 1988.

Fenton, Robert W. *The Big Swingers*. Englewood Cliffs, NJ: Prentice Hall, 1967.

Fury, David. *Johnny Weissmuller: Twice the Hero*. Minneapolis: Artist's Press, 2000.

_____. *Kings of the Jungle: An Illustrated Reference to "Tarzan" on Screen and Television.* Jefferson, NC: McFarland, 1994.

Glut, Donald F. *The Dinosaur Scrapbook.* Secaucus, NJ: The Citadel Press, 1980.

Griffin, Scott Tracy. *Tarzan: The Centennial Celebration.* London: Titan Books, 2012.

Hamilton, Edith. *Mythology.* New York: Warner Books, 1999.

Hansberry, Lorraine. *A Raisin in the Sun.* New York: Vintage Books, 2004.

Heins, Henry Hardy. *A Golden Anniversary Bibliography of Edgar Rice Burroughs.* West Kingston, RI: D.M. Grant, 1964.

Holtsmark, Erling B. *Tarzan and Tradition.* Westport, CT; London: Greenwood Press, 1981.

hooks, bell. *Reel to Real: Race, Sex and Class at the Movies.* New York: Routledge, 1996.

Lee, Ray, and Vernell Coriell. *A Pictorial History of the Tarzan Movies.* Los Angeles: Golden State News Company, 1966.

Lupoff, Dick and Don Thompson. *All in Color for a Dime.* New Rochelle, New York: Arlington House, 1970.

Lupoff, Richard A. *Edgar Rice Burroughs: Master of Adventure.* New York: Canaveral Press, 1965.

Malloy, Alex G. *Comic Book Artists.* Radnor, PA: Attic Books, 1993.

McGrath, Charles, and staff of Book Review, eds. *Books of the Century.* New York: Times Books, Random House, 1998.

McWhorter, George T. *Edgar Rice Burroughs Memorial Collection: A Catalog.* Louisville, KY: House of Greystoke, 1991.

Mitchell, W. J. T. *The Last Dinosaur Book.* University of Chicago Press, 1998.

Nayar, Pramod K. *Frantz Fanon.* London; New York: Routledge, 2013, first edition.

New Larousse Encyclopedia of Mythology, introduction by Robert Graves. Wingdale, NY: Crescent Books, 1987.

Nollen, Scott Allen. *Boris Karloff. A Critical Account of His Screen, Stage, Radio, Television, and Recording Work.* Jefferson, NC: McFarland, 1991.

Nollen, Scott Allen. *Boris Karloff: A Gentleman's Life.* Baltimore: Midnight Marquee Press, 1999.

Onyx, Narda. *Water, World and Weissmuller.* Los Angeles: Vion Publishing, 1964.

Perry, George, and Alan Aldridge. *The Penguin Book of Comics.* Baltimore: Penguin Books, 1967.

Porges, Irwin. *Edgar Rice Burroughs: The Man Who Created Tarzan.* Provo, UT: Brigham Young University, 1975.

Pringle, David. *Imaginary People: A Who's Who of Modern Fictional Characters.* London: Grafton Books, 1987.

Robinson, Frank M. *Science Fiction of the 20th Century.* Portland, OR: Collectors Press, 1999.

Robinson, Jerry. *The Comics. an Illustrated History of Comic Strip Art.* New York: G. P. Putnam's Sons, 1974.

Rovin, Jeff. *Adventure Heroes.* New York: Facts On File, 1994.

_____. *The Encyclopedia of Super Heroes.* New York: Facts On File, 1985.

Taliaferro, John. *Tarzan Forever.* New York: Scribner, 1999.

Thompson, Don, and Dick Lupoff. *The Comic-Book Book.* New Rochelle, NY: Arlington House, 1973.

Torgovnick, Marianna. *Gone Primitive. Savage Intellects, Modern Lives.* University of Chicago Press, 1990.

Ullery, David A. *The Tarzan Novels of Edgar Rice Burroughs.* Jefferson, McFarland & Company, 2001.

Van Hise, James. *Edgar Rice Burroughs' Fantastic Worlds.* Onaga Trail, CA: self-published, 1996.

Vernon, Alex. *On Tarzan.* Athens, University of Georgia Press, 2008.

Weissmuller, Johnny, Jr. *Tarzan, My Father.* Toronto: ECW Press, 2002.

Zeuschner, Robert B. *Edgar Rice Bur-*

roughs: The Exhaustive Scholar's and Collector's Descriptive Bibliography of American Periodical, Hardcover, Paperback, and Reprint Editions. Jefferson, NC: McFarland, 1996.

Periodicals and Pamphlets

Adkins, P. H. *Edgar Rice Burroughs Bibliography and Price Guide.* New Orleans: P.D.A. Enterprises, 1974.

Antiquarian Bookman. November 25, 1963. Whole issue on Edgar Rice Burroughs.

Bergen, James A., Jr. *A Reference and Price Guide to U.S. Books Written by Edgar Rice Burroughs.* Self-published, 1989.

Biblio. Aster Publishing Corporation, Sept.–Oct. 1996. Article by George T. McWhorter on collecting Tarzan and Edgar Rice Burroughs.

Burroughs Bulletin, New Series, 1990–present. Published by the Burroughs Bibliophiles. Editor, Colonel Henry Franke III (retired).

Crimmer's: The Harvard Journal of Pictorial Fiction. Winter, 1975. Interview with Burne Hogarth.

Day, Bradford M. *Edgar Rice Burroughs. a Bibliography.* Science-Fiction & Fantasy Publications, 1962.

Edgarmain Jr. fanzine, edited by John Martin. "Enjoying the Literary Legerdemain of Edgar Rice Burroughs."

The Gridley Wave newsletter, New Series, 1990–present. Published by the Burroughs Bibliophiles; editor Colonel Henry Franke III (retired).

Library Review. University of Louisville, May 1980. Editor, George T. McWhorter. Whole issue devoted to Edgar Rice Burroughs.

Smithsonian, March 2001. Article titled *Tarzan the Eternal* by Bruce Watson.

Satellite Science Fiction. Renown Publications, October 1958. *The Amazing Edgar Rice Burroughs* by Sam Moskowitz.

True. Fawcett Publications, September 1966. *He Put Tarzan in a Tux* by Arthur Whitman.

Video Watchdog, #114, Dec. 2004. Tim & Donna Lucas. *Tarzan Lord of the DVDs* by Bill Cooke.

Websites

Academy of Science Fiction Fantasy & Horror Films. (www.saturnawards. org).

ERBLIST. Website created by David Bruce Bozarth. Highly recommended. (www.erblist.com).

ERBzine. Website created by Bill and Sue-On Hillman. Also highly recommended. (www.erbzine.com).

Philip José Farmer Web Page. (www.pj farmer.com).

Geppi's Entertainment Museum. (www. geppismuseum.com/Home/7/1/52/ 500).

Heilbrunn Timeline of Art History. The Metropolitan Museum of Art (www. metmuseum.org).

Lambiek Comiclopedia. (www.lambiek. net/home.html).

Museum of Modern Mythology and Pop Culture. (www.modernmythmu seum.com).

Museum of Pop Culture. (www.popcul turemuseum.blogspot.com).

Wold-Newton Universe. (www.pjfarm er.com/woldnewton/Pulp.html).

Index

Page numbers in **bold italics** indicate pages with illustrations.

Index

Index

Bull Run 9
Burnett, Carol 148
Burr, Raymond 136
Burroughs, Abner Tyler 17
Burroughs, Danton 113, 173, 178, 186–187
Burroughs, Edgar Rice 2, 6, 9, 10, 11, *12*,
13, 14, 15, 16, 17, 18, 19, 21, 22, *23*, 24,
25, 26, 27, 28, 29, 30, 31, 32, 33, 34,
35, *37*, 38, 39, 41, 42, 43, 44, 46, 47,
48, 49, 50, 51, 52, 53, 54, 55, 56, 57,
58, 60, 61, 62, 63, 64, 65, 67, 68, 69,
71, 72, 73, 74, 75, 76, 78, 79, 80, 81, 82,
83, 84, 87, 89, 90, 91, 92, 93, 94, 95,
96, 97, 98, 99, 101, 102, 103, 104, 105,
107, 108, 109, 110, 111, 112, 113, 114,
115, 116, 118, 119, 120, 121, 123, 124,
126, 127, 128, 129, 130, 132, 134, 136,
137, 140, 141, 142, 145, 146, 147, 148,
149, 150, 151, 152, 153, 154, 155, 157,
160, 162, 168, 169, 171, 172, 173, 174,
175, 176, 177, 178, 179, 180, 182, 185,
186, 187, 188, 189, 190, 191, 192, 193,
194, 195, 196, 197, 198, 200, 201–202
Burroughs, Emma 12, 13, 16, 17, 18, 25,
27, 31, 38, 43, 51, 55, 63, 65, 71, 75, 76,
78, 80, 81, 113, 114
Burroughs, Florence *see* Dearholt, Florence
Burroughs, Frank Coleman 11, 18, 63
Burroughs, George Tyler 9, 10, 11, 12, 13,
15, 16, 24, 25, 34, 47, 98
Burroughs, George, Jr. 11, 12, 13, 18, 95
Burroughs, Harry 11, 12, 13, 16, 17, 18, 94
Burroughs, Hulbert 18, 50, 53, 71, 76, 80,
97, 98, 103, 104, 105, 108, 111, 112, 113,
115, 160
Burroughs, Joan 18, 50, 53, 54, 55, 56,
58, 63, 73, 81, 112, 113, 118, 173
Burroughs, John Coleman "Jack" 25, 50,
53, 55, 65, 71, 80, 83, 87, 89, 91, 93, 94,
95, 97, 104, 112, 113, 115, 118, 121, 126,
150
Burroughs, Johnny 113
Burroughs, Mary Evaline 9, 10, 11, 43,
67, 112
Burroughs, Studley 17, 65, 68, 71, 73
The Burroughs Bibliophiles 58, 132, 140,
144, 146, 148, 150, 151, 158, 160, 161,
168, 170, 173, 175, 178, 184, 186, 187,
189–190, 193, *194*, 195, 199
The Burroughs Bookies (fan organization) 187
The Burroughs Bulletin (fanzine) 44, 121,
122, 129, 132, 134, 137, 145, 146, 151,
154, *174*, 178, 185, 186, 195, 196
The Burroughs Newsbeat (fanzine) *37*

Burroughs-Tarzan Enterprises 78, 81, 83,
90
Buscema, John 178
Businessmen's Military Training Corps
(BMTC) 103, 104, 105

Caesar, Julius 15
Cagney, James 67
Caine, Michael 135
The Caine Mutiny (1954 film) 137
SS *California* 33
California Aqueduct 101
Callies, Sarah Wayne 194
Calloway, Cab 93
Calumma tarzan (chameleon species)
196
Cameron, James 195
Campbell-Ewald Advertising Company
55–56, 60
Canaveral Press 149, 150, 152, 154, 155,
160
Capone, Al 70
Captain Underpants 5
Carlton, Ivy 44
Carmen Jones (1954 film) 131
Carradine, John 145
Carson Napier 74, 75, 89, 97, 192
Carson of Venus (magazine story) 89
Carson of Venus (novel) 91
Carter, Lin 174
Carter, Miki 139
Cartoonists Across America & the World
(art project) 5
Cartoonists and Illustrators School 123
Casino Royale (1954 TV show) 124
Cassia County, Idaho 13
Catman Comics (comic book) 170
Caudron, Shari 201
The Cavalier (magazine) 27
The Cave Girl (magazine story) 28, 34
The Cave Man (magazine story) 34
Cazedessus, Camille "Caz," Jr. 145, 158,
178
Celardo, John 136
Celeste, Olga 118
Chabon, Michael 5
The Champ (1931 film) 67
Chandler, Raymond 104, 135
Chaney, Lon, Jr. 114
Chaney, Lon, Sr. 22, 109, 120
Chaplin, Charlie 67, 157
Charleston, South Carolina 9
Charlie Chan 52, 64, 83
Charlton Comics 152
Charteris, Leslie 120, 130
The Cheat (1915 film) 30

213

Index

Index

Index

fandom 1, 3, 4, 5, 6, 7, 33, 37, 48, 54, 55, 56, 58, 59, 62, 63, 73, 74, 77, 82, 92, 94, 110, 119, 120, 121, 122, 125, 126, 132, 134, 140, 142, 143, 144, 145, 146, 147, 148, 150, 151, 152, 154, 155, 157, 158, 160, 162, 164, 169, 170, 171, 173, 174, 175, 176, 177, 178, 182, 185, 186, 187, 193, 194, 195, 198, 199, 200, 201
Fanon, Frantz 179
Fantastic Adventures (magazine) 93, 97
Fantasy Review (magazine) 178
Faraday, Michael 20
Fariss, Evelyn 43
Farmer, Philip José 87, 129, 137, 140, 141, 152, 164, *165*, 166, 168, 172, 173, *174*, 175, 184, 186, 187, 192
A Feast Unknown (novel) 164–*165*, 166
Fechin, Nicolai Ivanovich 89
Fellini, Federico 136
Fenton, Robert W. 109
Ferguson, Al 60
Fiction House 136
Fielder, Brigadier General Kendall 99, 103, 112, 113, 118
Fields, W.C. 160
A Fighting Man of Mars (magazine story) 63
A Fighting Man of Mars (novel) 67
Filmation 177, 178
Films in Review (magazine) 160
Fimmel, Travis 194
Finger, Bill 92
Finlay, Virgil 97
Finn Family Moomintroll (novel) 116
Fitzgerald, Barry 99
Fitzgerald, F. Scott 78
The Flash 123
Flash Gordon 67, 76, 125, 137
Fleming, Ian 124, 200
Florey, Robert 124
Flynn, Errol 160
Forester, C.S. 164
Fort Grant 16
Fort Sumter 9
Foster, Harold "Hal" 60, *61*, 62, 63, 67, 87, 160, 170, 173, 178
Four Color (Dell comic book series) 119, 121, 132
Fox Pantages Theater 73
Franke III, Colonel Henry G. (retired) 195, 196
Frankenstein 6, 25
Frankenstein (1910 film) 26
Frankenstein (1931 film) 55, 67
Frankenstein Meets the Wolf Man (1943 film) 114

Frazetta, Frank 147, 150, 155, 160, 168, 170
Freeman, George 190
Freemasonry 11
Freese, Gene 145, 148, 151
Fu Manchu, Dr. 7, 75, 137, 173
Fury, David 46, 144, 161, 187

Gable, Clark 54
Gahan of Gathol 46
Galsworthy, John 51
Gambatese, Jenn 195
Gamley, Douglas 143
Garcia, Raul Angel 124
Garden of Allah 78
Gatling, Richard 11
Gehring, Philip-Sebastian 196
Gene Autry (comic book) 132
Germany 7, 33, 34, 39, 43, 45, 51, 79, 93, 109, 114, 120, 176, 199
Gernsback, Hugo 132
Geronimo 55
Gerson, Villiers 140
Gettysburg 10
Gianni, Gary 187
Gifford, Frances 109
Gilbert, Edgar 55
Gilgamesh 193
Gilmour, William 151
The Girl from Farris's (magazine story) 27
The Girl from Hollywood (magazine story) 46
The Girl from Hollywood (novel) 49, 169
"Gitarzan" (record) 162
Glendale Playhouse 56
Global Perspectives on Tarzan: From King of the Jungle to International Icon (book) 33, 137
Goddess of Fire (magazine story) 97
The Gods of Mars (magazine story) 25
Goebbels, Joseph 79
Gold Key Comics 148, 152, 154, 170
Gold Star Books 152
Golden Lion Award 151, 168, 170, 173, 175, 178, 184, 187, 190, 193
Golden Multitudes (book) 120
Goldman, Emma 52
Gollub, Moe 14
Goodall, Jane, Dr. 180, 189, 198
Gor (novel series) 175
Gordon, Alan 196
Grand Army of the Republic 11
Grant, Cary 118
Grant, Douglas 58
Graves, Peter 192
Greeley, Evelyn 43
Green, Brigadier General Thomas H. 103

216

Index

Index

Index

Lambert, Eddie 73
Lancaster, Burt 118, 130
The Land of Hidden Men (magazine story) 67, 71
Land of Terror (novel) 112
The Land That Time Forgot (magazine story) 32
The Land That Time Forgot (novel) 50, 52
Landon, Brigadier General Truman H. "Ted" 111, 121
Lang, Freeman 73
Lansdale, Joe R. 187
Lara, Joe 184, 188, *189*
Larson, Wolf 184
Last and First Men (novel) 49
Laugh, Clown, Laugh (1928 film) 121
Laugh It Off (newspaper column) 99, 101, 103, 112
Laurel and Hardy 118
Lee, Don 131
Lee, Robert E. 10
Lee, Stan 4
The Legend of Tarzan (2016 film) 200
The Legend of Tarzan (TV series) 193
Leiber, Fritz 155, 156, 187
Lemmo, David 198, *202*
Lesser, Sol 76, 77, 89, 90, 108, 109, 110, 111, 114, 116, 118, 119, 124, 125, 126, 127, 130, 132, 135, 137, 138, 139, 140, 142
Lewis, Bob *see* Lubbers, Bob
Liberty (magazine) 78
Lichtenstein, Roy 4
Lightning Strikes West (1940 film) 53
Li'l Abner (newspaper comic strip) 130
Lincoln, Abraham 41, 75
Lincoln, Elmo *35*, *36*, 38, 44, 46, 105
Literature for Composition (college textbook) 154
Little Bighorn 16
Little Caesar (1930 film) 67
Little Orphan Annie 67
The Living Dead (magazine story) 97
Llana of Gathol (novel) 126
Lombard, Carole 54
London, Jack 13, 32, 41
The Lone Ranger 4, 74, 83
Long, Ray 32
The Long Beach Independent (newspaper) 147
The Long Goodbye (novel) 135
Long Sam (newspaper comic strip) 130
Looney Tunes (cartoons) 87
Lord Greystoke 27, 33, 39, 123, 155, 175
Lord of the Trees (novel) 166

Lord Passmore 44
Lord Passmore of Ghenzi 44
Lord Tyger (novel) 168
Lorraine, Louise 46, 177
Los Angeles, California 2, 31, 32, 35, 38, 41, 50, 53, 73, 80, 101, 110, 118, 119, 120, 125, 129, 131, 152, 156, 173, 177, 178
Los Angeles County Art Institute 152
Los Angeles Farming and Milling Company 41
Los Angeles State and County Arboretum 109, 110, 111, 120, 130
The Los Angeles SubERBs (fan organization) 187, 193
Los Angeles Suburban Homes Company 41
Los Angeles Times (newspaper) 41, 131, 160
Lost on Venus (magazine story) 74
Louisiana 34
The Lovers (novella) 141
Lowell, Percival 18
Loy, Myrna 114, 120
Lubbers, Bob 130, 132, 136
Lugosi, Bela 67, 109, 124
Lupoff, Patricia 149, 150, 199
Lupoff, Richard A. 101, 148, 149, 150, 151, 154, 186, 198, 199
RMS *Lusitania* 34

Macan, Darko 188
Macauley Company 49
Machin, Will 34
Mackenzie, Joyce 177
MacLaine, Shirley 143
MacLane, Barton 114, 120
Macready, George 131
The Mad Ghoul (1943 film) 124
The Mad Goblin (novel) 166
The Mad Hatter 164
The Mad King (magazine story) 28
The Mad King (novel) 54, 187
The Mad Kings (fan organization) 187
Madonna 201
Magazine and Book Illustration Award 130
Magnus, Robot Fighter (comic book) 155
Mahoney, Jock 145, 146, 148, *149*, *150*, 151, 155, 158, 159, 177, 178
Mainliner (magazine) 171
Malibu Comics 185
Malone, Nancy 159
The Man from Earth (2007 film) 87
"The Man of a Thousand Faces" *see* Chaney, Lon, Sr.

Index

Index

Index

Index

Index

Index

225

Index

Index